THE PAGEANT OF THE NEW WORLD

The Pageant
Of The New World

STANTON A. COBLENTZ

diablo press

Copyright 1968 by Stanton A. Coblentz

PS3505
.0144
P34

Published by Diablo Press
Box 7084, Berkeley, California 94717

Library of Congress Card Catalog Number 68-56166

Contents

The Pageant of
the New World

I. Before Columbus

"While fear and distance still, like star-gulfs, sever
The New World from the Old . . ."

"Time's grandest epic never has been told
By Homers marshalling corps of tramping verse—
A story big with fate, millenium-old,
Yet modern as the skies where jets rehearse!"

So, in a trumpet tone,
A voice within me spoke; my glance
Fell on a varied zone
Vast as the arc from Borneo to France,
Where two long continental quilts of land
Circled from pole to pole.
Range beyond range I saw domed mountains roll
Above the foam-reefs of earth's lordliest seas,
With many a timbered ridge and white neck-band
And blowing plains whose grassed immensities
Might nourish empires; jungles with the coils
Of anaconda streams, and canyoned woods
Where pines, colossus-high, clustered and soared,
Marshes of cypress, spiny cactus soils,
Bush-lands, and gorges where Niagaras poured,
And glistening isles where seals' gray brotherhoods
Splashed in a swinging world that frothed and roared.

9

And in those vastnesses cloaking half the earth,
Were galaxies of creatures, winged and furred:
Gemmed hummingbirds that whirred
And flashed like elves, bison of bullish girth,
Moose in the shadowed fir-woods, elk and deer
Innumerable as the tinted leaves of fall,
And alligators where the swamp-streams crawl,
And mountain sheep where spiky pinnacles rear,
Red-waisted cardinals, green parrakeets,
Jabbering monkeys, geese triangling high,
And passenger pigeons whose long shimmering sheets
Darkened the summer sky.

Yet over all that planetary span,
From the clear Fraser's pools of glacial blue
To where brown Orinoco's torrent ran,
Few humans wandered; and among those few,
Most were but wild men, roving bold and free,
Appareled in hides, or dyed and plumed for show,
Or naked as the salmon in the sea,
Scouting for heads, scalping the tortured foe,
Plucking the beans and corn,
Dancing to gods of rain,
Chanting song-magic in an old refrain,
Challenging beasts and storm-fiends.

Still, not all
Were children of the waste. In condor heights
Under the bald, flint-ridged Andean wall
I saw stone palaces and ramparts rise,
And tape-like roads climbing in spiral flights,
And terraced slopes marking the enterprise
Of multitudes of toilers. Proud the reign

Of the Lord Inca, servant of the Sun,
Guiding the millions of his peaked domain
Down to the labor of the lowliest one,
Who hewed the cliffside rock,
Who wove the tapestry,
Who herded the llama flock,
Or fashioned the gold or silver filigree.
Though few were rich, I saw no ragged poor,
And none need beg, and daily maize was sure,
And the Inca, like a Jove, ruled over all, secure.

II

Far to the north, in jungles of Yucatan,
Rose picture-monuments of massive stone,
And charactered pyramids, and busts of jade
For snake-mouthed deities from that unknown,
Astute, deft-weaving race of Mayan man
Who watched the stars, and measured the wheeling year,
Yet wooed, by maidens drowned, the rain-god's aid,
Sculptured and worshipped, spun and sowed and prayed,
And founded cities doomed to disappear
Utterly as a whisper.

On plateaux
Burning and vast, beneath the threat and frown
Of tall volcanic cones whose ageless snow
Looked grimly down,
I saw another folk of strange renown.
Color, in peacock flames, lay everywhere—
The scarf, the shawl, the many-patterned dress,
And the long feathers mottled lords would wear,
Strutting with an imperial haughtiness.

And in the village square
Where blanketed women flocked
For a market day or fair,
Big golden gourds and scarlet fruit were stocked;
Enameled jars, and herbs, and quilts of gold,
Axes of brass, and puma skins were sold.
Color and light and majesty possessed
Mosaic walls and courts of Mexico,
Its towering architecture which expressed
A grandeur like the Pharaohs used to know,
Where pyramids, darkly red,
Causeways, and bridges, and blue lakes were spread,
Canals like Venice, and a mountain rim
Framing a capital of sparkle and joy,
Though, in the temples, living hearts were fed
To cannibal gods, which brooded goblin-grim
While populous life buzzed on and free men found employ.

Now once again I scanned
The wide dark bosom of two continents,
And saw how all the land,
Wearing its seas as timeless armaments,
Was fringed by brine rolling to Europe's coast
And isles of Asia. Look! the dragon prows
Of Viking ships that cleave the Atlantic waves,
While mailed, blond-bearded crewmen roar a toast
To Thor and Odin, bellow oaths and vows,
And crossing the waters, may be dashed to graves
Far-off, in chartless *Vineland*. Yet they make
Mere stabs and thrusts,
Flighty as summer gusts
Wrinkling the azure of a woodland lake,

While fear and distance still, like star-gulfs, sever
The New World from the Old, whose barriers seem forever.

III

High in the clouds that bounded the halves of the planet,
It seemed that I gazed upon beings who, mistily stirring,
With figures mighty as gods, and patriarch faces,
Were mantled in light, with trailing garments of vapor.
Many they were, and their brows were grave with reflection,
And sternly they gazed at the marvel of land and of ocean.
And one, with the whiteness of time on Olympian features,
Who seemed as the soul of the ages, thus uttered his wisdom:
" 'Let the waters divide!' was the ancient, the stirring
    commandment
Of Him who ordained the uniqueness of nations and peoples.
'Let the waters divide!' But time, in his rushing and flowing,
Demands that we see with new vision the crusted old order.
For now that the epochs whirl onward and man has arisen
To more than the plane of the bear and the fox and the badger,
It is ripe to throw open the gates and fashion the bridges
And bid him ascend to new peaks in his boldest adventure.
Let the seas become highways,
The harbors be hostels,
The fleets be his castles
To conquer the vastness!
Let him tremble, and wander
To ports of the sunset
In his bravest far-seeking,
His ultimate glory!
Thus man, newly plumed, shall be tested and tempered and
    proven,
If he ride on his way like a knight, heroic yet humble,

Or crawl like a beast in the swamp or a snake in the desert,
And squander the prizes that laboring ages have showered.
Behold! the waters no more shall be walls to divide him!"

High in the clouds that bounded the halves of the planet,
It seemed that I gazed upon beings who, mistily stirring,
With figures mighty as gods, and patriarch faces,
Were mantled in light, with trailing garments of vapor,
To flash me a sense of greatness, and epics unfolding
Where deep in the west there sparkled the star of the
           morning.

II. Explorers and Conquistadors

"Out of the flowered Indies"

Ginger and cinnamon and indigo,
Nutmeg and pepper, cloves and frankincense —
Here are the charms of harvests so immense
The dazzled centuries will watch them grow.
Here are decoys and bait
Dropped in man's shadow by old trapping fate
Out of the flowered Indies. Hardy fleets
Of ships, high-pooped and oaken-decked, will dare
The sea's unmarked Odyssean thoroughfare,
Where on the foamy blank the rover meets
No fellow but the dolphin and the whale.
And some will trim their sail
Down Africa's hot coast, and some will dream
Of spice, and silken-canopied Cathay,
And hauntingly on this theme
Fairylike myths and fables will portray
Great Khans and Marco Polos.

                              Nursed on these,
One musing youth, unburdened still by fame,
Seasoned among seafaring Genoese,
Stares at the distance with a witchfire aim:
To reach the perfumed eastern isles
By sailing west,
Shrinking immeasurable miles

In a novel quest.
Sturdy is he, and tall, and keen of glance,
And knows the ocean like a second home.
But more than courage, more than slippery chance
Must aid him to embark beneath the dome
Of unfamiliar stars. What destiny
Singles Columbus out amid the hosts,
Bidding him cleave the storm-ridged sunset sea
To strange new islands, undiscovered coasts?

    By the goad within his breast,
The vision that calls like song,
The flame of a fierce unrest
Unknown to the sparkless throng!—
By a dream unique and new
That is fueled night and day,
To captain a doughty crew
Over the western spray!—
By these, as though by barbs, he is spurred away, away.
Yet never will dreams suffice to clear a lane
Beyond the fogged horizon. Down the years,
Flitting through courts of Portugal and Spain,
He pleads, with little to show but promises and sneers.

    Upon how small a thread
Dangles the weight of empires! Now there breaks
A day when one invisible small strand
Might snap, and change the brow of many a land
Beyond the Atlantic rollers; and, instead
Of him before whose name a reverence wakes,
Some unknown John or Joseph might have led.
I see the wanderer, bleak though undefeated,
Packing his mule, leaving the jeweled court

Where the proud Spanish sovereigns have greeted
His pleas without the pledge he's tearfully sought.
Onward to France, to France!
With never a backward glance
He picks his way, when suddenly on his track
A clatter of hoofs, thudding from far behind,
Bids him to halt. A horseman fast draws near;
Displays an order. The Queen has changed her mind!
"Come back!" she makes command. "Come back, come back,
For now your way lies clear!"

        To us who travel in a patterned world
Whose flights are charted and whose trails are marked,
Whose mapless lands are few as uncrossed seas,
What voice shall utter the joy of sails unfurled
Where never a mariner before embarked,
Which might blow on to bright Hesperides
Or cannibal isles of Cyclops? Who shall limn
The glow, the agitation,
The wonder, and the fire of fresh elation,
The fear, like a wolf skulking, sheeted and grim? —
Fear of sea-serpents, fear of mountainous tides,
Fear of fanged goblins that the night-mist hides,
Fear of the waterspout, the death that rides
Screeching on hurricane wings; fear of the hush
Of petrifying calm; fear of the doom
Of venturing lost inside a billowy tomb;
Fear of the mysteries that bound, and crush
By Silence and vastness. Yet, above all dread,
The stinging urge, the everlasting lure,
Calling men to endure
Scornful of specters of the wave-washed dead.

All these the "Admiral of the Ocean Sea"
Dares with his crewmen, week on blustery week,
Trailed by the shadows of calamity
When over the swelling breasts of gray and green
The three small caravels bob forth to seek
A goal that seems remoter day by day.
Then day by day more querulous grow the men.
"When will we anchor?   *When?*
Reverse the rudders!   Head for home again!
Give up this madman's search
Before the deep, with one gigantic lurch
Shall bury us, or midnight monsters rise
With seven dragon mouths and snaky eyes,
And swallow us as lizards swallow flies!"

Threatened, beguiled, cajoled,
As westward the captain stares, and westward still,
The mutineers are controlled.
With desks washed clean by many a briny rill,
The vessels heave and wallow across the vast,
But ever beyond, beyond, new crests of white!
And then, a sign! a seabird fluttering past!
A fruited branch!   and, one tense fevered night,
Far-off, a winking light!

With wide, dark, luminous eyes,
Laughter and trembling and a tranced surprise,
The leather-brown nude Indians see the crew,
Decked with green crosses, wading forth to land.
Over them all, erect in shining mail,
Their master towers on the sea-wet sand,
Half like a god; the babbling innocents view,
Doubtful, not knowing whether to flee or hail

The regal visitants. But soon and well
The latter court them, win their guileless hearts
With caps of red, glass beads, the tinkling bell—
Magical baubles of the Spanish marts.

    Time's most enormous voyage has been made,
Pregnant with planet-shaking destinies.
But shadows and superstitions dim the light
Of the Caesar of explorers — mists of trade,
Mirages of rich-freighted argosies
And Kublai Khan's lush courts and salons, bright
A few isles distant. For his King and Queen
He claims the land, with that quaint western quirk
Which haughtily dusts aside the folk who dwelt
Perhaps since Abraham upon the scene.
Heathens are meant for tribute, cuffs and work!
So, while the captain reverently has knelt,
Thanking the wise Creator, in his mind
The germs already spread
Of terrors foul as typhus to strike dead
The simplest and the happiest of mankind,
Herding them forth from palm-green paradise
To drudge where dungeoned mines immure their sighs,
Or wilt on hot plantations, under the whip,
Till the heartsick worker dies.

    Oh, fabulous destiny, of spice and gold,
Which bore the New World greetings from the Old,
But to the island folk sent chains and graves,
Vacant tomorrow, and a tale soon told!

II

High in the clouds that bounded the halves of the
    planet
It seemed that I gazed upon beings who, mistily stirring,
With figures mighty as gods, and patriarch faces,
Were mantled in light, and trailing garments of vapor.
And out of the vastness a voice, low-toned with compassion,
Murmured, "O Man! we have acted! the portals fly open;
The path has been traced; no hand in all time shall expunge it.
Though you soar like an eagle, serene in your western
    far-seeking,
Are you clutching a fog when you might be enfolding
    a mountain?
Are you entering kingdoms of ashes, like Troy in her
    death-throes,
Your coffers made full and red from the blood of your
    brothers?"

Softly, by him who seemed as the soul of the ages,
With the whiteness of time on the crags of his Jovian
    features,
These questions were uttered; and softly the message
    continued,
"We who, cloud-pillowed, look down on human confusion,
May crave, as when ants go astray, to change your
    directions,
But man, having chosen his lamps, must follow their shining.
By the trails the discoverers make shall tomorrow be charted,
By the ridges or caves where they roam shall your sons and
    their children,
Long centuries hence, be haunted or blest or afflicted!"

The clouds, in a storm-fleet, drew round, and the
    figures had vanished,
And darkness lay deep on the ocean and prairie and summit,
But far in the west, through a shadowy rift in the ranges,
A light flickered weakly, rekindled, and slowly expanded.

III

New worlds to claim! New worlds beyond the sea!
Mountains of sapphire! Diamonds, pearls and gold!
Rose-tinted realms where towered Spain might be
Lost like one bloom in April's pageantry!
New worlds! New cities for the stanch and bold!
Avenues silver-paved, and mansions gemmed,
And people purple-robed and diademmed!

If having drudged in some poor town or farm,
You suddenly heard, sweet as a Siren strain,
This plea reverberating, would its charm
Not call you with a lyrical refrain?
Blue-rimmed horizons! glimmering wonderlands!
Colors that flashed innumerable as sands!
And many a virgin haunt
Of valley and forest, peak and waterfall!
And bouts of arms, gay as a gypsy jaunt!
And now and then perhaps the rollicking chance
To rise, a knight, a Roland of romance,
While saving your soul, you raised the Cross on high,
And bade the Church be hailed, and converts multiply!

In opening lands, by destiny's sad design
Rarely the bard, the scholar or the seer
Points an audacious prow across the brine

Or thrusts as conqueror or pioneer.
But they who drive and fight,
Venture and fend and slay,
Seldom have second sight
Piercing beyond today.
And thus with that swashbuckling, burly breed,
His Spanish Majesty's conquistadors,
Who cross the ocean, plunder the isles and shores,
And leave two continents to gasp and bleed.

IV

    Deep in a maze, through matted vine and thorn
Of an uncharted isthmus thick with trees,
Between the world's two most gigantic seas
Balboa's venturing band pushed on and on.
Clad in full armor, plagued by dripping heat,
Heedless of snakes twisting beneath their feet
And insects buzzing, sturdily they pressed
Where pallid skins were never seen before,
While rumors of water glittering leagues to west
Lured them like golden ore.

    And then — cool salty breezes, and a day
Time would remember! Climbing a hill alone,
The bearded captain stared
Where calm immense blue shimmering distance shone
Away, away, and far and far away.
Descending, he knelt, with pious head unbared;
By heaven's favor, for the King of Spain,
He claimed the sea, and all its ports and isles
Across uncountable miles,
Not guessing half the earth was covered by that domain.

V

A castle reared on termite-hollowed posts
Will sink more swiftly than a hut of clay,
Nor will it need a charge of Caesar's hosts
To strike the base away.
Proud Montezuma's kingdom, built on dread
And live heart-offerings of subject clans,
Buckled as though beneath a mound of lead,
And all the emperor's plans
Scattered and fell apart. Had his allies
Not fretted to escape his bloody vise,
He might have trapped the invading force, whose size
Was pygmy-small.
                              By some preposterous chance,
Wilder than any novel's scarlet weave,
Such as may color actual circumstance
With hues no mystery-reader would believe,
Old legends prophesied a god's return,
Pale-faced, black-bearded, from the eastern sea,
Just at the season when fate's weird decree
Called Montezuma, quaking, forth to learn
Of great white sails. On such a flimsy string
The life of tribes and dynasties may swing. .

"A madman's dream!   Worse than a madman's
        dream!" —
So the sane voice of prudence would have cried.
"A drunken sailor might have brewed the scheme! —
Four hundred men against the power and pride
Of a whole land!" Yet madmen's dreams may force
The rivers of time into a strange new course.

I looked on Cortes, fleeing the Cuban shore,
Hunted, an outlawed man
With ships that, like a robber caravan,
Wandered in hope of gold or silver ore.
Stern-browed, brilliant of eye,
With beard of pirate black,
Westward he voyaged on a chartless track,
His choice to dominate — to rule or die.
Armed with the bravery of the blind he went,
Swearing he'd venture to the sacred throne
Of Montezuma; swearing he would defy
The whole massed furies of a continent.
And well for him
That in the sovereign's mind the vexed unknown
Glowered, with questions shadowy but grim.
What if the god, Quetzacotl, should return
Incarnate in the Spaniard? He would be
Surely no guest to spurn!

Crowned by green feathers in a canopy,
Borne on a litter, gold and emerald starred,
With gilded mats, and flowers, and sweet perfume,
While nobles, with a reverent regard,
Trooped by in many a peacock gown and plume,
The monarch, Jove-like, perched upon his seat.
Long-haired, sparse-bearded, with pale ochre face,
He gestured with a slow, imperious grace
As four patricians spread a tapestry
And swept the ground beneath his sandalled feet.

Cortes, deferring to His Majesty,
Bristly dismounted from his chestnut horse
In a peaked helmet, with a bright steel dress,

And sun-tanned features whose assertive force
Equalled his manner's jaunty liveliness.
Freely, as when two old familiars meet,
He would have clasped the empire's holy lord,
Had not two servants, horror-faced, deplored
A move so intimate, so indiscreet.

    Yet none rebuked the wish. And who can say
What dark monitions bubbled up, to sway
Those deeper councillors even kings obey?
The emperor recalled
Stories of vast, miraculous Spanish powers:
Magical sticks booming like thunder showers
With vengeful lightning. He had heard, appalled,
Of maned man-headed stags dashing to fight
While the astonished earth shuddered in fright.
Rumors of massacre had stabbed his ears,
Of villagers prone beneath pale howling foes
As hail-storms of arrows and obsidian spears,
Feeble as straw, shattered on silver clothes.
And worse! with serpentine guile they had persuaded
Whole Indian populaces to their side,
Till Montezuma's vassal people raided
The mine of Montezuma's strength and pride.

    Still stranger the tendrils of fate,
Winding insidiously,
When later the potentate
Sinks like an axe-hewn tree,
Sinks groaning down the steeps of bottomless tragedy.
I see how resolution, daring all,
Puts shackles round the knees that waver in dread,
While the chained monarch cowers in the hall

Where once his feasts were spread.
I see him crumble, bleeding beneath a rock
Hurled by his riotous people; sag to earth
Less wounded by the stone than by the shock,
The mortal outrage to his royal birth.

Then, in the crimsoned central citadel,
I watch the white usurpers driven out
In a hooting, crashing bout.
Many, transfixed by arrows, stagger and yell,
Pulled down by gold they struggled to haul away,
And plunge like stones into the swallowing lake —
Less miserable than those the priests will slay
In furies of worship, clutching wrenched-out hearts
Low on the reeking altar-block, to slake
The insatiable war-god's thirst, and speed his gory darts.

After that dolorous night, a weaker chief,
Chin sunk on elbows, well might mourn his fall.
But stout-ribbed Cortes, built on princelier lines,
Traces new challenge bristling in his grief,
And by great toil and kingly new designs
Lives to announce another battle-call.

Among the towering tragedies of time —
Carthage and Troy, Jerusalem and Tyre —
When speared destroyers vomited steel and fire
And scattered ruin in a master crime,
Not least was Mexico. Behold the masses
Of natives heaving and tugging beneath the whip
Across the plain and over icy passes,
Dragging the parts of many a white man's ship —
A new-made squadron, soon to be assembled

On waters lapping round the Aztec throne.
And how the watchers must have stared and trembled,
Hearing the shrieking, swarthy braves who shone
In radiant plumes as Spanish sworn allies!

Vengeance that whooped like an abusive gale
Howled for these fighters, while the invaders' eyes,
Fastened on gold as on the Holy Grail,
Were savage as hawk-beaks. Now the old refrain
From cities stricken in a world gone by —
Seleucia, Nineveh and Babylon —
Sobbed on the wind their ageless grief and pain,
When hosts, in bloody quagmires, had to die,
And only death prevailed and famine won —
Havoc and desolation. Close the book!
Take not another look!
For the temples will soon be dust, the artisans hum no more,
The lakes will be drained away, the pyramids cease to soar,
And the tall white peaks alone will glitter as ever before.

The Aztec state, half like a fantasy
Of color and light, half like a bilious dream,
Had faded out — a ripple upon a stream —
And even the epic of its agony
Shrank from remembrance. Draw the curtain down!
Thus dies a world's renown,
And the glory of an empire and a crown!

V

Come, sing a song of conquerors,
Who govern with guns and brands,
And make of lily-petalled shores
Cratered and blackened lands!

Come, sing a song of conquerors,
Kissed by the lips of fame
For scarlet crumbling corridors
And barrens of smoke and flame!

Come, sing of conquerors, their arms
Laden with gold and ash!
Wreckage of capitals and farms
And spires of Romes they smash!

A dark example, like a luminous deed,
May plant itself in fructifying earth,
Scatter its fruit abroad, and sow its seed,
And come to life in many a far rebirth.
As Alexander, less a man than myth,
Lit flames beneath Napoleon's desire,
So Cortes, over several kingdoms' width,
Made a more ruthless ravager admire
His slashes of conquest. Ah, to emulate
Exploits that won him many a hundredweight
Of shining yellow metal! Such the thought
Kindled within Pizarro's wild-boar breast —
Pizarro, who had pressed
Balboa's murder, and had boldly fought
In seas and jungles.
                    Once a herder of swine,
He was of that fierce species sometimes met
In daggered Zulus and wild Mongol lords.
His passion was gold, his creed was spears and swords,
While raw ambition stirred his head like wine
And his crackling spirit scoffed at every threat.
Courting the King of Spain,
The Emperor Charles, whose dull-complexioned brain

Groped all in vain
To picture the argent West, Pizarro pleaded
Not only treasure vaults but souls to save.
And this devout appeal the sovereign heeded,
And grandly gave
What was not his — the right to seize Peru
And loot its wealth. So with the ringing name
Of Governor, Pizarro picked a crew,
Sailed south from Panama, and overcame
Natives and cactus spines. The rumor lured them
Of a bright monarch on a studded seat,
Ruling a kingdom which, the tale assured them,
Glittered with gold in every hall and street.

     Strangely, once more,
Must chance, blank drooling idiot chance, decide
If nations lived or died,
And random as a gust, swing open the door
To terror and doom? Old legends, well revered
By Incan folk, told of a deity,
Good Virococha, pale of face and beard —
And might the pallid wanderers not be
Sons of the god? — So would the questions go,
And doubts, like maggots, bred; while casual fate
Dealt in the dark a still more wounding blow:
Two royal brothers, fending to take the crown,
Loosened its whole foundations, split the state
Just when the conqueror bellowed at the gate,
And ripped it like some old wormeaten gown.

*   *   *

    Deep in the cordilleras, under a frosty sky,
Where the black alpacas wander and the condors wheel
    and fly,

The invading columns spiral, grumbling beneath their load,
With armored men and horses, strung on the Incan road.
And why does their Captain lead them forth to the world's
      bleak end?
And when will the tinkling showers of silver and gold
      descend?
After their strain and struggle with hunger and sickness
      and thirst,
By Christ!   they must not perish in the ice-cold wilds
      they've cursed.

      "Forward!" Pizarro cried, gritting his teeth.
"Forward! Let him who chooses answer, 'No!'
But he who fails me leaves his bones beneath
Andean rock and snow!"
So none dissented.   And there came a day
The pen of history would inscribe in red.
In Cajamarca, where stone stairways led
To a stone fortress, squatting huge and gray,
The townsfolk, wonder-eyed and hushed with awe,
Flocked to the mountain-shadowed central square,
And trembled as monsters bristled everywhere.

      But why the peril never a seer foresaw?
Why had the Inca shouted
No thundering command
When still he might have routed
The ravishers of his land?
Why had his arrowed legions
Not clustered against the foe
High in the crag-bound regions
And plunged them to gulfs below?
Surely, the Emperor could not conceive

What treachery befouled the white man's heart,
Nor, in his eaglelike hauteur, believe
He could not tear the barbarians apart
At a mere nod. And so was spun the net
Soon to entrap his feet; the tragic stage was set

Atahuallpa, who had wrenched his power
From a half brother, smiled with kingly grace.
A crimson headdress, like a blazing tower,
Loosed its long fringes over half his face;
Two feathers, black and white, betokened his high place.
And round his litter, in a reverent throng,
Vicuna-robed, pale blue and rosy-hued,
Nobles attended him, six hundred strong,
Though by his order, all that multitude
Came without arms. Thus would the strangers know
They might arrive in peace, safe from a lurking blow.

Close-ranged about the square, the people waited —
Brown friendly faces, doglike eyes of black —
And who of the thousands that participated
Could have foreseen the panther-sly attack,
As suddenly, swiftly made
As a sea-borne Viking raid?
Forward, with a great yell, the Captain sprang;
Chillingly on his lips the war-cry rang
Of "Santiago!" Then the world was dashed
To crazed confusion, with the rattle and clang
Of armor, where artillery boomed and crashed —
The fire of arquebuses, thrust of swords,
Clatter of horsemen, and the shrieks and screams
Of women and men fleeing in panic hordes
And falling by packs in oozy bright-red streams,
While chaos still wailed on.

                              The first onslaught
Might have unthroned the prince. But vehemently,
Almost with naked hands,
The gay-clad guardsmen of the litter fought,
Until Pizarro shouldered aside the bands
Of his shrill comrades, undismayed to see
His own hand bleeding. "Spare him!" he burst out.
And even amid the madman's rush and whirl
None could ignore his shout.
Down from a seat of parrot plumes and pearl
They dragged the Inca; tore his crown and robe.
Unwounded, stunned, in outrage and dismay,
He who had perched as sovereign of the globe
Was suddenly fenced within a spined array
Of swords and armor; saw a face of stone
Look haughtily down; heard his own terror say,
"Thus ends your reign and throne!
You are a prisoner!"
                              No grand design
Of statecraft, and no empire-founding goals
Inspired the conqueror, whose wolf-intent
Leered from the yellow fruitage of the mine,
Though sanctimonious talk of saving souls
Was strangely blent
With moans and wails of a looted continent.
Midas himself might well
Have turned an envious green
And writhed in covetous rage could he have seen
What now befell.
If the Inca packed a hall
Brimful from wall to wall
With gold, bright solid gold, it was agreed
He would be freed.

And so he promised. If the fools desired
Far more than ever a mortal man required
Of this gross rock they crazily admired,
Let them receive it! Scour the land, and bring
The golden crab and beetle, bird and ring!
Now they'd release him! . . . But when he had filled
The room neck-high, Pizarro's order shrilled:
"Atahuallpa, traitor, has conspired
Against our safety! Let him then be killed!"
Surely, great God above,
Fount of benignity and well of love,
Never had heard His name more vainly spoken
Than by this bloody-sleeved kidnapping gang —
Robbers whose pledge, like belts of sand, was broken —
Assassins who, without a throb or pang,
Battered an empire down. Yet in His name,
Hear holiness declaim!
Behold the stake piled high, where lustral flame
May burn the sinner clean!

And now the grisly culminating scene,
Like some macabre vision Goya drew.
Gripped in brute hands, dragged to the stake, and tied,
The Emperor wore a weight of chain, and knew
Life's frenzied tragedy was almost through.
Yet he could hear wry tongues of irony
Mocking him through the tatters of his pride
While priest-lips bargained. Gracious charity
Would ease his torment if he but espoused
His persecutors' creed and thus insured
His soul from deathless pangs. So was he lured
To the new faith, so let himself be doused
In holy water. With his dying gaze

He watched the judges drown his last dim hope,
When mercy spared him from the roasting blaze
But choked him with a rope.
More than a man was murdered. For the hand
That pulled the strangling noose, had toppled down
A tower no conqueror could understand —
A whole society fell with the crown.

To gold, all-conquering gold, the praise be given,
That one more nation had been gouged and riven,
Its art-works lost or melted, its subjects scattered,
Its terraces dust-smothered, its temples shattered —
To gold, all-conquering gold, while squadrons, sailing,
Tap a new treasure-trove that seems unfailing —
Faint, faint and far, who hears a people's wailing?
Let weighted argosies
In kingdoms overseas,
Give nurture to new wars, new victories —
Faint, faint and far, who hears a people's wailing?

VI

And yet a few did rise in saintly white
Above the wolves and foxes, bears and boars
That dashed, fang-snapping, to the New World's shores.
High overhead I saw them lift a light
Of pity through the dark, for those sad hosts
Scarred by the boot or brand, or lashed to whipping posts.

Bishop Las Casas, born the princely heir
To lands and slaves, startlingly saw the truth:
How servitude, sharp as a dragon's tooth,
May strip man's spirit bare.
For he had learned what all the enlightened know:

That not from slant of eye or shade of skin
But from the sunlight of the self within
Our living values flow.
And he had witnessed, like a father pained,
The requisitioners of bleeding hearts
Herding the captives, stoop-necked, roped and chained,
Down to the labor marts.
In mines where beaten slaves, with heads low-bent,
Drudged in the heat, blistered like fiends in hell,
And on plantations where the masses went,
Too grieved to last, too hopeless to rebel,
He saw men's nerves and brawn and selfhood offered —
Blood-sacrifices, even as victims proffered
At reeking fanes of Babylonian Bel.
Deeds so unhallowed, scenes so vile, he swore,
Must foul the world no more.

Low on his knees in Spain before the King,
I heard him argue for the persecuted,
And to the colonies I saw him bring
Balm for the torn, and treasure for the looted.
Surely, one man against a world's great need
Was but a fragile reed
To halt the tentacles of rage and greed.
But through the years of toil and vain appealing,
At last he brought medicaments, and healing
Like sunbeams filtered through a sooty ceiling.

* * *

But healing, love and mercy could not win
The slaving captains, tracing the things to be,
Who stole the Negro from his shack and kin
And hustled him off to sea.

Far out, across the white-capped vast, I heard
In England, Spain and Portugal, this word:
"Grow rich!   Grow rich!   A mountainous treasure haul
Is waiting for all, for all!"
So tortured hearts beat fast, and gave no peace.
And vessels, on the South Atlantic swell,
Plowed up a lengthening wake that would increase
For centuries to come,
Witnessing scenes of weird delirium
Wilder than Dante's hell,
When chained black thousands, squeezed into a press
Like hens squawking in coops on market day,
Sweltered and groaned in sweaty nakedness,
While the tossed ships swung on the dancing spray
And sharks slid round them wide-mouthed, waiting for prey
Hurled lifeless overboard.

                                    And who took heed?
Why waste a thought, indeed?
Cheap was man's flesh, and more and more remained.
But far in isles where cane and cotton grew,
And deep in mines that must renew, renew
Their breathing fuel, workers might be chained —
So let the slave-ships cleave the merry blue!
In the name of trade, trade, trade,
The trappers and tamers of men
In many a pirate raid,
Must plunder and slash, and then
With the booty trailing low
In a hooped and roped parade,
Deal the limb-wrenching blow
In the name of trade, trade, trade.
In the name of trade, trade, trade,

Push on! push on! although remembering time,
Which sees tomorrow's huts and mansions reared
On hills we gouged and timberlands we cleared,
Will not condone one sin, forget one crime.

III. Colonists, Warriors and Trappers

"Such challenge as rarely was met . . ."

Like a dream it returned, a dream that recurs and
  refreshes —
The vision of cloud-mantled beings who, mistily stirring,
With figures mighty as gods, and patriarch faces,
Were mantled in light, with trailing garments of vapor.
And out of the vastness a voice was upraised, clearly speaking:

"Behold! where the mountains and streams of the
  north, and the prairies
And deserts reach out, and forests and lakes are extended,
Such challenge as rarely was met since the cave-folk
  migrated
From thrust of the cold or dread of the wolf or the grizzly,
Awaits your descendants! such challenge of peril and
  courage,
Of hardship and patience, starvation and terror and striving,
As gauges the depth of a man and the breadth of a people!
But not in a day, and only by epochs and cycles
Shall we, from above, count ultimate credits or losses.
Go forth! as the trustees of lands, but not their despoilers,
Creators of cities and states, whose glory and fortune
Are the pulse and the surging and light of the manhood
  within you!"

38

Far in the clouds hanging low over half of a planet,
Shone beings, Olympian-browed, who murmured,
  "Oh, witness
New vistas unravel, and ever new vistas beyond them,
And ever new vistas, new struggle, in strangeness and
  wonder,
Of life brightly kindled. — Oh, gaze at the drama
  unfolding!"

                    * * *

I saw the whole gray-green Atlantic span
Crisscrossed with lines as in a mariner's chart,
And on those lines, seeming without a plan,
I watched the small exploring craft depart
From Spain and England. Some, mist-belted, roamed
To Arctic barrens where the sea-fowl shrieked
And icebergs glared in mountains, white and beaked;
Some dared the waves that treacherously combed
Islets and headlands. From the creaking decks
The wool-clad captains gazed forlornly north,
Sometimes past shoals and wrecks,
Looking to see clear channels beckon forth
To sunrise lands beyond the sunset fires.
And roamers of the burning South, in quest
Of Cibola's cities, peaked with golden spires
And golden-palisaded, pushed to west
Through purple heights and mesas. Mythic lore,
More than the hard rock-truth, exclaimed, "Explore!"

Yet brave, more lion-brave than we today
Can hazily estimate,
And stanch and spined with hardihood were they
Who dared to emigrate.

Think! with no houses, crops or measured bounds,
No certainty from Indians, health or weather,
No likelihood except of burial mounds,
To band with strangers, rolling all together
Week after week through chartless vasts!   I saw
Again the ironic law
That rules us by the things we do not know;
Bids ignorance swagger, trumpeting of a might
Wisdom would never show,
As when two roosters, driven to bloody fight,
Are unaware of spurs.   Then may we be
Dupes of veiled powers that no man understands,
Striking with arms that slash invisibly
To goad us onward to new seas and lands?

     "Virginia!" rang the cry.   "A coast as fair
As ever the westward-turning heart could ask!"
And like rash boys, men leapt to meet the dare,
Not seeing the skull-bones through the rosy mask.
Now came impetuous Raleigh, sanguine-lipped,
Dreaming the birth of buzzing colonies —
Foretelling not the roofless wanderers, shipped
To famine, Indian scalp-knives and disease.
Yet many stayed alive
Where most were swallowed, sinewed by that will
To conquer and survive
Through which alone the sons of man fulfill
A place above the scorpion and the snail.

     And one there was among the common crowd
Who seemed rock-fortified, a knight endowed
To battle and prevail —
John Smith his homely name; his face as strong

As a mountain bear's; sharp humorous eyes that peered
Out of a straight-nosed face; a brushy beard,
And voice fire-edged to overcome the throng.
Of him strange tales were spoken: shipwreck, fights
With sworded enemies he battered low,
Slavery in Turkey, and daredevil flights,
And hot romances when he played the beau
To Oriental belles.   And stranger still
The story often told, of that dread day
When blades were levelled to kill
And Princess Pocahontas, slim and young,
On a passionate impulse, flung
Her own lithe quivering form between, to stay
The executioner's hand.

                              Fiction and fact
Here meet and mingle in a radiant haze,
And hard it is for even the keenest gaze
To pick the fable from the living act.
But this men swear: John Smith was hewn of oak,
Such timber as has tamed a continent,
And deep in woods where wolf-packs howled, awoke
A striding spirit and a steeled intent.
Like the tough skipper of a mutinous bark
I saw him stalk at Jamestown, shouting abroad
The orders all must hark,
Till sluggards worked, the country was explored,
Corn had been planted, whips and chains lashed down
On wranglers, friends were made of Indian foes,
Who came with laden arms, and houses rose
In a palisaded town.
Had Smith remained, the question vainly runs,
Under the checkrein of this able master

Might not Virginia and Virginia's sons
Have skirted the quicksands and defied disaster?

    If ever nature raised a hand
To pick the true and best,
She sifted with a deft command
The stalwarts sailing west.

    She shuffled off as incomplete
The settlers who would sow
Tobacco in the central street
But had no corn to hoe.

    She flung aside the drones who leaned
Idly on brothers' arms
And ate the grain their brothers gleaned
From common plots and farms.

    With tomahawks and knives she slew
Hundreds who learned, dismayed,
That hate and wrong would only brew
The screaming Indian raid.

    Yet, they who, struggling, met the test,
They were the breed of man
By whom, in many a burning quest,
A nation's rise began.

II

    White were the breakers on a rocky shore,
And white the ground beneath bare creaking trees,
And white the look the new arrivals wore,

With prayers, and sighs, and veiled anxieties.
But thankful the tears and murmurs that, at last,
After long bouts with scurvy and despair,
After rat-crowding in the cavelike hold
And weeks of tossing on the fluctuant vast,
And groans, and tight-lipped vigils weighed with care,
The *Mayflower* found the port that all foretold.
Brave would he be, but blind
And reckless and contemptuous of grief,
Who even in his relief
Looked to the morrow with untroubled mind.
And well that none could know
That when the spring, with azure innocent sky
And bursting buds, replaced December snow,
Half that courageous company would lie
Mute underground. But still men battled on.
I saw them staring, staring at the sea
Whose ridges and swinging gray immensity
Reminded them bitterly of all things gone,
Kindred and home, while mist-banks gathered round
Or the storm-trumpets made a shrilling sound,
And never on earth could lonelier souls be found.

How iron-ribbed is faith, whose preachments bring
Settlers to capes and islands overseas,
Beckoned by ghosts to far adventuring
From guarded ports and ease!
They who went pitching in the Pilgrim barks —
I saw them, straight of lip, disdaining mirth,
Like Noahs driven in rude private arks
Across a flooded earth.
I watched them in the plain, high-seated church,
With guns and prayer books, hunched against the cold,

Awed at the pastor's brimstone words, his search
For grace and spirit-gold.
A startling mixture — thunderclouds and ice,
Blooddrops and flint within the same hard pew,
Hickory sinews, flame of sacrifice,
Clods of the common earth, and vials of rue,
The wild bird's passion to go soaring free,
The zealot's cry for God, the zealot's fire
That scourges freedom as iniquity
Unless it wear his gyves, his squeezing wire.
Yet mark the strength to rear
Mansions and counting houses! Mark the will
To strive with grinding teeth, to persevere
Though storm-banks gather and the gale blows shrill.
Here are good solid strands
To weave into the fabric of new lands!

For folk so gray, drab-mantled and devout,
The unseen weavers of the abusive years
Patterned in devious cloths with varied shears
And hues sometimes arresting as a shout.
I watched the doors swing wide
For coppery comrades bearing fish and maize,
But saw a gust of arrows whizz and blaze
Against the hut which women, screaming, tried
To barricade, even as the whooping foe,
Dancing like hell-flames, swinging tomahawks high,
Circled more near . . . I saw suspicions grow,
Noxious as broths that poisoners apply,
And one nightmarish dread
Suckled at Salem — dread, and its daughter, hate:
That witches, ghastly as the risen dead,
Riding on midnight brooms, would congregate

With demons of Satan.   Hear that wrinkled dame
Gibbering to herself — for shame, for shame! —
She mumbles spells of blackest wizardry!
For she it was who summoned the northeast gale
To sink the floundering brig!   And who but she
Ordered the babes to die, and crops to fail?

So the commotion grew, the trial court rose.
Both sexes, old and young,
Were shaken and unstrung
By pointing fingers, deadlier than blows,
And gossips hissing, muttering, who declared
They saw the Dark One come, his brew prepared.
Crazed as the bomb-scare of a later age,
Fear, evil councillor, demented guide,
Seethed in the minds of able men and good,
Stormed over them like an inrushing tide,
Extinguished pity in a swirl of rage,
Where, grim with fruit, the new-built gallows stood.

And now a scarcely less ill-omened scene:
Anne Hutchinson, severe and matronly, faced
Gray persecutors in a growling court.
And what, they snapped, did her mad capers mean?
Not that she was intemperate or unchaste —
She whose sweet charity had often brought
Balm to the ailing! — but they asked to hear
How could she claim the right to sermonize
To other dames of Boston?   God, all-wise,
Granted the weaker sex but one career.
Besides, she erred in doctrine.   Let her then
Be banished, clearing thus the town's fouled air!
But stoutly she retorted, "What, good men,

And who was wronged?" They answered with a stare
Of stormy scorn. And so she had to live —
She and her children — where the wild deer strayed,
Leagues from her friends and home, a fugitive
Till felled at last beneath an Indian blade.

Harried like Anne, and driven from the fold,
Was Roger Williams — preacher true and tried,
Whose claims, men thought, were dangerously bold
And quite unsanctified.
Proving him darkly on the Devil's side,
He urged an impious right: to disagree,
With man's own conscience crowned as sovereign, free
To judge, undisciplined as a flying bird.
And hear these vaporings, not less absurd:
"What of the Indians?   What of *their* claim?
Remember that their fathers' bones were here
Ages before we came,
And to their hearts ancestral fields are dear.
Even with royal orders, what our right
To land their tribe bequeathed them?   If they fight,
Who first found haven in the law of might?"

"Out! Out with him! Out, heretic! Traitor! Out!"
Clamored the elders, with a hounding shout.
Deep was the rogue's transgression: to deny
Assumptions few had ever thought about.
And so the Ismael went
Forth to the wilderness, the wind and snow,
Roaming the night without a crust or tent,
Living by struggles God alone could know.
Ragged and wan and thin,
Gratefully he would find a dwelling-place

In smoky wigwams of the forest race,
Whose sons he hailed as kin.

But soon a mightier drama flashed to view.
Blown by a storm across a white-capped bay,
Showered with spray,
Fearing to capsize, yet propelled by need
Like that of one who sees his house afire,
Williams rode forward in a bark canoe.
Long, in a heated powwow, he would plead
With Narragansett friends: "Put out your ire,
And scorn the Pequots!" While the Pequot chiefs
Plotted a thrust, haranguing in disdain
Of settlers and their rabbit-souled beliefs,
Williams foresaw the peril all too plain:
The slithering approach, the mass attack,
The howling braves, the village slashed and black,
The blood-red victims arrow-pierced and scalped,
The prisoners tortured, all New England racked
By raids and conflagrations. From the worst
Of this vast doom, the people now were saved,
Rescued by him they cursed —
This outlaw at whose sins the preachers railed and raved.

Now I observed him stand
Waving a paper with a solemn smile
Among a feathered, deerskin-wearing band.
And not by force or guile
But armored with understanding rarely known
Between the savage traders and the whites,
He gained his land, with clear and open rights,
Where Providence would be a city grown,
And stout Rhode Island, among the colonies,

Would rise, a fortress tower of liberties.
And yet — as when an actor walks the stage
Before the watchers at a pantomime
Wearing the costume of too late an age,
Oddly the shifter of the scenes of time
Miscast the rebel, cloaking him in views
His grandsons would embrace, and his brothers would abuse.

III

A rapier at his side, and richly decked,
His long hair hanging loose in wavy strands
Over his shoulders in a foppish mode,
He was not one the observer would expect
To cleave deep pathways into trackless lands
Or shape a nation-building episode.
Yet see young William Penn
Staring defiance of a red-faced sire
Who'd doughtily led a squadron, braving fire
In the Dutch wars. The father's fists are clenched.
"Perhaps you'll tell he, then,
What means this? Had you gambled, drunk or wenched,
I might forgive you. But to be cajoled
By fools! by spineless Quakers! Son, give heed!
Be strong of arm, and bold
And valorous like fighters of our breed!
Put off this folly!"

But he might as soon
Have argued with the wind to change its tune.
For some are born as though immutable ends
Have stamped their hearts; as though some mightier will
Commands them to fulfill
Missions of love to which their whole life trends.

Beneath that regulating destiny
Which bids the snowstorm nurse the sprouting grass,
In time it came to pass
The Admiral, not by his wish, would be
The sinews of a Quaker colony.
For his great riches, which death little heeded,
Offered young William means that William needed.

Many a seer, before and after Penn,
Has drawn bright pictures of a happier earth,
Where truth and justice are the law for men
And virtue the barometer of worth.
But only to few has poker-playing fate
Dealt out the cards to fructify the dream,
Erect a commonwealth, and populate
The wasteland with a burgeoning new regime,
Where, scorning the tyrant's ancient power-thirst,
Not government but man is honored first.

Vast was the lift and spread
Of his green paradise, a sylvan zone
Of lake and plain and mountain watershed,
Greater than many kings could call their own.
And what of the Indian who claimed the land?
Unlike those lords who, crying "Slay!" and "Seize!",
Hoped their contemptuous words would countermand
All titles of the aborigines,
Here was a royal leader who would treat
Redmen as mates and equals. Not by force,
Whose very triumph brings the soul's defeat,
But only by brotherhood he'd steer his course.

So did he promise. He whose missile clove
A native skin, no less must make amends

Than he whose irresponsible bullet drove
At the white brethren, truly known as "Friends."
"Come, seal a pact!" he urged . . . Under the shade
Of a tall elm, his legate Markham smoked
The pipe of peace, and piously invoked
The Great White Spirit's supernatural aid
To bless the treaty. "While the moon and sun
Flame in the sky, and green spring branches bud,
Never we'll shed a drop of Quaker blood,"
The Indians chanted. And the years went by,
And spouting crimson streams began to run
In sadder colonies, but where the law
Of Penn endured, no settler had to die
Transfixed in arrowy war.

      Only to him who comes with peace in hand
Peace shall be given — such his rule of life.
And he who enters with a gun or knife
Bids terror, like a maniac, snatch command —
Here is the simple creed
Penn carried like a scripture; here the seed
For lack of which great lands and tortured centuries bleed.

IV

      But rare as bards in a boiler mill
Captains like Penn appear,
And rare the man so tempered of will,
So selfless and sincere.
Far from his sage example, splashes of red,
Crisscrossing many a smoking town and farm
As from a ceaseless hemorrhage, were spread
To distant trail-ends, after the sharp alarm,
"The redskins come! They come! Defend! Defend!"

I gazed on slim and mocassined padding shapes
Like phantoms drifting down the forest track —
Shadows with which the leaf-shades seemed to blend —
Each in a leader's footsteps, stooped like apes,
With bow or tomahawk poised for sly attack,
And dark eyes staring. Then the screaming clash,
The fiery arrow, and the scalping blade,
Bawling and yells of children, muskets' flash,
And oaths and shrieks of folk who fought and prayed . . .
Till there remained only an empty glade
Spattered with black and scarlet. Now and then
I marked pale weeping women driven along
To forest wigwams, mates of savage men;
But not on one side only was the wrong.

    I heard that merciless call,
Older than Baal, by which the guiltless fall
In retribution for the bloody sin
Charged to their kin.
Chilled and agape, I saw
White raiders gathering clotted scalps for fees,
White blades unlimbing even the babe and squaw.
I watched again the age-old act rehearsed
By which all man's advancement is reversed
And war ignites old wildcat savageries.
I looked on redmen swinging the hunters' bow
With paleface comrades; redmen, snaky-eyed,
Smiting their wisest and their best, who died
In some mad Brutus blow.
But even had they joined their wide resources
And struck the whites with congregated forces,
What of the end? . . . There came the tramp, tramp, tramp
Of disembarking warrior hosts who told

That, almost as by ordinance of fate,
Death had impressed his stamp:
Muskets and numbers must predominate,
And Europe's flags would float where wigwams stood
      of old.

V

    I turned to quiet of the northern lakes,
Across whose meditative summer mood
Scarcely a murmur, scarcely a ripple breaks,
While trees, like pictures, line the solitude.
There, where the waters glisten clear and cool
As though delivered from earth's primal springs,
And rarely a paddle dips into a pool,
And rarely a sound but of a passing school
Of wild geese jars upon the dateless dream,
I found the trigger of earth-shaking things.
Bordered by woods, I saw the shallop float
With bearded passengers; and paused to note
The arquebuses' sullen steely gleam,
While squadrons of birch canoes
Pushed in the wake, their bronze harsh-featured crews
Gaudy with war-paint, knifed and hatchet-bearing,
Arrowed and feather-wearing.

    "Hurons, rejoice! The Great White Father's thrust
Will send your enemies sprawling to the dust!
Follow my lead! In me, Champlain, have trust!"
So spoke the paleface captain. Then they rode
Into a lake where scattered tree-clad isles
Jutted amid the azure glimmering miles,
Breasted with mountains, like a king's abode.
There, in a Merlin spell,

Peace should forever dwell,
Peace and her partner beauty. And yet there,
Where silence seemed forever, men decreed
Clamor and puff and flare —
Ensanguined strife — the shrill bone-shattering deed.

One evening, far across the clear expense,
They saw canoes — a sudden warrior fleet
Low in the water! and they rode to meet
The enemy's advance
Hooting raw insults. "Iroquois!" they yelled.
"Black wolves of Iroquois!" Still hurling jeers
They paddled close, till they almost beheld
Their rivals' haughty lips wrinkling in sneers.
"Then will you fight?" . . . "Being men, we'll fight,"
    they shouted,
"Tomorrow when the sun-god lights the shore.
Let mouse-hearts flee today! Else you'll be routed
And your thin blood will pour
As foam upon the sand!" And while this gibe
Screeched from the challenged tribe,
The Iroquois moved landward. After dark,
When fireflies gemmed the shore with blinking lamps,
Many a signal-light and spiralling spark
Rose in the brooding camps.

Straight-limbed and tall, the nude brown warriors
    stood
With arrogant eyes defiant as a bear's,
Contemptuous in their strength and hardihood,
Scourging their enemies with taunting stares.
And did no monitor within the breast
Warn of the ambushed peril coiled to smite,

Whose angry nemesis would be expressed
Often in blood-streaks of a later fight?
Three chiefs, with plumes of white,
Led on the host, without presentiment
That pitiless strategies
Of hairy battle-lords from overseas
Would change a continent.

Under a robe within a beached canoe,
Champlain lay waiting for the signal cry.
Then what a prodigy shot into view!
Truly, a spirit from the sun-bright sky,
A veritable god,
With shining breast-piece, and a shiny rod
That roared commandments in the crash and crack
Of thunder, while men watched in stiffened dread
Lightning spout forth . . . till suddenly, on his back,
A chief lay gasping and red.

Undaunted by this dastardly bolt, which seemed
As though great heaven itself had joined the fray,
Might not the Iroquois have still redeemed
Their honor, saved their name, and won the day?
But what new apparitions flashed to being!
From other beached canoes, two giants sprang;
More thunder snapped and rang,
And soon the fire-raked tribesmen all were fleeing.
Screaming, the foe pursued them; many fell,
Writhing in Huron hands,
And roped in deerskin bands
Were noisily carried off; and stakes arose;
And mocking the victims' dying groans and throes,
The captors capered and danced like fiends in hell.

And it may be, as some maintain,
That thus the French unlocked
A doorway to the north domain
Which Hurons might have blocked.
Yet deep the shadows that descend
When treachery and murder blend
To cull however prized an end.

And palisades of France would fall,
And forts and farms be scarred,
While by the fierce Five Nations' gall
The trail of France was barred.
Yes, there may be rich crops to reap,
But never the ghosts of vengeance sleep
Where treachery and murder creep.

VI

To woodlands where the wide Saint Lawrence runs,
And westward, close to those fresh-water seas
That feed Niagara, rushed the well-armed sons
Of France, throughout adventurous centuries.
Yet never adventure drew the rovers forth
More than the pelts of beaver, bear and fox,
Marten and mink — a bottomless supply!

But others, ranging the forests of the north,
Had simpler aims: to teach the brown-skinned flocks
To serve the Just and High.
I watched the long-robed Jesuit Fathers mix
With murmurous children of the wigwam, armed
Only with Holy Book and crucifix.
And many went unharmed —
Alas, not all! Devouringly on some
Would fall the fire of courted martyrdom.

Courage was theirs, courage beyond demands
Of warriors storming castles. Thus I saw
Father Le Jeune, whose lacerated hands,
Smitten as by a crocodilian jaw
In Indian torture bouts, did not suffice
To hold him from the missionary trail,
Although he pictured well the grisly coming price.

And then, beloved by all
Whom his paternal care would never fail,
Father Brébeuf, a figure huge and tall,
With smiling countenance and long soft hair.
"Enchon," they dubbed him, an affectionate name,
And gladly his friends the Hurons would exclaim
To see him towering near — his graybeard form
Which hour on hour, along a leafy track,
Would bend beneath a pack
In sleet and rain, in snow or thunderstorm,
Or paddle whole summer days in heaped canoes.
And yet — his childlike cheer
Was overshadowed by a gloom, a fear
Which he would shrug away but could not lose.

Long, with solicitous grace,
He ministered to the children of the wild,
Till the snug mission houses were in place
And tended acres smiled
With apple trees, and grain in yellowing crops;
And kitchens steamed, and proudly he gazed on shops,
Chapels, and half-built forts . . . Then they were trapped
By that dark fury fuming in man's heart
Which, ever since the first Sumerian dart
Smashed down on townsfolk as they toiled or napped,

Has cursed our species. An audacious plot,
Malign as witches' potions, had been brewed
In the long houses of the Iroquois,
Whose eagle-feathered braves had not forgot
Their tribal enmity, their hissing feud,
And now were like coiled vipers to destroy
The Huron nation. At the fell first stroke
Chaos erupted, and the whirlwind woke.

Chaos erupted when three Hurons ran,
Crazed-eyed and gasping, into the settlement.
"People, O hear us! Hear us! Hear! O, hear!
Our homes lie splintered — charred! No breathing man
Stirs at Saint Ignace now! The foes' descent
Was swift as the wolf-pack's on the cornered deer!
So flee! Flee! Flee!"

Almost as though the ground
Jarred upward in an earthquake's savagery,
Women and children shrieked, flew round and round,
And scattered with a loud commingled tone
Of terror; while, with stoic brows of stone,
Stood eighty Hurons, brusquely challenging,
"What! Fear the Iroquois? We're strong as they,
And do not shake like hunted does! We'll swing
Brave tomahawks, and stay!"

And Father Brébeuf? Joining the panic flight,
Could he not scurry to a safe retreat,
And by a guarded hearth one day recite
The tale of massacre and dire defeat?
Not by self-conscious will, but by the flame
Of his life-mission, his entire life-aim,

His course was kindled when the crisis came.
He'd not desert his children! Long and shrill,
A whoop broke horribly through the air, a howl
As of all hell's accumulated ill,
While watchers saw, below,
Topknots of lean marauders on the prowl.

    But Enchon and a gaunt old brother priest
Remained, and never ceased
To salve men's wounds, and stanch their bright red flow,
And bless the dying as the fray increased,
While the wide-billowing onpouring hosts
Leapt like weird shadows bounding beyond the Styx.
The Hurons, seeing feathered shafts transfix
Their kin, and dozens bleeding, lashed to posts,
Waited their grim last chapter.

                       Enchon, too,
And his brave fellow fighter, felt the cords
Of moosehide sink into the flesh, and knew
All dread forebodings now were coming true
Just as he'd long foretold. Pull down the screen
Upon the blistering torture, like a scene
Staged in madhouses of some rabid world
Where lunatics are lords! Fury wiped clean
The village and the mission; dashed to dust
The Huron nation, yet could not erase
The memory of a calm, gray-bearded face,
With eyes upraised in trust
To One whose princely purposes explain
And justify all loss, all martyrdom and pain.

VII

But what of the miles upon measureless miles
      outreaching,
Cobwebbed with rivers and lakes and coated with forests,
And spreading to mountains and prairies immense as an
      ocean?
There, for the true and brave-hearted, a summons, a
      challenge
Was calling, a beacon to distances burning with wonder,
Where danger and death were entwined, and courage was
      godhood.
There, out of the clouds, great beings, mistily stirring,
All mantled in light, with trailing garments of vapor,
Commanded, "O Man, over ruins of ramparts and towers,
Press on! through meadows once dark with the shapes of
      the fallen!
Press on to new channels, new highways, new harbors, new
      summits.
But see! how like clouds as they drift round the head of
      an Atlas,
The actors appear, are applauded and dazzle and vanish
In a drama immortal as time and young as tomorrow!"

      And now another form, as on a screen,
Stalked in that wild northeast of white and green.
His hat was plumed, the scarlet brim down-turning,
His mantle silken gray beneath the wig.
His eyes, hawk-bright, were steely and discerning;
Sharp was his chin, his nose was ridged and big.
The Comte de Frontenac and retinue
Of armed retainers, stood about a deck
And watched some rock-bound houses rise to view,
Lost in the waste of river and wood, a speck

He came to govern, and would govern well,
And dominate as with an emperor's spell —
The fortress town, Quebec.

Behold the river conference he sought
With the Five Nations, and his lush display
And pomp as of a court,
His peacock-feathered men, their tall array
Of burnished armor, jeweled glittering swords,
Sashes of red and sable, soft as plush,
And the great flag, with golden flecks on white,
While over the braves a reverential hush
Has gathered, and they view the French as lords
Almost of Jovian might.
For Frontenac perceived, as all perceive
Who lead the rabble in pre-reckoned ways,
That men are children, and the thoughts they weave
Stem from the infant as he wails and plays —
Tinsel enthralls them, straw-gods woo their praise.
He even called them children — they, the grave
And doughty Iroquois! In awe they heard
The Great White Father speak, whose every word,
Solemn with thought, proved he was strong and brave;
Who smoked the calumet as friend to friend;
Gave wampum gifts; bade mutual trust increase
With pacts of trade; shored up the rickety peace
With skill no other even could pretend,
Since none beside so neatly turned the key
To all man's snarls and tumults — power to see
Deep in the heart of vexed humanity.

VIII

To Frontenac came one of thrusting mien,

Long rapier face and great projecting nose,
Brows slanted like a bloodhound's, and a haste
As from dark fires that raged within, unseen.
"I'm Cavelier La Salle, and I propose
To penetrate the wide untrodden waste
And found an empire!"
                         Some deep-probing sight
Informed the Governor, "Here walks a man!"
And though his knowledge of the youth was slight,
Their partnership began.
I followed brisk La Salle as pioneer,
Swinging the axe, breaking new land to sow;
And watched him rising to his true career
In pathless woods, and by the swirl and flow
Of rapids, and on rivers yet unmapped.
But while his skin-clad, beaver-hatted band
Sought golden furs in regions still untrapped,
A power that prodded, seared him like a brand
Blazed in the leader's breast —
The fire of that magnificent unrest
Which drives to bottomless pits or heaven's peak.
To seek, to seek, seek, seek,
Throb at chain-lightning dreams, and plan and dare
In skies where castled purple visions swim
And any ridge may be a thoroughfare
Straight to the rainbow's rim!
Down serpentining bends, and round the isles
Of a vast river, brown with sediment,
I saw him paddle, and in green defiles
Where never before a pale-skinned ranger went,
Till, in the swamps and cane-brakes of the south,
Three channels opened and he felt a breeze
Salt-flavored with the breath of unknown seas,

And saw the river mouth,
And in high exultation, like the joy
Of a new Magellan in a world new-found,
Claimed all Louisiana's verdant ground
For the French king, and swore he would employ
Builders of forts and settlements, that none
Might seize what France had won.

    Majestic as the peaks, and brilliant-starred
The path he took! But he was of that corps
Whose fires burn brightest when the way is barred,
And who, when stumbling, only shine the more.
I heard him at the throne
Of gilt and gems where glorious Louis reigned,
Painting so gorgeously the silvered zone
Of Mississippi mine-lands that he gained
Approval of his scintillant fantasy.
The King, more treasure-bent than nimble-witted,
Had four small vessels fitted
To bear the fortune-seeking band, and be
Foundations of a fat new colony.
But oh, the chequered story,
Scarred by a thousand woes,
When luck was desultory
And constant were their foes!
Shipwreck and brute desertion,
Capture by fleets of Spain,
Fever, year-long exertion,
And comrades lost or slain!
Whipped from without and hollowed from within,
Buffeted round and round, they strove to win
Their dreamt-of port and goal
Where delta torrents of the Father of Waters roll.

But torn by the sneering winds of fate, marooned on
a houseless beach,
La Salle has missed the prize he sought when it dangled
within his reach.
Instead, a land of brine and marsh where no sweet fruit
redeems
The rattling in the perilous grass, the alligator streams!
With casks and wreckage of a ship, driftwood and tattered
sail
And broken timbers they erect a refuge from rain and gale.
And savages slink about the fort; dissent within flares hot,
And women and men, red-eyed, bemoan this cursed, malarial
spot.
About them turkey-buzzards wheel and wildfowl scream —
but why,
Among these burning brakes and dunes must humans mope
and die?

Still, still the captain stalks apart, stoical, silent,
grim,
And who shall say what thoughts, like ghosts, at midnight
torture him?
With a scheme as wild as Hannibal's where the icy Alps
expand,
He'll dash to distant Canada, and save his threatened band!

But ah, the fangs that dart unseen, the viper in the nest!
See how his followers skulk aside, growling in sour unrest!
Generals aloof as Ludendorff, who rule with an iron glove,
May govern a world by barbs of fear but rarely by light of
love.
Like hunters in an ambuscade when deer or elk are slain,
The traitors aim the bolt of fire that pierces their leader's
brain.

Yet well for him that he could not survive
To see his ruined fort, its wreckage black
On the red sands, and not one soul alive
To tell the dread of the whooping last attack.
But if the measure of a man be found
In kindled dreams, the striding will to fight
Heedless of thunder-skies and sinking ground,
Even in failure he had sparked a light
The centuries may dim but cannot cloud from sight.

IX

When in a wooded earth no man molested,
Fond nature wove the beaver's warm sleek coat,
Surely no tongue of irony attested
How dire the cost in ages still remote,
Nor how a hunger after soft fur-booty
Would carve the features of a continent,
Erect stockades, make ash of flowering beauty,
And summon war's profane disfigurement.
Yet had no small dam-building worker dwelt
Deep in the wonderlands of spruce and pine,
Nor any creature with a man-prized pelt,
Then history would have changed her whole design —
Her law the whining shot, the cruel snap
And claw-hold of the lacerating trap.

Across the silence of a mirror pond
Bordered by woods no axe had even shaken,
Down nameless rivers, and beyond, beyond
Amid a world as virginal and forsaken
As Adam's children knew,
I followed the glidings of a large canoe
Paddled by rovers of a nameless type,

Coureurs de bois, brown forest gypsies, lured
By loon-calls of adventure, and inured
To hardship, hunger, cold and bears, and ripe
For storm and peril. Chanting a resonant song,
Or telling weird stories of the *loup garou* —
Wolf of the sky — I saw them float along,
A lean and moccasined crew,
Swift as a tethered dog to fight, and swift
To oaths and laughter as they plod and drift,
Kindling their camp-fires by remote lake-beaches,
Bearing their birch canoes and furry loads
Across rock-shouldered, cataract-threaded reaches,
Or riding the rapids' white uproarious roads.
But rarely pausing, on and on they press
To pierce the tangly maze like open land—
Scouts and trail-blazers of the wilderness,
Who point the pathway with a piloting hand
For later generations.

                    Where a ring
Of birch-bark hovels, low and small and round,
Clustered like mound on mound,
I saw three *coureurs* flit and dance and sing.
Beside them, near a broad fresh-water bay
That circling spruces plumed and dignified,
Savages decked in painted coats of hide
Gathered to watch the white man's queer display.
And while the strangers' glances restlessly ranged,
Long pipes were passed and twinkling gauds exchanged.

    "Fur! Bring us fur! Bring fur!" I heard the cry,
Urgent and shrill and loud.
But the flat-featured, stoic-mannered crowd

Grunted no clear reply.
"Fur! Bring us fur!" Then from a beached canoe
One of the whites, with tempting gestures, drew
A big and bulging cask,
And pressed a flask
To a waiting pair of lips. And soon the throng
Cried out in laughter, in hilarious song,
And the husky visitors, with smirks and smiles,
Joined them and left a half-filled vat instead
Of the furs that suddenly came forth in piles.
And little could they foresee,
Little perhaps they cared for the tragedy
Of groveling men and broken lives ahead.

Yet far, and far, and far away,
In many a thick and roadless wood,
I saw them friendly-tongued and gay,
With redmen clasped in brotherhood.

Not kin to the planting southern breed
Who hunted tan-skinned folk like deer,
They knew that shots were only seed
For crops of massacre and fear.

But all across an empire's length
Of looping trails and leafy shade,
Few smoldering lodges drained the strength
Of them who came to see and trade.

Now in their path, across two hundred years,
I saw the crews of great explorers glide,
Fur-hunting through the northern countryside,
Even when traps of English pioneers

Replaced the French. I watched, amid the blanks
Of broad gray tundra, bold Mackenzie press;
And through the ridged, coniferous wilderness
Where ice-peaks spired in pyramidal ranks;
And over crests where white men never before
Had stood, and in the lean canoes that rode
Down glacial streams against the cascades' roar,
Until at last he strode
Under a cliff upon the foamy shore
Of the north Pacific, knowing that it meant
A summit in time, a pivotal event —
Man's first triumphant thrust across the continent.

IV. The Genesis of A Nation

". . . weaving the knotted woof of a mighty destiny"

Like processions of clouds that wind on the brow of a
    mountain,
Assemble, and darken with sinuous streamers, and vanish,
Like processions of clouds were the wanderers flocking to
    settle
In forests and prairies remote beyond shores of the
    sunset —
Like processions of clouds whose billowing, weaving and
    passing
Have left but the print of a feather, the weight of a
    shadow,
While still from above, in the darkness faint-stirring, a
    Watcher
Peers forth to the cities and farms of a peopled tomorrow.

I looked upon a land of lakes and pines,
Dark cypress swamps and dripping Spanish moss.
And there, where torridly the summer shines,
I saw, of old, the bloodied sword and cross.
There vision-goaded Ponce de Leon strayed,
Seeking the clear miraculous spring of youth;
And there de Soto, musket-bearing, preyed
On Indians slaughtered without check or ruth.
There wandering de Vaca flashed as god
For moonstruck groveling natives; there I scanned
Grave Huguenots, who on the warm, rich sod

Claimed a new home . . . till, scorched by blazing brands
Of duelling faiths, they heard the yells and rush
Of Philip's warrior bands,
And fell beneath the halberds' drive and crush.

Behind its sea-wall, I beheld it rise,
The oldest Spanish town, Saint Augustine.
I saw the packed and balconied houses lean
Above dim alleys under hot blue skies.
I paced its river sand
And heard the great Atlantic thresh and moan;
And entered, far away, a magic land,
A vague enchanted zone
Of riches shaming fabled Samarcand,
Which man's delicious fancy paved with gold,
And where, the bright, rose-haloed legends told,
A highway to the Indies might unfold.

II

Broad as a lake, bitter with salt-sea brine,
Low-walled to east with green in blended shades,
And to the west a long and level line
Of rocky palisades —
It seemed less river than an ocean arm,
Leading perhaps to Burma or Cathay.
So Henry Hudson, slave beneath its charm,
Ranged the far reaches of the waterway,
Bequeathing it his name. Along the shore
I watched canoes of feathered Indians glide,
And white-winged vessels sailing to explore
Regions as fair as ever a crew espied,
Marked southward by an island ridge of trees,
Manhattan, on whose every cliff and hill,

Brooklet and pool, shone verdant draperies,
While in some grove or glen
Villages with slow smoke-trails, small and still,
Sheltered the forest men.

    Scanning the island's crowded tip, I viewed
The high-stooped houses in a gabled clump,
The fort, the windmill, gardens many-hued
With patterned beds, the docks, the village pump,
Where, bit by bit, man started to intrude.
But time moves darkly. None could see in this
A modern Babylon, the genesis
Of a vast-towered world metropolis.
Yes, time moves darkly. And the conquering Dutch,
Who weighed the scenery in the scales of trade
And reckoned pelts acquired as progress made,
Counted their laden ships, nor cared for much
Beyond the clinking deal. I saw them go
In peaked, tall-pointed hats, sedately gray,
And heard their great fat governors growl, "Obey!",
Red-faced at self-assertion from below.
I saw land-barons strut, with claims that spread
Wider than Flanders' sweep of shore and plain;
And watched as arrows whizzed and cows fell dead
When Indians, snarling, fought to save their grain;
Watched, too, revengeful musket fires spout
And skulking warriors retaliate
On some lone farmer with a whoop and shout
Of rage and hate.
And rage and hate rebounded when a corps
Of Dutch, beneath the cloak of night, sneaked down
Cat-footed on a slumbering native town,
And after a screaming pandemonium

Left eighty braves twisted in their own gore,
While tensions swelled and swelled like a red mangled
       thumb.

    And later came a day
When sleek black English frigates, stoutly gunned,
Rode bristling in the bay
And Stuyvesant, the one-legged governor, stunned,
Grumblingly signed his province all away.
And what the English rights? No more than those
Of Caesar's troops against the Gallic foes,
Or Genghis with his kingdom-splintering blows.
But thief robs thief. And time will soon forget
The wrong and right. At dawn what man remembers
Last evening's dying embers,
The torn cloud-streamers of a day that set?
Already hands that moved invisibly
Were weaving the knotted woof of a mighty destiny.

III
    Unchecked for centuries the current ran,
Dark with the drift and crush of human freight,
As though its tides obeyed a cosmic plan,
A fixed decree of fate.
From stone-ribbed farms, meandering hawthorn lanes,
Low crooked streets, the dairy and the shore,
Old misty fishing-towns and pasture plains,
Forges and mines, behold the migrants pour! —
Groaning in pestilent ships,
Huddled in leaky holds, shaken in storms,
With pinched cadaverous cheeks and prayerful lips,
While the fanged waters swallow sheeted forms;
And trailing to new-won homes

In hamlets that the ragged woods surround,
Or stooped above a furrow, spading ground
In bouldery fields where some white freshet foams.
Swept by a power like the torrential drive
That lifts the southward-winging geese or sends
Lemmings in legions from their nests to dive
Into the sea, they seem to follow ends
Not of their making. Wave on wave, they press
Forth to the green and summoning wilderness.

    And see them with burdened backs
On forest trails that twine
Slenderer than goat-tracks
Through snarls of bush and vine!
And over oozy bogs
Where mules may slip and drown,
And crossing streams on logs
Where ferny gulches frown,
Dreading the snake whose rattling numbs the feet,
Challenged by bears that growl from dusky caves,
Shelterless in the snow, the gale, the sleet,
Naked to arrow-bursts of ambushed braves!
But on and on they plod,
Up hills, down river valleys, circling lakes,
With axes swinging; when raw hunger wakes,
Their saviors are the gun, the fishing rod.

    Then, blessed recompense for trial and strain,
Healer of wounds and hearts, the Promised Land!
See the log cabin stand
Low amid stumps of oaks and maples slain.
Within its small one-windowed single room,
Roofed by rough timbers propped on stones or poles,

Even the firelight's welcome orange flare
Cannot expel the gloom
That reaps sharp tolls
With memories of home and kin elsewhere.
No neighbors but the panther and the deer,
And small dawn-singers in a migrant flock,
And savages sneaking close with scalping knives! —
A world of strife and fear,
Of hardihood like gnarled old mountain rock,
Where he alone survives
Who rips aside the wall of generations,
Roams trails his fathers' skin-clad sires pursued,
Shrinks at their terrors, pants at their elations,
Recovers the courage and path-breaking mood
Of a primal earth now curiously renewed.

IV

    Freedom, whose witch-fire sparkles through the night
For pilgrims blown upon Atlantic gales,
Burns from no window of unwavering light,
But sometimes blinks, and flutters low, and fails.
Not only in price-tags of the auction-block,
Where flesh, warm palpitant human flesh, is sold
Like lettuce, loaves or stock,
Tremulous hands and spirits are controlled,
But clamps grip clawlike in New England pews.
Shaken at sermons of hell's blistering host,
All settlers must attend who would not choose
The public pillory or whipping-post.
And then the youths or maids
Wall-bound or roped, cringing at blows and sneers,
Indentured captives leased like mules for years,
Perhaps self-bartered for the passage price,

Or, writhing and grappling in kidnapping raids,
Dashed aboard ship like bags of corn or rice.
And "Freedom!" has a sneer, a rasping ring
For crowds the African trading vessels bring,
Dealing in rum and dark-skinned folk, who feel
The cold chains clanking and the lashes' sting.

    Yet freedom, though it burn to soot and ash,
Recovers phoenix-like. Through many doors
I saw it shine — a beacon that would flash
A signal and a promise to all shores.
Now, among shifting scenes, I was aware
Of a disdainful face, a high-ridged nose,
Light eyes down-looking with a ducal stare,
Long rings of drooping hair,
And mien as positive as a sultan's pose —
Sir Edmund Andros, whom the King has sent
To rule New England for its royal lord.
Let all obey! Let colonists be bent
And squeezed as by a cord!
Their rights? To bow, to hail their masters' reign,
To work, pay taxes, and seal tight their lips
Against seditious speech and dangerous quips
As censors may ordain!

    Then were they serfs in some rude barony,
Cowed by brute custom to the sovereign will?
No! for they knew the tang of liberty,
And their complaints were trumpet-tongued and shrill.
On Boston streets I saw
A rabble pluck the Governor's sleeve; pursue
The wig-crowned minion of imported law
With many a hoot and boo.

I heard him, one historic night, demand
The charter of Connecticut, the gauge
Of people's rights . . . when, like a sequel planned
For actors on a stage,
The candles flared and failed. Tumult rang out,
Mutterings, yells and curses in the dark,
Thumps of great bodies in a threshing rout,
Before, at last, a scraping and a spark,
And candles rekindled! But on Andros' face
The crimson of rage! Where had the charter fled?
All stood unhearing, tongueless as the dead,
And none recalled the document's hiding-place
Deep in the hollow of an oak nearby —
Itself with oaken sinews not to die.

    At last a morning dawns
When drums reverberate; a signal warns
The folk of Boston, to the tramp and thud
Of marching feet. And how the people surge
Forth on the street, an ever-deepening flood,
Gather in loud assembly, and converge
Upon the Governor's house! Behold him dragged
Like a caught bandit, hearing threats and jeers
Scream in his ears,
While his face whitens and his knees have sagged.
Later that day, terror has made him rash;
Robed in a woman's long disguising dress,
He plots, with an adroit confederate's aid,
To slip around his sentries in a dash
To freedom and safety. But he is betrayed
By one small carelessness.
What! Those a lady's shoes? A guardsman's sword
Blocks him, and ends a power all abhorred.

V

In woods once shivering with the battle whoops
Of Mohawks and Mohegans, now there came
Redcoats and swords of musket-swinging troops
With tinder lit from Europe's white-hot flame.
Hundreds of miles along a green frontier
I saw the French and scuttling dark allies
Rain down like bolts from innocent blue skies
On the English pioneer.
In treachery and massacre and dread
The strife began; and one who watched could see
How dread and massacre and treachery
Would grow and spread,
While many a settler on a new-cleared farm,
With wife and children, cattle and corn-bags, fled
In tumult and alarm.

Viewing the wind that swirled
In scorching gusts, the cindery clouds that rose
Over the host who crouched with guns and bows,
I saw two nations wrestling for a world.
Keen-eyed, with jaunty air and dominant height,
Two thumbs stuck cockily in a scarlet vest,
The eager aide-de-camp, George Washington,
Descanted on tactics of a forest fight,
While Braddock, the graying general he addressed,
Smiled as upon a son.
The youth, already versed
In the hard lore of trails and scouting foes,
Had felt the wrench of wry defeat, the thirst
For victory that every soldier knows.
Now, with the expedition Braddock led
To batter their adversaries, white and red.

He hoped to smite the French pretensions dead.

But slow, slow-plodding through the timbered deeps,
The squadrons lumber on, with wagon trains,
Cannon to drag, and herds that close the rear.
Breaking a trail, the vanguard barely creeps;
Cursing the swamps and streams, fierce suns and rains,
They pause, and crawl, and groan, and persevere.
But in those tramping hosts, are there not some
Who hear, like throbs of an unearthly drum,
The muffled knockings of a doom to come?

Sickness, whose gray bedraggled wings droop low
On many an armored camp, has worked its will
With Washington, who, prostrate, has to go
In a jolting cart that makes him yet more ill.
But when a huge defeat
Falls wolflike on the troops, he leaps to horse
And battles on a spurring, galloping course
To check disaster though it seems complete.

Unwarily through the woods the British rode,
Like children unsuspicious of a trap.
Then, where a form in Indian deerskins strode
With French insignia on his shoulder strap,
Suddenly as the snap
Of a pine-trunk in a gale, a crouching band
Opened sharp fire, and terror snatched command.
Brilliant in crimson coats, with streaks of white,
The English stared like targets on display,
While marksmen, slithering barely out of sight,
Pressed to the oak-boles, waited for their prey
Amid the shadows. Gaudy line on line

The English came, and line on line they fell,
Heedless of bullets' whine,
Screams of the hurt, the Indian whoop and yell.

    Forth at their head, his brandished sword swung high,
Calling his troopers forward, Braddock dashed;
Five times a horse beneath him sagged and crashed;
Five times he mounted another, with the cry,
"Onward to victory!" In vain, all vain!
Bleeding he dropped, and finally lay at peace.
Then, seeing the maimed, the prisoners and the slain
Increase, and still increase,
And watching the beaten run,
The men felt panic seizing crazed control.
The new commander, brisk young Washington,
Undaunted by the foes' victorious roar,
Charmed as a god, miraculously whole,
Rode back and forth along the shell-torn wood,
Spurring his men; and his rare hardihood
Saved shards and tatters of Braddock's tragic corps.

VI

    Empires that fall upon the battlefield
May be dismembered less by blades or guns
Than by the bursting of their human shield,
The moral grit and sinew of their sons.
Hollowed from deep within
By rat-teeth of officials hot for gain,
And punished for the sin
Of the cat-comforts of a yawning reign,
A state may totter. So decay that spread
From gold-leaf salons round the Bourbon throne,
With faith a fading ghost and honor shed,

Gathered unseen, unknown,
And after all the dawn-glow and romance
Of planters and settlers of a brave New France,
The country could not halt its foes' advance.

Strong were the English chieftains. Strong the hand
Of Pitt the Elder, lord of colonies;
And strong his youthful general in command,
James Wolfe, bold architect of destinies.
I saw him, lithe and lean,
Red-haired and hawklike, glittering falcon-eyed,
Who, with mercurial mien,
Darted and dared, and challenged and defied.
Hollowed of frame, and bony with disease,
He towered at Quebec, where, loud and rash,
He captained a madman's dash
Up precipice walls, whose fences of felled trees
With limbs spear-pointed, and a chaos of posts
And matted boughs, tangled the climbing hosts.
I watched him, among the first
Of his hard-panting troops to gain the top;
And while red death mowed down a grisly crop,
He led the daredevils in a thunder-burst.
A bullet tore his wrist; but still he pressed
Forward against the Frenchmen kneeling low
With smoking muskets levelled. Then a blow
Like a sledgehammer's thumped against his breast.
He staggered; he gasped and sank,
And as his blood, unnoted, crimsoned the soil,
And round him the din of charging rank on rank
Stormed to crescendos, England took for spoil
A giant realm, a continent-spanning prize

Of forest, stream and lake, where mansions and mills would
    rise.

    Knowing his rival Montcalm slipped to doom
On that same flaring day,
We ask: in shadowlands beyond the tomb
May chieftains such as they
Meet and confer, and meditate and sigh,
And gently question, "Why the feud? Ah, why?

    "Ah, why the terror, agony and waste,
The smashed and starving town?
And what to us who perish is the taste
Of glory and renown?
Was there no room for peace, for brotherhood
In the wide pavilions of the northern wood?"

    Perhaps, amid the gloom, with clasping hands,
The two war-leaders strolled,
While to their ears the drum-beats and alarms
Of distant bugles rolled,
And round them, where huge cloudy phantoms surged,
All men, all peoples, and all nations merged.

VII

    He who has dread of burglars in the night
Will not bemoan the coming of the police.
But after the robber band has taken flight
His welcome to the shielding corps may cease.
So with the Colonies, when vise-like fear
No longer gripped a gun-patrolled frontier.
Now, like a youth who grows
Intolerant of the brusque parental nod,

In widening power the Colonies arose,
While pursed lips asked, "Can royalty be God?"
See, in the fogs of coastal isles and bays,
The smugglers' boats dodging to foil the Crown!
And notice, in a thousand waterways,
Vessels the buzzing native yards laid down!
While forges clang and glow
And shops are loud with work,
The products mount and flow,
And notary and clerk
Bustle to serve the few large towns that rise
With close-walled streets and rattling enterprise.
And villagers far-scattered
Build lives as free and bold
As if no movement mattered
In lands remote or old.
And townsmen scan the pages
Of Locke and Diderot,
While judging with those sages,
A master is a foe.

Then ominous the growls and clamoring
Where muskets of the marching redcoats swing —
What! are they not slave-herders for the King?
And fierce the undertone of oaths that flame
At taxes which the royal lips proclaim —
Not taxes merely! bullets taking aim
At freedom's heart! Woe to the man assigned
To pass the English stamps for revenue!
I saw the mob pursue
With lashes snapping, ropes that trailed behind,
And shouts of "Drown him!", "Hang him!" I beheld
Bonfires of stamps, while rebels danced and yelled

To view stamp-masters burned in effigy,
Their houses wrecked, their yards and cellars plundered.
I heard the multitude roar like the sea
As onward it rushed and thundered.
In Boston I watched it bursting open the door
Of Governor Hutchinson; it raged and smashed,
While tatters of busts and vases strewed the floor,
And manuscripts written in the heart's own blood
Were seized and dashed
Outside into the obliterating mud.

Like children pulling switches in the dark
May be the men whose furies and dissents
Scoop out the channel of immense events,
Or like half-blinded sailors who embark
On oceans pierced by devious shoals and straits,
Where never a master pilot navigates
And none can even conjecture what awaits.
I watched new tumult spout
When Boston mobs, with bluster, oaths and blows,
Struck at the troops. I heard the order, "Fire!",
Break over them in a panic-stricken shout;
Then saw the redcoats whirl around, retire
While five men, falling, squirmed in deathly throes.
And then, as if to prove
How pinhead episodes may elbow great,
I heard one syllable move
The populace like a creed, and agitate
The whole roused coast. A cry of "Tea! Tea! Tea!
No English tea!" throbbed like a pious call —
The voice of a people balking a foreign wall
And daring to be free.

Again in Boston, one December night,
I marked the rebel companies far-flung
Like Vigilantes mustered for a fight.
Masking as Mohawk braves, with blankets slung
Over their lean bare shoulders, skins dark-stained,
And tomahawks and feather-crests, they strained
Forth to the bay, where laden vessels swung,
And while onlookers jammed the wharves to view
They mounted the decks, exclaiming, "Tea! Tea! Tea!",
And sometimes aided by a cowering crew,
Plunged down the hatches; seized the cargo; threw
Case after open case into the sea.

And who among the insurgents could foretell
The screams of revolution just ahead,
Knowing that violence reaps with sword and shell
And chases reason from his hearth and bed?
And who perceived, with shadow-piercing eyes,
The radiance of that never-followed path
Where peace bids pride and fury compromise
And thought is arbitrator over wrath?
Propelled in loops and spirals, like a snake's,
Man moves, but seldom sees the road he takes,
Or pictures dawns beyond the day that breaks.

VIII

But some there are who, with an eagle vision,
Gaze on remote tomorrow — who, endowed
With sight to lead by many a sage decision,
May live whole centuries beyond the crowd.
One such I viewed, in whose reflective eyes
Contours and lights of simmering schemes would flit —
A round full face, and ways urbane and wise,

Toned by experience, and sparked by wit.
Many a year before
Beacons of revolution first had flared,
I saw a luminous project Franklin shared,
Which might have lanced away the festered core
Of brooding trouble. Nobly in his mind
Flickered foreglimmers, pale and half defined,
Of a great nation Providence designed.
Unite the Colonies! not with intent
To balk the sovereign will of Parliament,
But under its wing, and blest with its consent! —
A towering plea that looked
Across man's fences and the day's confines
To the clear uplands of a world remade!
But few have ever brooked
Obliteration of dividing lines
Until the iron of the barricade
Has all but crushed them. So the plan was killed,
And with it the hope of peace died unfulfilled.

I heard knife-edged denunciations ring
When Patrick Henry, thin and leonine-eyed,
Sneered at divine assumptions of the King,
Shouted of tyrannous Tarquins, and defied
The British Crown. I heard the mutterings grow,
With growls and warnings of catastrophe,
When cod of Boston harbor came to know
The taste of English tea.
Such raw rebelliousness must be restrained!
So huffish George the Third, wounded and riled,
Like a hurt mother with a fractious child,
Wielded the whip that most severely pained,
And surely not once inquired

If what he most desired
Were provocations that sizzled and back-fired.

IX

Lashed through the town by some demonic force
The rain, in swirling gusts and wind-borne sheets
Came pelting down on Boston wharves and streets,
Where every gutter housed a watercourse.
With coats turned up and wide-brimmed hats pulled low,
The citizens ran hunched along their way —
All but the riders who, in disarray,
Paced forward heedlessly, almost as though
Their floundering horses did not have to wade.
Soon, at the docks, where men in scarlet coats
And close white breeches lined with golden braid
Returned their greeting from the waiting boats,
The cannon rumbled and roared,
And rumbled again and boomed in welcoming accord.
And yet — beneath the patterned courtesy,
Sharp as a storm that hooted evilly,
I heard the rasp of veiled hostility.

But who in human flesh
Would not be hostile now,
Feeling a prison mesh
Fast-closing round his brow?
Sent at the King's direction, General Gage
Was here to nip the burgeoning port, and write
Black bars on freedom's page,
While men could feel, descending like a blight,
A gloom so deep they almost heard it groan.
Few carts were creaking on the street; the bay
Was but a wood of silent masts; dismay

Wailed a bleak undertone
Where, mumbling and cursing at their empty hands,
Sailors and carpenters and clerks slouched by.
The shops lay idle, and the bakers' stands
Bare of a bread supply;
And sharp-ribbed famine, with a skeleton grin,
Haunted the town.
                                   But now I saw the sheep
Driven in droves from neighboring colonies,
Saw fish and flour and money flowing in,
So that the rebels, close beset, might keep
Their faith, and know their brothers' sympathies.
Sadly the King would learn
An insurrection only half suppressed
Will smolder on, and burn
Even more fiercely for the long-drawn test,
For by restraint that piled on cruel restraint
He poured out oil to feed the whole complaint.

"Workers! Bring workers!" was the General's call
To laborers who, hands deep in pockets, stood
Waiting, and never seemed to hear at all —
As soon find zebras in a British wood!
And sabotage, the masked destroyer, stared
From broken carts and bridges; patriots dared
To tread dark byways, scattering brick and straw,
And halt the needed barracks Gage prepared,
While, snarl for snarl, they answered martial law.

A few strong wills and minds may blast the way
Thousands will follow, half without intent,
Till bit by bit the ancient props decay
Through small, slow-gathering actions, scarcely meant,

While borne upon the drift
Of great events they hardly can perceive,
Men watch the current shift,
And, trembling, stand on revolution's eve.
Thus, when the fiery-throated pamphleteer,
The crackling Thomas Paine,
With white-hot phrases tingled the nation's ear,
He seemed a throbbing country's nerves and brain,
And proved again a laden thought may wield
Charges more potent than a battlefield.

X

    Stern faces, sober manners, solemn tongues
Joined when the Continental Congress met,
And with the end not plainly pictured yet
Lifted the Colonies precarious rungs
Closer to union. Meanwhile sparks were flying —
Warnings of conflagration. "Quick! To arms!
The redcoats come! To battle!" men were crying.
And Paul Revere rode forth to night alarms.
And patriots gathered, and a fight was won;
And then the red affray at Lexington,
Spouting Colonial blood; and next I saw,
At Concord, like a dragon long restrained,
Now suddenly unchained,
The explosion, the fury and the flame of war,

    From firing squads behind stone walls, concealed
By barns and houses, fences, earth and trees,
Came puffs of smoke; fighting without a shield,
The advancing scarlet-coated companies
Were thinned by many a gap. But who could press
Against invisible enemies that fought

Like Indians skulking in the wilderness,
And rarely darted into view, and wrought
Blind death from ambush? Here was not a fight
Planned like a game in patterned English ways,
But like guerrilla wars of later days,
Aimed but to track the enemy, and smite
And scuttle to safety. Now, with scores of slain,
The British saw, too murderously plain,
The Colonists were not mere chaff to scatter —
They faced a tigerish test, a fierce campaign.

    And yet, who could foresee
The trial by fire, the gray and withering years
Before at last bugles of victory
Gave comfort, and assuaged the waste and fears?
And if they could have known —
Those farmers and those tradesmen seizing guns —
How they would droop and bleed and lose their sons,
Would they have dared to strike against the Throne?
But man's protection, as time's storms drive by,
May be the things he cannot prophesy.

XI

    When solemnly they bowed their heads and signed,
Their scratching quills sent echoes round the earth —
They who left dear familiar fields behind
To certify a rebel country's birth.
If ever a paper rattled at the door
Of time, and governments still unconceived;
If ever a bravely planned pronouncement bore
The stamp of hope and liberty retrieved,
This Declaration spoke like holy lore:
That men could now go forth

Free and with equal rights,
And south and west and north
The common folk might rule by their own lights,
With their own Congress. In a world where lords
Sported trim mincing retinues, and swords
Of kings and emperors cowed the vulgar hordes,
Here was a blazing goal
In man's old war for man's unshackled soul.
So let the praises swell!
Ring, ring the Liberty Bell
For a new nation where free men may dwell!

But hard the birth-throes while a host stood by
Saluting the flag of England. Peril racked
And tore the Colonies, where myriads lacked
The will to mortify
Spirit or flesh, or stand against the Crown.
Then was it only chance that gave us one,
The war-tried colonel not without renown,
Well-armed to lead the battle just begun?
I looked on towering, straight-limbed Washington,
Riding commandingly in buff and blue
Of his Virginian uniform, with mien
Stern as a lion's, in his eyes the hue
And glint of steel, toned by a melting sheen
That won the watcher. Not for gold or fame
He'd left the peace of his estate, and come
To whirl in war's grotesque delirium,
But only with one aim —
To offer of himself.
                              Yet he required
More than the wizard gift to master men —
A stone-ridged will, a patience near inspired,

And faith and hardihood enough for ten.
And ah, the long ordeal
When rattling skeletons, in every gale,
Gibbered, "Defeat! Defeat!"; when every trail,
Red with the mangled heel,
Warned him, "Turn back!" And ah, the troops hurled low
At Valley Forge by that limb-shrivelling foe,
Starvation, and its blind confederate, snow!
The bleeding men bare-footed in the ice
That cut like scalpels! dumb and huddled forms
Hunched around camp-fires, which could not suffice
The blanketless and shirtless in the storms!
And ah, the frozen amputated feet!
The typhus victims trucked away! — a brood
Of terrors that pursued, pursued, pursued,
Till only an Herculean fortitude
Could stave off tragedy final and complete!

Now other visions rush upon my sight
Like pictures in a weird kaleidoscope.
Creeping against a dim Long Island slope,
Phantoms with knapsacks glide across the night,
Scatter like Stygian shades, and stumble and grope
Down to the bay. There tiny boats and sloops
Lie tossing in the fog, whose shadowy zone
Mantles the thinned-out lines, the fleeing troops,
While General Washington walks mute, alone,
The last of all to join the escaping groups.
As when at Dunkirk, in a crueller age,
An army runs before the Nazi rage,
The evacuating force will live to wage
More potent battle.

                    In a later act
I see, at night, the sleet-swept Delaware
Duskily swirl, spotted with drifting floes —
Great ice-packs, beaten round and round and packed
In crunching isles. The cold that grips the air
Tortures like hell-pangs; numbs the feet, the nose.
And yet, in open boats, band upon band
Of men with guns courageously are borne.
I notice Washington, arms waving, stand
Urging his stalwarts on.
I see him landing under blustery skies,
And with the night and ice-storm for disguise,
Dash into Trenton streets for victory
That stabs the revelling Hessians with surprise.

    Still other episodes of blood and flame,
Like cinematic scenes, are flashed to mind —
Triumphs, retreats and routs that went and came
Through slow devouring years as hope declined —
Skirmishes, night assaults,
Treason whose stench made sour the atmosphere,
Delays in snowy camps; long chafing halts
More trying than even fury's mid-career;
Plaints of disheartened farm-boys. Scantily fed,
Half armed, half sheltered, all untrained at first
But valorously led,
Fighting with freezing gales and heat and thirst,
Famine and sickness more than animate foes,
Time upon time they conquered when hope's gate
Narrowed and seemed to close.
And could it be that tantalizing fate,
Resolved to test men's spirits, drew them taut
Until they almost snapped,

And then released them with a glad report
Of enemy power sapped?
At Saratoga, like a turning tide,
I saw long ranks of British laying down
Their swords, their flint-locks; oddly, only then
Came tidings from the irresolute French Crown:
"Hear Brothers! Side by side
We'll wage the fight! We'll send you ships and men!"

    Strange marriages are made in war. And strange
The mating of the plush-bound monarchy,
Its goldfoil and its frayed nobility,
And the free people in a swirl of change.
And when, in later years, all France was shaken
By revolution's red eruptive burst,
Some of the sparks that lit the fuse were taken
From forges that the New World tested first.
But this was not divined
By Louis or his ministers, as blind
As most who guide mankind.

    Fixed and familiar, like a native peak,
May be the landscape of a great event,
And yet another ridge or monument
Might have replaced it by a chance or freak.
At Yorktown, with white handkerchief in hand,
A messenger walked blindfold, with a tender
Of victory or surrender.
But what of the fleet of France that, strongly manned,
Battered the British with a cannonade?
What of the aid
Of serried Frenchmen, standing row on row
In sleek white broadcloth, while Cornwallis' sword

Was passed to Washington, and many a foe
Helplessly watched them? True, a just reward!
Yet if all wars since arrowed raids began
Had ended justly, then the whole world-plan
Would show new contours for our eyes to scan.

XII

To win a war is not to found a nation,
And brighter than the triumph shines one fact:
Out of the fury, out of the conflagration,
A people rose intact.
Long centuries before, when Greeks impeded,
With arms close-linked, the rush of Persian blows,
The cities fell apart as fear receded
And struck again the old belligerent pose.
And later, in the riddled Netherlands,
When William the Silent balked the swords of Spain,
Not all the provinces joined fraternal hands
Or rose in freedom from the oppressor's chain.
Then brighter in time's chambers shines the feat
Of thirteen colonies that might have drifted
Like Balkan states to chaos, and yet lifted
A common flag to make their victory complete.

History, like the captain of a team
Who picks his players for their special roles,
Sometimes appears to fabricate her scheme
With planned requirements, deliberate goals.
So did it look at Athens' purple hour,
And so in Florence when Lorenzo led,
And England of Queen Bess. One might have said
The chiefs were named by some beneficent power
Who weighed their qualities and chose their parts

In statecraft, or as shepherds of the arts.
And so the one-time Colonies, combined
In a loose band
Whose props were putty and whose links were sand,
With columns that no architect aligned,
Soon might have pushed their leaning edifice
Down to a blank abyss.
But saviors, iron-armed and bulldog-willed,
Solemnly rose to build
A new majestic structure. In a hall
Of grave, stern lines where stern, grave delegates meet,
Notice how Washington, sedate and tall,
Presiding in a high-backed central seat,
Hears arguments that broach the one solution —
A citadel of rock, a strong new Constitution.

XIII

The barge was gaily bannered. Men in white
Stood round it in an ornamental corps.
And thirteen cannon, in re-echoing might,
Boomed out as they approached Manhattan's shore.
Buzzing as thick as bees
On every wharf and street, watchers assembled;
And bunting shone, and streamers tossed and trembled
In every breeze.
And when night came, red-orange bonfires glowed,
Exalting General Washington, who rode
Forth from Mount Vernon, his beloved abode.
So let men's cheers be lifted, honoring
This warrior chief who would not be a king!

High on the flag-decked balcony he stood,
And took, in resolute tones, the oath, "I swear

To serve the people and the country's good,
So help me God!" And suddenly the air
Was shaken with applauding cries, "All hail
George Washington, the land's first President!"
And in a growing gale
Those cries went forth, "All hail! All hail! All hail!"
And myriad voices, blent
In one long call, echoed "Our President!"
And startlingly it seemed
What patriots fought to win and seers had dreamed
Was crowned by one superb accomplishment.

* * *

High in the clouds that bounded the halves of the planet
Strangely I looked again on mysterious beings
With figures mighty as gods and patriarch faces,
Apparelled in light, with trailing garments of vapor.
And a voice with a rising and falling like tones of an organ
Vibrated among them, and chanted a solemn pronouncement:

"O Man, you have mounted one more of the cliffs, of
    the ridges
That wrinkle all time; and thence, with far-seeing vistas,
May climb to resplendent new domes, new gardens and
        park-lands,
Where freedom will float like a bird that circles blue heaven
And your hands will be gripped by the hands of all men, your
        brothers.
But beware of old pitfalls and cages! old ruts and old nooses!
The cord in the dark! the snare for the feet at the crossroads!
Beware of the mold of the thought of the dissolute kingdoms
That people the earth! the ways of the dukes and the barons,
Slavedrivers and herders of men, usurpers of nations,

And shedders of blood for the glory of houses and titles!
Be yours the original highways! the trails forward-looking
To blue-misted ages when wisdom and love and compassion
Shall conquer the spirit and mind of man, the unconquered!"

    High in the clouds that bounded the halves of the planet
Strangely I looked again on mysterious beings
Who pointed and pointed, in dayshine and distance and
        shadow,
On roads that were forked, that meandered and looped and
        divided,
And growing remote as they broadened, were lost in the
        sunset
Under glitter of peaks that shone like the pledge of a nation.

V. Adventurers of the South

"... trails to fabled lands"

Like some Gargantuan snake that holds
Half of a continent in fee,
With slithering twists and wriggling folds
The river pours to meet the sea.

And broad its arms as an ocean bay,
And lush the swamps its torrents flood,
Where razor-jawed pirhanas prey
And vampire-bats are gorged on blood.

And where the jungle drips and steams
And filtered light is green and pale,
Numberless are the feeding streams
As leaf-flecks on a forest trail.

Here, while the jaguar makes his den
Beneath the palms' thick humid press,
The Indians haunt, alone of men,
The Amazonian wilderness.

But even here the white adventurers came,
Devil-may-care as Viking crews of old;
Always with eyes that plumbed for gold, more gold,
They staked their claim
To dank unthreaded jungles in the name
Of Portugal's king. A mixed and swarthy breed

Who laughed at codes and laws,
They wooed compliant copper-colored squaws,
And scattered their kin and seed
In woods and ranches. When the slave-ships bore
Black Africans in chains, to groan and sweat
And irrigate with blood this torrid shore,
The masters would beget
Still other hybrids, while the mold was set
For those blent races that would sparsely fill
The huts and river hamlets of Brazil.

But when that nation was not even a dream,
And when the New World still remained so new
Columbus was recalled by not a few,
Behold! the conquest of earth's mightiest stream!
From the wild mountains of remote Peru
The wanderers' course was taken; all unguessed
The ultimate goal, the meaning of their quest,
As though the fates, by some sly stratagem,
Had bidden the expedition master them.

Not that they aimed, with rash exploring hands,
To pierce this continent, as yet unwon.
They courted trails to legendary lands
Of gold and cinnamon —
Bright Eldorado, whose bejeweled booty
Lit preparations neither love nor duty,
Honor nor faith nor beauty
Would have inspired. Far over hills and fields
I saw the Indian burden-bearers cower
Under the lifted whip, the snarling word;
And watched the Spaniards swaggering in power
With arquebuses, flashing mail and shields,

While all around them browsed an uncounted herd
Of horses and llamas, packs of foraging hogs
And big ferocious dogs
To gather game and hunt and terrorize
The forest people.
                              Bristling at their head,
Gonzalo, brother of Pizarro, rode,
Heedless as even his kinsmen of the cries
Of dusky women weeping for the dead,
And porters staggering beneath the load
Piled high on beaten backs. But where, ah where
Did yellow spires of Eldorado stare?
Only the shadowy sweep
Of river and wood, canyon and mountainside,
With neither food to grasp nor gold to reap,
Where the heart-weary Indian drooped and died,
While hollowing hunger slunk on every trail,
Toothed like a grizzly.
                              Now the Captain spoke
To one he honored: "Are we worms to fail?
All our ambitions only rings of smoke?
Not if our blood flows red! So this I've planned:
You, Orellana, with a vessel manned
By our steel-sinewed best, will aim to find
That kingdom, richer even than Mexico,
Where silver paves the streets, and gold is mined
Freely as quarried slate. Now hurry! Go!
I'll wait for your return!"
                              With glad new zest
They built a brigantine, and sailed away.
And fifty-seven men pursued the quest
Amid a mesh-like green where, day on day,
Rain-torrents droned. Soon — soon as they won food,

Back they would hurry, knowing their brothers chewed
On weeds and roots. But weeds and roots were all
They too could pluck. And some would gasp and groan,
Poisoned by herbs unknown,
And some, so weakened they could barely crawl,
Would boil shoe leather.
                                   Guns pointed, forth they creep
Around the low, leaf-shingled forest huts,
Scatter the people like stampeded sheep,
And plunder the fish and manioc, maize and nuts.
And then — the throb of drums!
Dugout canoes! A daubed war-party comes
With many a waving spear,
And five witch-doctors at their head appear,
All painted white and blowing clouds of ash . . .
Followed by arquebuses' crack and flash,
Fierce screams, and prone forms bleeding! Raiders seize
The village produce — turtles, fruit and grain —
And hanging some captives from the river trees,
Annex the country for the glory of Spain.

        Down, down and down they ramble, down and down
Past swamps and muddy isles
Where boas loop and coil, and crocodiles
Stick their long snouts from banks of scummy brown.
And near miraculous the sequel seems,
As if some great Jehovah's magic arm
Beckons above them, and a guardian charm
Leads them across that land of bogs and streams,
Of heat like steam-baths, fever's fiery bite,
Insects, and poisoned arrows that pursue.
At last they push their way from far Peru
Round numberless river turns, and come in sight

Of Atlantic billows, where, in ships that bear
Cordage of vines, and strips of sailcloth sewn
From blankets, they exchange the vast unknown
For safe, familiar scenes now shining doubly fair.

II

    In long canoes they paddle, the hunters alert for prey,
Curving on nameless currents through forests of twilight
        gray.
Score upon score they voyage, with nooses and spears and
        guns,
Dark-browed and bearded rovers who pillage like Avars
        or Huns.

    In the jungle-shaded clearing where manioc roots
        are sowed,
They charge with the panther's wildness the big palm-thatched
        abode,
And to the crash of gunfire, the sizzling of torchlit flame
The hunters hold a round-up of the howling human game.

    In chains and ropes, with stripes across the back,
Lashed in canoes, their hunched-up shoulders bare
Beneath the drag of sorrow or disease,
The victims of the brigands' slave-attack
Are carried off, not knowing why or where,
And sold in settlements of the Portuguese,
They who survive — less numerous than those
Of whom a ghastly liberator will dispose.

    Now every European could be king,
With Indian slaves to plow and hunt and fish,
To blaze his pathways, fight his wars, and bring

Wood from the forest; humor his maddest wish.
And so decay began
Like infection in a tooth — the rot that grows
Wherever preying man
Finds pleasure or capital in human woes.
Soon, with the African as well in yoke,
The backbone of man's will and spirit broke
In languor and corruption that awoke
As in war-glutted Rome an age before.

Meanwhile the tall lush cane,
With honeyed juices in its succulent core,
Harnessed the laborers to bend and strain
As beasts of burden drooping at the mill
That crushed the stalks and crushed the workers too,
And, dragon-like, would chew
Others and others, others, others still.
Then, in the later years, that timeless curse
So many lands, enduring, have extolled
As though they valued riches in reverse,
Fell on the country — and its name was Gold.
Gold! — and that syllable lit
Tinder within the mind, till man became
A thrusting terror, with but little wit
And less of shame —
A beast of bottomless frenzy and desire,
Awed by a metal's shine, pledging his bones for hire.

As when the rats and children in the fable,
Enamoured of the sweet Pied Piper's song,
Like needles drawn by magnets, were unable
To keep from drifting with the dazzled throng,
So friars and merchants, herders of cows and sheep,

White men and red and black, dashed forth to reap
The lustrous booty. Now the fields lay bare,
And shafts were sunken dangerously deep,
And moiling in the dark beneath the flare
Of torches, slaves were lashed in groaning lines,
Half naked in a heat that choked and killed,
Passing from hand to hand the buckets filled
With hard and heavy fruitage of the mines.
And in the dust-swirl of the treasure hunt,
When civil war blew past with flaming throes,
And plenty edged the fleshless arms of want,
And the wild sons of Sao Paulo fought
With knives and musket shots and cutlass blows,
What was the prize, I wondered, what the loot
Whose capture or pursuit
Was worth the rubble that the gold rush brought?

III

Back to a high-ridged coastal land I traveled,
Where long, in great rock-walls, the Incas reigned.
And though the empire's woof had been unraveled,
Rebellious fires remained.
"Come! Hurl the despots down!"
Thundered the Inca Manco, royal heir.
"Tyrants who've smashed our doors, usurped our crown,
Outraged our daughters, stripped our temples bare,
Thrown out our brothers for the dogs to tear,
Burned us, enslaved us, mocked our gods, and made
Our country like a hut that eagles raid!
Hear, kinsmen! Rise, and drive
The monsters into the sea! None, none shall stay alive!"

The speared and arrowed braves were thousands strong,
But more than weapons armed them for the fight —
Cracklings of fury at their people's wrong,
Which they alone could right.
Forward to Cuzco! central city, site
Of ancient glory! To possess this place
Will be to crush the snake, the pale-skinned race!

I wandered to the town's wide public square,
Its palace, with a gate in many tones
Of colored marble. Every thoroughfare
Held a stone conduit, and was paved with stones
And flanked by houses in rectangular zones.
But most was I impressed
By the huge Temple of the Sun, which wore
A coronal of gold, while golden plates
Coated its heart as feathers coat a nest,
And golden thrones, with golden sun-rays, bore
The mummies of old reverenced potentates.
Surmounting all, a three-banked fortress stared,
With triple towers projecting, hewn of rocks
Massively joined in elephantine blocks,
With tunnels and ramparts skillfully prepared
To balk assailants. Lacking this retreat,
No invader's triumph could be made complete.

As when the lowering purple storm-clouds burst,
The legions of Manco hurled their grand assault
With screeches like the tortured and accursed
In swarms innumerable as locust packs,
And guns and barricades were chaff to halt
The torrent of their attacks.
As though on wings they flew, and in a wind

That puffed and sneered and dinned
Till it outyelled the raving battle cries,
Cinders and sparks cascaded to the skies
From roofs of reeds and straw; the smoke-braids curled
So black and dense
Men gasped for air, while in hoarse turbulence
Forward and forward still the rebels swirled.

    Fighting in courts and streets,
Scooping deep pitfalls to entrap the foe,
Pouring out cataracts to overflow
With inundating sheets,
At last, exultantly shouting, they had taken
All but some houses and the central square.
And then the Spaniards met, droop-lipped and shaken,
With drawn gray faces trenched by pain and care;
And heard a plan. Soon, while the rebels yelled
In wild cavorting antics, what the sight
That suddenly they beheld
To choke the paroxysms of their delight!
What shapes, like beetles, in a clinging crawl
With ropes and ladders up the fortress wall!
Now, on the ramparts, how the battle raged!
But pace by pace the attackers crept ahead,
Till, where in smoke and blood the fight was waged,
A tan-skinned chieftain, circled by his dead,
Groaned that the gods had failed him; turned and fled.

    But one there was who, with unvanquished will,
A dark Leonidas, with club swung high,
Strode round and round; challenged that he would kill
All who would not remain to fight and die.
Finally, with a parapet-daring lunge,

He leapt, he vaulted over the fortress rim,
And by that fatal plunge
Proclaimed no Spaniard ever could capture him
In body or spirit. Vain heroic deed!
Then had some overseeing power decreed
The revolution should not quite succeed?
Or was it maniac chance,
A hair's breadth in the knot of circumstance,
Which shaped the victory,
And altered all things to be,
And crushed forever the native bow and lance?

IV

Great-domed, and white with everlasting snows,
Elbowing miles above an eel-thin plain,
The sovereigns of the southern Andes rose —
A long, deep-canyoned chain.
Under their knees, in woods and meadowlands,
Clustered a half nomadic folk, who raised
Corn and potatoes, while small hunting bands
Wandered in valleys where vicunas grazed —
The Arauchanians — tall, and slant of eye,
Broad-headed, spacious-breasted, scarcely draped,
Fierce as Apaches; few they seized escaped
Ordeal by torture that might pacify
The gods in sacrifice. Their warrior corps
Kept them secure when weaker tribes succumbed,
And from beyond the River Maule, they thumbed
Their noses at the Incan conqueror.
But now a sterner foe,
Before whose fire less doughty bands withdrew,
Burst down like Tatars, spurred by overthrow
Of the princes of Peru.

Pedro Valdivia, Spanish knight who aimed
To stride in Cortes' and Pizarro's track,
Might have been jewel-crowned and richly famed
Had templed cities towered for his attack.
But he must comb a barren countryside,
Till what he most desired was most denied.
In fastnesses where ribboned glaciers glared
And limbs froze solid, or where deserts rolled
And men, with dry tongues lolling out, despaired
In broiler heat, his hand was bold and firm . . .
Then, after a dragging Purgatorial term,
His armored horsemen hewed and gashed their way
To a river where, with arrows, clubs and spears,
The high-cheeked tribesmen of the plain and wood,
Ranged in a fenced array,
Defiantly stood.
He saw the shields of hide, while in his ears
The war-hoots shrilled. Should he assail this host
And dare inglorious death for all his band?
And yet — the Spanish boast
Remained: no force could stand
Against their valor. "Forward!" rang his shout.
Plunging across the stream, he ordered, "Fire!"
And the guns bellowed with a murderous spout,
And, dazzled, he watched the bleeding horde retire.
Deep was the Arauchanian dread and wonder,
For who could battle when the gods made thunder?

Forth to new triumph, with their guns and horses,
The conquerors rode, but piled along the route
Blank fury, raw antagonistic forces
That bore a poisonous fruit.
Raised in the heretic-burning home tradition

That made the Spaniards crueller than a snake,
Valdivia, in icy self-ambition
Tripped on a blind mistake.
See! Indian captives freed
Only to sigh and moan,
With stumps   that gape and bleed
Where living hands had grown!
And hear the people wail
When the mangled men return —
The sparks will hardly fail
To light new fires, and burn
For vengeance, vengeance that will unify
All Arauchanian clans to battle, bear and die.

It was as though the tigers, fanged and clawed
In slashing brotherhoods,
Had organized beneath a chief, and warred
To save their hunting woods.
I watched the raiders scuttle down, surprising
The Spaniards with a sudden arrowed flight,
Leaving but stones and shards, and smoke arising,
And ashes at a town's new-founded site.
And then I saw a leader, famed in song,
Who, like a nemesis, a lashing fate,
Loomed iron-breasted, to retaliate
Against a mountainous wrong.

Heedlessly as his side, Valdivia nursed
The Indian lad by whom his life would be
Defeated and accursed;
Who, watching the Spaniards face to face, could see
They were but men, not sons of deity.
Mark him! Lautaro, with the bit and rein,

A slave-boy grooming horses of his lords.
But in his eyes there blazed a whole campaign
Of clashing swords.
And having viewed his masters long and well,
One day he vanished; and I saw him stride
Where Arauchanian huts of poles and thatch
Clung to the bare, rock-crusted mountainside.
"Hear me! This upstart power is but a shell
Our courage can more than match!"
I heard him pleading; and a voice replied,
"Our courage can more than match!"; and men drew round
As to a prophet luminously revealed,
And swore they would not bend, they would not yield
One pebble of native ground,
And armed with clubs and bows, streamed forth to halt
Valdivia's conquering surge by one combined assault.

Strange that the lordly civilized domains
Far to the north, crumbled with cloud-like haste,
While the rude huntsmen of the southern waste
Tenaciously fought as old sword-swinging Danes.
Not in their simple lives the secret rests,
For simple folk may be the first enslaved.
But by the fire and steel within their breasts
Their fields and homes were saved.
Still thrusting on, still battling to despoil
The Indians of their loved ancestral soil,
Valdivia won his way with mulelike toil.
Then, in the marsh of Tucapel, a fight!
Trapped in an ambush on the miry plain
While horses floundered, he must face the might
Of a brave captain showering bolts like rain.
Charge upon charge, the arrowed hundreds whirled

Against the Spaniards in a mass attack.
Charge upon charge the arquebuses hurled
Impetuously back.
But suddenly, with a flash
As of a lunging lance,
Lautaro led the dash
Against the foe's advance.
Like imps the warriors seemed,
Like devils they swung about,
While men and horses screamed
In a crazed nightmarish rout.
All over the bloodied pools and reddened ground
Of the marsh of Tucapel,
Men wallowed and reeled and fell;
And some, borne under by hooting foes, were bound;
And finally the fiendish, trumpeting sound
Shrilled a new note, shrieking the overtone
Of victory; the Indians strode alone
Save for the captives, tied
And slashed and torn, muddied and desolate-eyed.

Among the prisoners, haughtily erect,
Valdivia stood, daring the scorching rage
Of a fierce leader, once his stable boy.
And little compassion could a man expect
Who'd been directing actor on a stage
Marked "Torture! Maim! Destroy!"
And some will have it that Lautaro said,
"Master, your eyes were always set on gold,
So of the molten treasure you'll be fed
All that a man can hold!"
But this we know: Valdivia sank from sight
After that last grim fight,

Though still in Chile, for two hundred years,
The Spanish guns faced Arauchanian spears.

  Out of the clouds one day a vision stared:
Lautaro, arrow-slain, with glowering form
And eyes that darkened like the thunderstorm,
While in his chest a blood-red injury glared.
"Press on! Press on! Press on!" they seemed to cry.
And with his image leading heaven-high,
The Arauchanians, through the centuries,
Were hardened to fight, to suffer and defy.

V

  The mission walls were shaped of whitewashed clay,
With long verandas, and the roof was tiled;
And, far around, the Indian cabins lay,
And fields were green, and garnered crops were piled.
Serving the patriarchal enterprise
Of the grave Jesuits of Paraguay,
The people, clad in frocks
Of baggy cotton, like some loose disguise
Meant for a mask, came forth to toil in flocks.
Yet merrily, and to the sound of flutes,
They tended the cows, and harvested the wheat,
And climbed the orchard trees for purpling fruits
In the mild autumn heat.
Simple their lives, and simple their regime,
And moneyless as some Utopian dream,
With prayer and work and festival the theme
Ever recurring: all was owned by all,
None starved while any neighbor's loaf remained,
And none need vainly call
For salve when sick, or shelter when it rained.

But liberty became a watchdog chained,
And white man's ways bred demons of disease,
And whether the plan was nearest to fulfill
A rose-bright favor or corrosive ill,
What voice shall answer after centuries?

Then, in the final act, a swirl and dash
Of armed adventurers, crying, "Diamonds! Gold!"
The earth-walls of the mission crack and crash;
The Indians, writhing in chains and ropes, are sold.
And while the chorused sighs
Of captives mount beneath unhearing skies,
Long in a world that tumult sways and hate
Has reddened, memories of the Jesuit state
Will bless like visions out of paradise.

VI

Brightly the sparks were flying
From lands that would be free;
From ancient kingdoms dying,
And nations yet to be;

From cold New England waters
Where patriots rose, and swore
To save their sons and daughters
From clamps that squeezed and tore;

And from the red upheaval
Of France in storm and blood,
Where out of death and evil
Surely new worlds would bud —

From these, and writs of sages
On all men's equal birth,

The Latin rebel gauges
Hopes of a fairer earth.

Vague in the background, pack on shoulder, looms
The Indian with the sorrow-tautened face;
The half-breed that a scowling fortune dooms
To jeers and lashes for his mongrel race;
And settlers of Caucasian blood, who glower
When Lisbon's lords or grandees of Castile
Flout them like beggared cousins; flaunt a power
As over dogs they train to trot and heel.
Many the winds that, could one truly read,
Might seem to scatter revolution's seed,
And now and then a brave, soon-muffled deed
Told of volcanic fires that lunged beneath
A thin concealing sheath.

* * *

The lightning's devil-dance, the thresh and moaning
Of trees uprooted where the night-gusts blew,
Startled the jungle, when a weird intoning
Spoke of dark hundreds in a rendezvous.
Baukmann, witch-doctor, robed in flowing red,
With features twisted, waving sword upraised
And long gesticulating arms outspread,
Stood where a fire, crackling with resin, blazed
Under the rock-eaves of a precipice.
Poised as the thunder snarled hoarse emphasis,
He droned, with hollow rumblings, "Friends and kin,
Black men of Haiti! for three hundred years
Our people have been cursed by blows and sneers.
But now deliverance comes!
Now we will snap our chains!
Hear how all heaven, with a roll of drums,

Joins in our just campaigns!
Hear how the crashing rains,
Hurled from above by high invisible powers,
Threaten the tyrants! scream in winds and showers!"

    Then, from the listening horde,
A long, deep, ululating chorus rose,
Loud with the wail of ancient wrongs and woes.
And while the leader crazily flashed his sword
And the lightning leapt in ever dizzier throes,
And the bonfires, like convulsive demons, flared,
And a huge rock-altar showed
Fresh stains where blood of a goat and deer had flowed,
A maiden came, her body all unbared,
And drank of poison; then, with ecstasy,
Chanted of glories destined yet to be —
A people risen — joy — equality!
Soon, with a gasp, she staggered; she fell, she died.
And through the forests of the night there poured
Fresh lamentations of a host that sighed
And groaned and wept and cried.
"Oh, strike our shackles off! Lord, Lord! Unchain us,
    Lord!"

    Speechless among the crowd stood one whose goal
Would be to make the frenzied dream come true.
I saw him, massive-domed, with skin like coal,
Small mouth, thick sensuous lips, and teeth that grew
Close-packed and sparkling in defiant white.
Once to his mind, men say, a vision came:
A radiant woman, garbed in scarlet light,
Perched on a cloud-bank, strewing flowers of flame,
While unseen trumpets voiced exultant song:

"You, Toussaint, you shall rise,
A Spartacus of the hosts that men despise,
To smite away the old, back-blistering wrong,
And teach your flock to laugh beneath kind skies!"

Before me fluctuating pictures played
Of an imperious, proud-striding soul —
More than a Spartacus — one who essayed
The part of Washington, a Cromwell's role.
Not like a liberator, drilled to lead,
He'd passed his nursling years;
With shackles on his wrists, though finally freed,
He knew the scourge that sears.
I saw him slinking on a forest track
Like an avenger of dead centuries,
Guiding his ragged pale-clad companies
As a wolf may guide a pack.
And slashing like a wolf, he slipped away
With red plume lifted. Where the palm-leaves lay
In stewing jungles, I observed the fray;
And after fire and shot had scoured the isle,
I saw him glitter on a seat of state
In blue and gold, in grand monarchial style,
A reigning potentate,
A man of sparks and steel
Who scattered magisterial decrees
For roads and industries
And, hammer-fisted, sought the people's weal . . .
Until, like many another who is numbed
By his own God-position, he succumbed
To foes the bristles of his pride brought down.

Not lightly a long-acclaimed dynastic king
Would have provoked the great Napoleon's frown.
Yet Toussaint dared to fling
Stark challenge in his face. Oh, brave and rash!
Soon came the sequel in the approaching sails
Of French invaders — cannon's boom and flash,
And tramping squadrons that, like hurricane gales,
Cut swaths across the island. Then the end,
After red battle and an earth scorched bare —
The Negro sovereign fell,
Caught in a web as treacherous and unfair
As ever the wiles of spiders could extend.

There was a cavelike, narrow, ice-caked cell
High in a fortress on an Alpine crag.
And in the dimness and the damp and cold,
He who was child of light and warmth must drag
His hours away in pain's long, clawing hold.
And he who bruised his heart that freedom's flag
Might never fold,
Now on a frosty foreign mountainside,
Banished from friends and kindred, and denied
Fire and light, and even a healing word,
Must writhe and suffer like the crucified.
And yet — if in the leader's dying ears
Gravely the Angel of the Judgment spoke,
"And what the gain, the fruitage of your years?",
He might have shown: a people's happy tears,
A chain that crumbled, and a cast-off yoke.

VII

The church-bells pealed with slow reverberations,
And pealed and pealed, a rolling, echoing plea,

Calling the people from their occupations
As at a lord's decree.
Armed with long bows and muskets, clubs and knives,
They packed the church, and crowded far around
The village square, and through the burial ground,
And at their side were swarthy sons and wives —
Barefooted, ragged-sleeved,
The disinherited, the butts of fate,
Some vomited from the jail, just now relieved
Of a sad human freight.
And still the bells tolled on, their urgent mood
Timed to the mutterings of the multitude.

And when at last the pealing faltered, ceased,
The swarms swirled round, their murmuring but increased.
Grimly before them in black robe and cross,
With hands upraised, beckoned a grizzled priest
Loved by them all for his benignities,
Making of silk, growing of olive trees
To slacken the claws of Spain's monopolies.

"Children of God! Hearken my words!" he cried.
"For I, Hidalgo, bear the Lord's command,
Tender as ever a bridegroom's to a bride,
To succor your homes and mine. Hear me! Our land
Today is not our own!
In olden times, robbers from distant shores,
Taking our soil like taloned predators,
Swarmed down, and stripped our country to the bone!
So let us rise! and with the Lord behind us,
Hurl out the oppressor! burst the cords that bind us!"

Fierce as a stream in spate,
The rabble seethed and roared.
Screeches of rage and hate
Dinned from the milling horde,
And banners flashed and soared,
"Virgin of Guadalaupe!", and the sign,
"Down with bad government!" Forward they went
Loosed in abandonment,
Many a broken group and straggling line,
Women among them, striking villages bare,
Scooping up maize, raiding the fruited tree,
Driven as by a drunken ecstasy
To gouge wide lanes of havoc everywhere.
All things they swept before them, but they moved
Less as an army than a wild-beast swarm,
And, even as Europe's peasant rabbles, proved
A mob may rave more terribly than a storm.

Batter and pound and hack!
Ravage and loot and slay!
Hear now the raw attack
On a city along the way!
Bludgeonings at closed doors! fragmented walls
Down-crashing! red of fires! screams and pleas
Of doomed men, and the pack's hyena calls
As they unclothe the dead, or dash to seize
Fabrics and vases. For the long-abused
It was as though a steaming monstrous pot
Had burst its lid, and vapors scalding hot
Took vengeance for the chains that bound and bruised!

After a time, the fighting priest had led
Tempestuous thousands to a mountain place

Where, miles below, gleaming in gemlike grace,
The spires and roofs of Mexico were spread.
Like Hannibal when he surveyed afar
The walls of Rome, Hidalgo now observed
The prize of his ambition, yet some bar
Was built to leave him fluttering or unnerved.
Or was it that he feared
His wild-beast followers, who might have burned
Or battered to dust the city? Back he turned,
And while he wandered on through crowds that cheered,
His was the figure of the Seeker, barred
After the golden gates have beckoned wide,
When he beholds their splendor glistening-eyed,
Then stumbles on and on where rocks are sharp and hard.

    And yet, though dour defeat
Would smite, and his rude swarms could not endure
Against drilled battle troops, and he would meet
A destiny that from the start was sure,
When he must stand before the cold, bare steel
Of levelled muskets, he would still become
Honored like many whom a bright ideal
Has pitched to martyrdom,
Remembered less for glories brought to be
Than for his echoing bid to a people's liberty.

VIII

    As just before a heralded king has called,
A spell, an expectation seemed to reign
In Guayaquil, upon whose river plain
The twisted earthen streets were wooden-walled.
There, when a ship came in, upon the dock
Were two who met with ceremonious bows,

Seeming to mate no more than fire and rock,
And yet alike as neighboring mountain brows.
One, weighted by the years, was grave and gray,
Frugal of speech, though of commanding mien;
The other, lithe and gay,
With quick, thin figure, an ebullient tone,
Moods like the wind, and black eyes dagger-keen,
In which a flame, a magnetism shone.

    "Hail, San Martín!" the cry
Blithely rang forth. "Bolívar!" came a cheer
In swift reply.
"Twin liberators!" Would it not appear
As when two crashing canyoned torrents merge
And thunder seaward with a mightier surge,
These dominant two would mate in one career,
Stronger for mingling forces? But not so!
The deeper currents of man's spirit flow
With many a secret swirl and undertow,
Beyond our probing. Some immense divide
Sundered the pair. The elder man departed
Silent and somber-hearted
After the toasts, the banquet glow had died.
I saw him moodily voyage overseas,
To roam the streets of Paris and Boulogne,
One of a crowd of outlawed refugees,
Unhonored and unknown.

    Yet time would recognize
José de San Martín, who fought to wrest
His pinioned people from the Spanish vise,
And marched straight forward to accept the test
Careless of puffballs of the world's applause.

Far on the western Argentinian plains
Of Cuyo, under white Andean chains,
I heard him summon warriors for the cause.
I watched the women bring
The jeweled case and ring —
Long-treasured heirlooms, while their mates and sons
Were melting church-bells, fabricating guns
In foundries he constructed. Then I marked
How, like the troops of Carthage when of old
Bowmen and slingers challenged Alpine passes,
He gathered mules and horses and embarked
Amid a resolute force into the cold
Of flinty peaks, whose beaked and glacial masses
Glared warnings high above. Twisting up trails
Miles in the sky, where cattle reeled and sagged
And men were massacred by winds like flails
Ripping at lungs, the hang-necked horses dragged
Artillery wagons. On precipitous slopes
Impassable to hoofs, the men must haul
Dismantled cannon piece by piece with ropes
Up ledges smooth with ice, compelled to crawl
Round blank crevasses. Many would complete
The long, grim trek on some deep shelf of snow;
And of the beasts, far less than half would eat
The grass of plains below.

    But up and up and on
The general pushed, across the gale-whipped rise;
Then with his troops, grown thin and travel-worn,
Wound to the lowlands. Swooping by surprise
With rapier-sudden sallies
Upon the Spaniards in Chilean valleys,
He plucked the fruit on which so long his eyes

Had fastened; gained a flaming victory,
And waving aside all honors, scorning gifts,
He smiled to watch the clouds, through widening rifts,
Let in the sun-rays of new liberty.

IX

"Never I'll rest until the bonds are broken
That tie my nation! Witness, God, my vow!"
In dedicated tones these words were spoken
By one upon his knees, with hatless brow,
High on the Aventine. There, far unfurled,
The arches and columns of the Roman world
Called from their ruins to his eager youth.

"For I, Bolívar," bravely he reflected,
"Will pull out tyranny like an aching tooth!
No more my kin will cringe like curs, directed
By masters overseas!" It may be well
He could not pierce tomorrow's citadel
And with a clarifying lens, foretell
Death-grips, and epic tramps beneath bald peaks;
Battles with wild horse-fighters of the plain
Who wheeled like flanking archers of Tamerlane;
And that decree, cruel as hawkish beaks,
Which struck against the guiltless, with the cry,
"Fight at my side, or die!"

But after flaring years
Fitful with steep descents and high rebounds,
Clashing colleagues in envy-stained careers,
Ruses, escapes, and smoking battle grounds,
Gallantly in the end he would achieve
Laurels that rarely emperors receive,

And count, to mark his fame,
Four nations freed, and one that took his name,
And yet, upon his crag of hailed success,
Almost as when a sky-borne pilot rues
Engines that sputter, balk, and fatally lose
High altitude, he'd stare on emptiness.
Groaning, he would discern
What men in saddened later lands would learn
After eruptions of red tragedy:
A nation has to earn
The bright pavilions of democracy.
For when a people, generation-long,
Is ruled by ropes and scourges from above
And laws that squeeze it like an iron glove,
How can the ignorant throng
Lead with the wisdom of a Pericles?
Blown by cyclonic animosities,
Flung on cross-currents of tumultuous aims,
Bolívar would lament, "I have but plowed the seas."

    But though his sword would slash away ten ills
To bring nine others, and the Promised Land,
Calm in an aura of harmonious wills,
Would seem remote as temples Thutmos planned,
Still we who look afar on human deeds
Know they are built on more than steel or stone,
And often a tower in the mind succeeds
When eyes detect no walls, and ears no tone.
Bolívar, dying early, racked by sorrow,
Might still look out, and in a long tomorrow
See how he'd hewn a trail, had marked a path
Which through the fog and nettles, tears and grime,
His people would pursue in their slow, winding climb.

X

Like some antique Crusading brotherhood,
They pushed through houseless valleys and plateaux;
Through deserts where the barrel cacti stood,
Any canyons under shelves of rock and snow.
On horseback and on muleback, forth they rode,
Franciscan padres clad in blue and gray,
Tribesmen in deerskin, soldiers splashed with red;
And sometimes, where the deep hill-chaparral spread,
A scout, with raised machete slashing, strode
To clear the path. Then, near a fair blue bay,
Under wide ranges by the western sea,
In a charmed land where winter never came
But where the mountain shoulders were aflame
With golden poppies, and a tapestry
Of flowers like the roses of Castile,
They knelt with hands upraised to One above,
That He, in light and love,
Might smile indulgently on their ideal.

Surely, great faith had moved them, and the sense
Which fires apostles of a thousand creeds,
That theirs alone is true beneficence,
And theirs the single key to spirit-needs.
Limping among the pilgrims, cross in hand,
Came Junipero Serra — priest who blest
The earliest mission in this sun-warmed land
Of the paradisal West,
This Alta California. What he saw
Was but a brushwood hovel, with a roof
Of reeds; but he required no better proof
Of God's eternal law
That yet would save the heathen.

                          Far to north,
Beyond long valleys, antelope-dotted plains,
Oak and madrona woods, and mountain chains,
The Fathers pushed. I watched their missions rise,
Tile-roofed, adobe-walled, with bell-towers reared
To sound a chorus to the listening skies;
And round them green, far-spreading acres, cleared
For maize and barley, fig and apple trees,
And purpling vines. Before the mission gate
The traveler, though unknown, might leave his mount
In sun or storm, at early hours or late,
Knowing that he could count
On plain, warm-hearted hospitalities —
Board and a room — if he desired to stay,
Lulled by the shrubs and flowers, the fountain's flow,
Lounging and resting through the sunny day
In the arched corridor or patio.

                    *   *   *

    Now on the mild coast Indian fell the prod
Of alien orders and a scowling god.
Now, after lives free as the fox or bear,
Threading day-long the forest undergreen,
Catching the lizard, climbing the tall rock-stair;
After the acorn-gathering routine,
Grasshopper hunts, searches for seed and roots,
Trapping of fish, and plucking of wild fruits,
And warless lives in huts of bark or grass,
Suddenly came to pass
A revolution — foreign strange pursuits
To puzzle and harass.

    Whip-lashes of pontifical control —
Work by compulsion, faith by high command,

Laws like harpoons for some dim holy goal,
Hot fever-fiends few bodies could withstand —
Struck at the redmen. On the mission grounds
I watched, with wooden plows, the captives strain,
Or driving sheep or cows in sun or rain;
I saw the women mope like kenneled hounds,
Bolted indoors while stocks clamped tight the shapes
Of men and squaws accused.
And there were midnight flights and rash escapes
Of victims striped and bruised;
And soldiers galloped after, shots rang out,
And some, regained, were brought with snarl and shout
Back to their masters' mock-benignity.
Lost was the tribal life, since Spaniards tore
And ripped away the roof that served before,
Leaving them dazed as men adrift at sea,
Making them houseless on their native shore.
Not that they meant it thus; they could not halt
A law that even in Xerxes' day was old.
We may take towns and temples by assault,
But cannot match men's hearts to our own mold.

Yet like a dream of blest Hesperides
Would seem the padres' old simplicities
In after-time, with missions in decay,
The Fathers leaving, and the Indians freed —
Booty for bloated lust and fat-jowled greed —
To swagger with the tinkling glass, and play
With dice in plush-green parlors, and to steal
Horses and cattle in the whirlwind raid.
How rivet down their lives upon the wheel
Of white man's industry and white man's trade?
But brute reprisals struck, like retribution

Of Hunnish blood-feuds — ruffian chiefs who held
Annihilation was the sure solution,
And hunted as for wolves or rats, and felled
Old men and young; dropped women as they fled;
Shot down the babes; and dashed with scalping-knives
To end still-struggling lives
Or desecrate the newly fallen dead.

   And what if soiled survivors — wretches left
Grubbing in wild ravines like things bereft
With stones and digging sticks — might still intrude
Upon the whites, haunting the farms for food?
Round them all up! Ignore their plaints and pleas!
Herd them to reservations! Settled there
In plains of spiny brush or desert-bare,
They may take flight, or wither of disease,
Famine, or heart's unease.
But in the valleys where they stalked the deer,
Harpooned the salmon from the riverbeds
And lit their fires in groves of oak or pine,
Old tribes and nations soon will disappear,
And in museums leave their only sign
In patterned baskets, pots and arrowheads.

VI. Building Blocks and Blows

". . . the surging and flowing of peoples"

Vast as the threshing of tides in the foamy Atlantic
From Florida's keys to headlands of Spain and of Norway;
Vast as the roll of the billows, the combing of breakers,
Is the surging and flowing of peoples from islands and
    empires.
Westward they swirl to the shores of a fledgling republic
As though at the throb of the same universal propulsion,
From ancient stone cities whose streets are twisted like
    tendrils,
The muddy farm-road, and the peat-bog and pasture and
    forest.

Crowded as hen-coops to their bulging bows
With freight of immigrants and refugees,
Small are the ships, almost as cramped as those
That heaved the earliest Pilgrims overseas.
Weeping and laughing, dusty throngs embark;
Singly, or mixed with garrulous family groups,
The voyager, weighed down with bundles, stoops
Awkwardly to the hold's dense reeking dark.
And soon the sails are spread, the pitching craft
Points her long bowsprit to the sundown shore.
Each with his bag in barely a two-by-four,
Swung like a drifter on a wind-swept raft,
Brushed by the rats, feeling the vermin crawl,
Cooking a meager meal by smoky fires,

128

And bearing, for the endless passage, all
The bread and meat and bedding he requires,
The traveler may be racked by coughs, or lie
Shaken with fever, fearing he will die,
While gusts blow shrill and waves curl castle-high.

But at last an end of dread
After the long, long night!
His glad eyes see, ahead,
The land of hope and light:
The steeple-cloven green
Of Boston's twining ways,
Or a brisk Manhattan scene
Of horse-drawn carts and drays!
Yet there the migrants, with their mounded goods
Beside them on the wharf, may droop forlorn
As lost dogs circling for the master's trail.
And some, where jackals nose, are snatched and torn,
While agents of benevolent brotherhoods
Smile upon many; lead them to a haven
Sad-eyed, in shreds and rags, unwashed, unshaven,
When other hostels fail.

Almost as though the waves that bore them west
Were driven on a planetary tide,
Thousands, on reaching harbor, cannot rest,
But seek a far and savage countryside.
There, mingled with the ever-widening streams
Looping through mountains to the rough unknown,
I see them hitching mules and packing teams
With the few sticks and wares they call their own,
And plodding mapless miles
Under great trees whose overarching aisles

Drape out the sun. And where shy antlered faces
Or furry snouts accost them from the green
That juts in walls, they throw up dwelling-places
Of clay and logs deep in some mossed ravine
Or lake-rimmed hollow. Then the thud and thump
Of axes smash the silence; and the fields,
Dotted with many a log and splintered stump,
Are streaked with straggling yields.

From sparse New England's stony beggared soil,
From southern dunes and pine-lands, wanderers flock,
And, heaving and tugging in bone-wrenching toil,
Battle and die. Slowly the towns are born,
Till Cincinnati, with her hog-pens, stares
Where the immense Ohio surges on
And wood-fed steamers churn on thoroughfares
That seek the Gulf. But where the towers will soar
Of State and Dearborn Streets, one still would miss
All promise of a proud metropolis —
Some cabins and a fort, alone on a long green shore.

Yet who that scans the tale
Can confidently balance gain and loss?
An empire opened, and a bloody trail
Of scalps, and wigwams seared without remorse;
And bears and bison slaughtered till they passed
Utterly as the tribes of ancient Thrace;
And forests charred, or felled as by a blast
Of a comet out of space;
And hills gouged out, lake-basins clogged with silt;
And rivers that gray wastes pollute and choke;
Soil that laborious centuries have built,
Now gullied deep, the grave of elm and oak.

Ah, great is progress, and our pride and light.
But oh that man, from his sultanic height,
Would cease to line its way with bones and ash,
Would cease to hack his trail with dynamite!

II

    As one who, with flood torrents at his breast,
Valiantly strives, and rears a knee-high dike,
So still some dusky champions would strike
Against white raiders of the north and west.
Predominant and proud, there flashed on me
A man stern-featured — glowing eyes that stared
Out of twin pits of ageless tragedy,
Yet with the bright hawk-glint of one who dared —
Tecumseh, Shooting Star,
First of his people, son of a Shawnee chief,
Upon whose chest was marked a double scar
Of irremovable grief,
Recalling the regal Cornstalk, who had died
In a faithless paleface plot,
And his own father, arms flung high and wide,
Reeling beneath a white man's treacherous shot.

    Shove after shove, he saw his people driven
Out of their homes, their ancient hunting grounds,
Two meadows snatched for every meadow given,
While they were harried as by hawks and hounds.
But a great vision blazed across his mind,
A continent-spanning dream: that all his race,
All nations and all tribes, must be combined
Within the safe embrace
Of one alliance, rearing thus a wall
Against the whites. An Indian state would rise

Which none could batter down, and none despise,
And it would flourish like the valley oak,
And live at peace with all. —
So ran the dream. I saw him, loud with zeal,
Range from the Gulf to Minnesota woods,
And where round tepees stood with curls of smoke,
Discourse with scintillant speech of his ideal
To men who heard in stone-eyed brotherhoods
Of strange magnificent goals they could not feel.

        And not alone in speech,
In eloquent action I beheld him fighting,
Leading his thousands like a whirlwind smiting
The regiments of the foe with many a breach.
"Battle like men!" he cried. I gazed at him
When with a blazing face, convulsed and grim,
He saw war-hatchets flash
At fettered captives. With a shout and dash,
Fierce as a grizzly charging, he flung low
One of the murderers, and swept aside
Others with an infuriated blow.
Yet none could be more grave and dignified.
Bright in his war-paint, cheeks all daubed with red,
In moccasins and breechclout, he appeared
No more than any chief the paleface feared,
And yet, in British uniform, he led
A British corps against the United States,
Not knowing he could place no more reliance
On any white alliance
Than on the casual dicing of the fates.
One day he passed amid the battle's blare,
And all his visions, smokelike, fled in air,
Brilliant chimeras doomed before they started.

But he will live among the mighty-hearted
As long as dreamers struggle and despair.

III

Although I saw a newly wakened land
Reach out, expand, and yet again expand,
While steeples, wharves and cattle yards were planned,
Still the first right, prime fruitage of its shores —
That all men should be free
In a free society —
Reeled under mass attack. Inside its doors
The wreckers stood with crowbars, and their blows
Smashed columns with a patriotic pose.

Rotund and short, with plump and sober face
And disputatious mien too sure and proud,
John Adams, in the Presidential place,
Was bountifully endowed
As diplomat and scholar; without blame
He'd broken knightly blades in freedom's name.
And when the riotous rabble rose, and cried,
"Down, down with France! To arms! To arms!
        To arms!",
And clamored with rude alarms
At fancied wrongs that hatred magnified,
Adams was steeled against the oncoming clash:
Drums did not roll, nor sabres stab or flash.
But when a fire, round his official seat,
Smoldered and smoked, with freedom in retreat,
What demon of weakness gagged him, tied his hand?
What satyr of folly forced his life's defeat?
Strangely, he signed the law against sedition —

Let none henceforward voice profane suspicion
Of governmental failing or omission!

Howling, the mobs streamed forth; and judges yelled
In bedlam courts against defendants daring
To name the Constitution's Bill of Rights.
And if an editor, doom-flouting, held
All views deserved the same impartial airing,
Grim deputies might rap his door when nights
Were stormiest and darkest; like a wretch
Dragged forth for treason, he might serve a stretch
With thieves and murderers in a moldy cell.
And snoopers, garbage-hunting, combed and clawed;
The great and wise, as by rat-teeth, were gnawed;
Famed Jefferson himself was forced to dwell
Like one outlawed, while burrowing stealthy eyes
Ferreted through his papers. Now no more,
Even in church, his followers would be free,
Nor was he seen upon a salon floor
For fear of buzzing spies
And swaggering toasts, "Death to democracy!"

        Then, swiftly as a storm-wind's savagery,
The fury ebbed; and perched as President,
Jefferson swung aside the prison bars,
And forth in flocks the beaten victims went
To save the Stripes and Stars,
Yet knowing well what crouching monsters wait
Behind the doors of even the sanest state
In fuming bias, veiled and sputtering hate.

                        IV

        From the great mansion on the mountaintop
A call arose, and black folk clamored out,

Ran down the slope, and in a noisy rout
Raced to the carriage lumbering to a stop.
"He comes! He comes! The Master comes!" they cried.
And many laughed or shouted; others wept.
Black fingers clutched the door; and one inside
Felt loving arms around him, and was swept
Eagerly from the large upholstered seat —
A staid, tall man, with face unmarked by guile,
Long sandy hair, kind speech and courtly smile,
Who seemed as glad to greet
His fond old slaves as they to hail him back —
He who for days, on the jogging homeward track,
Had longed for good home faces, white and black.

Few, as they watched him, could have known that here
Was one the world would idolize, "the sage
Of Monticello," famed in his own age
And later times as statesman, scholar, seer.
Now, as I glanced at Jefferson's career,
I saw that birth was fate,
Which could devise for him and dominate
His devious branching paths. But something more
Presided as the captain of his days,
That spokesman hidden at the being's core
Which every life obeys.
I viewed his father's green Virginian land
Rolling in heights and thickets; and the son,
Who early took command,
Might have grown lax with idleness, the fun
Of the fox-hunter with his hounds and horses —
Except that more illuminating forces
Kindled his mind. Beneath the oil-lamp's glow
While the full-moon dropped steeply down the sky,

I saw him, with tight-furrowed brow, apply
His thoughts to Sophocles and Cicero.
Then from old bards and thinkers he would turn
Searchingly to the world about his door.
I watched him stalking on a courtroom floor,
A gangling young attorney yet to earn
His laurels, ruddy-cheeked, his gray eyes stern
And hazel-spotted, while with arms flung wide
He pleaded for a trembling octoroon.
"See him, a man like us! but one denied
Freedom's all-precious boon
Because his father's father's mother wore
A colored skin. So let him be released!"
As well preach Buddha's creed of light before
Drum-beating cannibals drooling at a feast!
And yet this episode
Bespoke his life's whole upward-winding road.

    I followed him, a giant striding high
Above the flushed horizons of his land,
School-keys and books in one far-beckoning hand,
And all tomorrow in his lifted eye.
I saw him swing a quill of fire to mark
The dome of still-unrisen centuries
For a stanch people daring to embark
Upon the squally seas
Of freedom from old bullying monarchies.

    Far to the south the Presidential gaze
Had traveled where the Father of Waters flowed
Past New Orleans — a strange and colored maze
Of many a bright or pastel-hued abode
Of brick or clay, with intricate iron grills

And crescent balconies. He threw his glance
Covetously across the rolling spread
Of river and wood, of bayous, prairies, hills,
Which far away, in battle-clouded France,
Appeared a hot, moon-barren waste that bred
Wild Indians and mosquitoes. "Let it go!"
Ordered Napoleon, and thus decreed
A grander, more reverberating deed
Than Ulm or Austerlitz would ever show.
And all Louisiana's lush domain,
Which charging Khans or Caesars might have fought
Through barricades of brick and fire to gain,
Was given easily as an uttered thought.
And gates were opened wide
To an adventurous clan,
The trapper and the guide
In an ever-rising tide
Of westward-pushing man;
While in green valleys where the bison strayed,
And on the rock-scarred, piny mountain slope,
The covered wagons, in a long parade,
Would roll to bloodshed, tragedy and hope.

V

First the explorers hack their way — as daring
As even an astronaut adrift in space —
Who, after years of triumph and despairing,
Might come, as strangers, to their starting place.
And how men looked, with daily expectation,
To find a waterway from east to west,
A Mississippi carrying navigation
From the mid-country to the splashing breast
Of the blown Pacific! When as yet this view

Called like a radiant reality,
Jefferson summoned forth an able two
To reach the sunset sea,
Lewis and Clark, whose names would be of note
To states unheard of then and times remote.

   Obscure as Africa's lion-haunted heart
Remained that fabled country from whose deeps
The swirling yellow-brown Missouri sweeps,
And into this misty vast, without a chart,
I saw a band of forty-three depart —
Three laden boats, one with a great square sail
And partly decked, and all with heaving oars,
While horses paced along high leafy shores
And sometimes galloped on a hunting trail.
In slow laborious weeks they might progress
Less than a modern car or rail express
Within as many hours. Ah, but that world
Of pristine sights and scents! the sunrise blazing
Garnet, or purple-domed, or mauve or pearled,
And wildflowers in bright crazyquilts unfurled,
And fenceless herds of elk and bison grazing,
And dams of beavers in the timbered streams,
And swamps and brush where fluttering bird-life teems!

   Over the billows of this virgin land
The men could stride breast forward, and withstand
All trials, all distance, all the snarls and bends
Of the long river. Then they had to pass
A winter where tall snowbanks, mass on mass,
Shadowed the wigwams of their Mandan friends
In blue sub-Arctic cold. And in the spring
Onward they ventured, while strange Indian fires

Smoked on the hills, and black and frosted spires
Jutted above them, and a thundering
Deep in snake-canyons summoned them, "Explore!"
And where the seething rapids twisted and foamed
Sometimes upon their stooping backs they bore
Canoes and arms and baggage, while they combed
Impassable recesses, bent on finding
A channel between the coasts. Yet what they found
Was a wide river's vastness westward winding,
The great Columbia. Skirting the soggy ground
Of Brobdingnagian forests, on they sped
Down a swift current, whose huge drifting trees
Threatened their craft; and finally were led
Past hillsides blurred with rainy draperies,
And heard the regular tramp and rush and tread
Of waves in unviewed seas.

VI

While the enormous West unlocked her doors,
Fury hit eastward with a falcon beak.
I marked, against the gray Atlantic shores,
The triple masts of the frigate *Chesapeake*,
Her Stars and Stripes, and square-rigged sails swung high.
And then the *Leopard*, of the English King,
Guns pointing, floated menacingly by,
And over the waves I heard an order ring,
"Halt! Halt! Our boarding crews
Must search you for deserters from our ships!"
And rapier-quick there snapped, from angry lips,
A resolute, "We refuse!"
Between the ships there billowed less of sea
Than might be traveled by a ball well thrown,
Granting the victim not a foot to flee

The sudden battle zone.
Three puffs of fire shot from the *Leopard's* side;
And balked by a burning sail, a toppled mast,
The *Chesapeake* replied
With only one flaming blast
Before the flag came down. Like pirates swarming
To snatch a prize, the assailants climbed the rail,
Swinging long swords about the deck, and storming
Down through the hatches in a yelling gale.
"Catch them, the slimy rogues!" A scuffling sound,
Curses and snarls came savagely from below,
And soon four squirming captives, slavishly bound,
Were prodded from the hold and forced to go
Down to the *Leopard's* boat and face the whips
And irons of His Majesty's fighting ships.

     Now peace hung trembling. "Shield our rights, our
         rights!"
Men clamored. "Crush the King!" And he, our chief,
The gentle sage who knew that war requites
Its author but in storm-blasts, hate and grief,
With wrinkling countenance and weary heart
Met the dilemma every leader knows:
Swept by a rain of unexpected blows,
Must he bow down? depart
From his ideal? No! for he clearly saw
The answer was not war.
Better decree that, as a last resort,
Vessels lie manless in the empty port.
Better the silent mill, the piled-up crates
Than shell-torn boys, the cannon's growled retort.
And so, though oaths and blusterings smote his ears,

No battle flags were waved. But less adept
Was his successor in more frantic years.

VII

In fleets and forts, by land and sea it blazed,
From Lake Champlain to where Gulf currents swept,
This war on which today we look amazed.
Wedged in the middle, like a puppy caught
Between two snapping bulldogs, we had strayed
Into a bout voracious empires fought
With truculent side-lunges at our trade.
And were wars made by logic, then our lance
As justly might have showed its edge to France
As to our mother, England. I could see
A figure scholarly and cool and bland,
One of the last of the great dynasty
That built a nation in a virgin land,
James Madison, daring to throw the dice
In time's most hazardous and heady game,
Staking his own astuteness with the aim
Of making peace the price.

But politics of Europe, like a net
Snarled by Napoleon and British guile,
Had caught his hand, and so he missed the throw.
And annalists will tell you even yet
That had he waited just a little while,
He'd not have seen the smoke of conflict blow.
Striking in rage and darkness, not forewarned,
We writhed in a war that patience would have scorned.

With puffs of smoke and fire, the privateers
Scouted and prowled down byways of the sea,

And like old skull-and-crossbone buccaneers,
Bore high-pooped prizes to captivity.
And on the land, where boys untried and raw
Crouched to confront the redcoats, what a scene
Of arms flung down and fleeing shapes I saw,
As often when war's timber is too green!
And flares from captured Washington's charred roofs,
And painted braves down-sweeping on Detroit,
And a threatened burst from Canada were proofs
Of moves not always valiant or adroit.

    And yet — the breasts that swelled
With patriotic pride,
When men at home beheld
The foreign foe defied!
Till the war-spirit, flooding like a tide,
Washed over scattered states
In surges of hot elation,
With rivalries, and hates,
And terrors, and a loud new love of nation.
Unhappily, amid the flame and stress,
Somehow the trade we fought for was unsafe
As streets that columns of diving bombers strafe,
And docks again became a silent wilderness.

    That long-faced general of the fiery air,
The slashing Andrew Jackson, who had tracked
Armies of braves like grizzlies to their lair,
Captained the trained sharpshooters, and attacked
At New Orleans. I watched his followers creep
Behind gun-barrels, through a gray thick blank
Of fog, beneath a thrown-up earthen bank,
Where a protecting ditch was straight and deep.

And suddenly, as though
Nature herself enlisted as ally,
The fog drew open, and a shining sky
Stared at the British foe.
And rifles snapped and crackled; shrill and loud
The English clamored where the dead were piled.
And while their shots flew wild
And stunned commanders fell and marksmen chose
Their game like deer, survivors in a crowd
Of panicky stragglers, at the battle's close,
Went scuttling and panting for a safe retreat
To guns and bulkheads of the waiting fleet.
Surely, a resonant victory! Yet fate
Was smiling with a new sardonic quirk,
And with a sneer, a smirk,
Muttered, "Too late! Too late!"
He who outlived that gory day would find
The blind had lashed the blind.
Papers of peace already had been signed.

VIII

Impetuous as though a spring propelled
His life-maneuvers with a snap and flash,
The tides and torrents of his being welled
Forward with an impulsive rush and splash.
Born with a gun in hand, bristling to fight,
He made, it seemed, his entry on the stage
With the thrust and clangor of a jousting knight,
Compelled to wage
Continual warfare. I observed the boy
Among log cabins and in border mud,
Contentious as a nettle, finding joy
In spurred cocks battling with a spurt of blood.

Then, at a ripe thirteen,
Jackson beholds a more ensanguined scene.
Looks how he steals away
To join the Revolution's brave array,
A volunteer! Already thus he sips
The bitters of war. One day he sees a row
Of scarlet coats that ring him all about,
And raises his arms, a prisoner, with wry lips
And shoulders sagging low;
Then hears curt orders rasping; hears the shout
Of a jaunty captain; notes his kinglike air:
"Boy! Black my boots!" With an indignant growl,
Reckless as one unwarned who raps a bear,
He answers, "Black your own!" The officer's scowl
Is dark as storm-banks. "What! you surly scamp,
You mock me! Does your lordship then suppose
You've been declared commandant of the camp?"
The flat edge of a sword, with pummeling blows,
Beats down, and thuds against the rebel's head,
Which streams with crimson. Cuttingly, from that hour,
He'll bear a hatred he will never shed
Against the British; in his day of power
The wound, still festering, will cost them dear.

And now he roared across a later day,
A lawyer feuding on the green frontier.
I watched the duelling gun leap forth to slay,
And saw his rifled band
Take aim, with bright red tolls
From the long-bowed and kilted Seminoles
Where Florida's giant mossy oak-trees stand,
As earlier, in a battle with the Creeks,
He'd levelled his slashing blade at limb and heart.

True, right and wrong may change with him who speaks;
True, white men groaned from many a feathered dart,
And British counsel drove the redmen on.
And yet what strong, proud people would have waited
Until the axe and bullet legislated
And all their fathers' hunting grounds were gone?
I looked on Jackson, kindling fiery trails
To villages across whose log stockades
His rangers swarmed in pillaging crusades,
When huts were sacked and all the able males
Were clubbed, or shot like rabbits. Now what matter
If settlements which they had come to shatter
Harbored a friend or foe? I saw a pact
Made with the plumed and calumet-smoking chiefs,
Whose nations had been hacked
Like hulls ripped open upon spiny reefs.
Mountains and meadows, spacious as a state,
Streams they had fished from an unreckoned date,
Woods where they chased the deer, and banks and knolls
Where tepees stood, their people must vacate
At Jackson's nod.

                                    So they were pushed afar
To the wide undulating treeless blank
Of Oklahoma, and in hangneck files,
Like exiles banished to some alien star,
Bent under burdens, stooping rank on rank,
With squaws and babes, they dragged through miry miles
To wasteland lodges. Surging like a sea,
The settlers' inundating tide progressed,
And Jackson, more than other men, expressed
Its elemental thrust, its mass ferocity.

Yet there would flash to view, in startling shades,
The paradox within his heart and mind.
Many have pushed, like him, through barricades,
To make but shoddy leaders of mankind.
But only by storm and trial,
In unexpected tests, a man can show
The actual fabric of the self below,
Which leaves no register on an outer dial.
And Jackson, taking oath as President,
Had power within to make a quick ascent
To the wise decision and the great event.

"Old Hickory" they called him. For his arm
Had hickory's toughness, hickory's strength to smite
And stir the council halls of France with fright,
Or save the plowman or the clerk from harm.
Thus, as time drew him near
Those crossroads which a high and tortured soul
In stormier days would face, when states decreed
Each might pursue its own divisive goal
Though all must skirt the precipice, falling sheer,
He rose to the stature of the country's need.
"The Union will be preserved!" men heard him shout.
"Come, let the governors send troops!" And none
Who listened to his rallying-call could doubt
Which side had won.
The Indian fighter valiantly had saved
The nation from itself, with hands that waved
The flag of Jefferson.

IX

Forth to the Cherokees' prairie dwelling-place,
His shoulders overtopping most men's hair,

Dominant as a king, with striding grace,
He ventured, but his gaze held gray despair.
The Indians dashed about him, loud with cries,
"He comes! The Raven comes! He comes once more!"
The big white chieftain, brave and strong and wise,
Always was welcome at his brothers' door.
Not to these simple folk was he the great
Sam Houston, Governor of Tennessee,
Who'd quit his office, less by power of fate
Than by his own decree
After his bride of only twelve short weeks,
The yellow-haired Eliza, wildly burst
Out of his door. Her wet, contorted cheeks
Remained; her ghost still tortured and accursed.

Three years I saw him range the wilderness,
Sharing the hut of one his youth had known,
Oo-loo-te-ka. And then, in native dress
Of beaded buckskin, blanket carelessly thrown
Over broad shoulders, forth one day he went
To the head paleface village, where he pleaded
With Jackson, once his friend, now President:
"The Indians' land, their treaties must be heeded!"
Stirred by the fierce impetuosity
Of his appeal, the tribesmen in tense bands
Chorused their old demands
To halt the white man's growing banditries.
Alas, they might as well have flogged the seas!

Now, with a flare, a flash,
He shines in a new exploit,
Where border squadrons clash,
Audacious and adroit.

With guns and bowie knives,
Far over the Texan plain,
A raw-boned host arrives,
And Sam is leader of a brisk campaign.
"Remember the Alamo!   The Alamo!"
A cry blares forth, a long, reverberant call.
Let Santa Anna, lord of Mexico,
Shake in his seat, and fall! —
Red Santa Anna, whose assassin blade
Heinously struck to death a whole brigade
Of Yankee captives. To avenge this crime
He must be taken in a punishing raid!

"Remember the Alamo!" still rang the cry,
While the dictator, whose life panorama
Was like a page of purple melodrama,
Won new recruits. I saw his troops apply
The swinging gun and sword
To farm-boys herded, fearing to question why,
In a raw conscripted horde.
And so, with oil and faggots for the slaughter,
Onward he marched, vowing to give no quarter,
And it might seem to any good reporter
Soon he would sweep all Texas. Back and back
Sam Houston moved his hundreds. Was it, then,
His knees were quaking in terror of attack
By Santa Anna's men?
Soon would the answer come, as strange and gory
As in some fabulous heroic story.

On San Jacinto's fields, one afternoon,
The Mexican commander tossed and snored.
About him sprawled his soldiers, tired and bored,

Trail-worn and fevered, thankful for the boon
Of drowsing through the long, hot, dusty day.
Idly the sub-lieutenants shaved and dressed,
Sure that the foe — cowards by any test! —
Awed at their mighty host, would sneak away.
So, while their slumber-heavy lids were closed,
No sentinel bristled where the army dozed.

And never a watcher saw
Shadows that crept among the straggling trees.
Drilled in the ways of war,
Sam Houston thought, "The chance is mine to seize!"
Fleet as the hawk that swoops
Low on the chicken coops,
He climbed the breastworks; fell on the screaming troops
More in a slaughter than an ordered fight.

"Remember the Alamo! The Alamo!"
In panic at that blast of echoing sound,
Scattered like hens before a fox, the foe
Flies round and round.
"Remember the Alamo!" So mad the flight
And fierce the haste
That rifle butts are clubs men raise to smite.
And here and there a frienziedly fleeing knot,
Scuttling into the waste,
Is seized or shot.
And here tied captives stand at point of gun,
And here men dodge and leap and weave and run.

And Santa Anna? Seeing his friends have fled,
Away he scurries through the brushy lands.
Next day a fugitive in a shirt of blue,

White-pantalooned, and shod in carpet red,
Is seen by Mexican troops, who raise their hands
In prompt salute. And so they flash the clue
To searchers. "Rope! A rope!" dins forth the cry.
"Tighten his neck!" And soldiers swarm about
The cord-bound captive, bawling, "Let him die!"
But Houston, deaf to this bloodthirsty shout,
Holds him well guarded. He will live to be
Once more enthroned in pomp and treachery.

Texas, new nation, solitary giant
With far sea-reaches and wide-stretching plains,
Shielded by Yankee rifles, stood defiant,
While Mexico called, "Our union still remains!"
And Houston, seated high as President,
Then Senator, when after long debates
His country was embraced among the States,
Would have been stunned had some presentiment
Showed him the jutting city that would rise
With steel skyscrapers crowded close abreast,
Massive beneath the bright south-Texan skies,
Bearing his name whose every breath expressed
The bigness of the wild, the free and open West.

X

Guns smoking, swift as panthers, forth they rode
From hideouts safe beyond the Rio Grande,
With broad sombreros, and black eyes that glowed,
Sweeping the cattle from huge swaths of land.
And in retaliation, back there flashed
Blond rangers in a galloping foray,
Long-limbed and rifled, lawless as knights that clashed
In ages of fable in a clanking fray.

But small wars nourish great,
And great and small are born
When greed and fury mate
And ignorance suckles scorn.
Thus many a fighter, with gruff hunting cries,
Saddled his horse, and seized a knife or gun,
And empires of plain and peak became a prize,
Deserts and needled slopes were overrun,
And Californian vasts of shore and sun
Were taken without a shell-burst. Here again
War's camp attendants, chaos and disease,
Clawed at the fighting men.
I saw deserters sneak, on hands and knees,
From smoldering fields; I heard the sick man moan,
The starving whimper; watched the wounded bleed;
And I observed the bold climactic deed,
And frenzy scattered and suspicion sown
By victory itself. Through soaring passes
To Mexico City from the hot Gulf Coast,
I saw invaders circuitously wind
In coiling serpent files, while sky-rimmed masses
Of rock and snow frowned on the drawn-out host,
In places so inclined
That cannon were hand-carried up a slope
With whose precipitous steeps no mule could cope.

But why should warriors from cold northern shores
Be catapulted at a tropic gate?
Why, then, did Romans pound at Parthia's doors,
Or Turks go growling at Byzantium's strait?
The scenes are shifted, but man keeps alive
His old Assyrian urge, his trampling drive
To push with swords into his brother's house

And snatch at honey from his brother's hive.

So blades and guns leap out.
Sabre to sabre, hand to hand men fight
At the stone-walled redoubt
And under towers of the guarded height.
Down to the Mexican valley, corps on corps,
Victorious columns pour.
And there, with bayonets, all lanes are cleared;
There General Scott, perched on a great bay horse,
With plumed regalia and a well-trimmed beard,
Captains his troops; while, with a storm-gale's force,
The ragged thousands on the roofs proclaim
Curses and blasphemies, and in the streets
Daggered assailants, crumpled by sudden flame
And spattering shell-bursts, lie beneath white sheets.

XI

One of the mountain men, who made a track
To lands once private to the fox and bear,
Who piled his beaver pelts, and balked attack
By arrowed scouts, and plumbed the grizzly's lair —
One of the sun-tanned rovers who could read
Canyons and forests like a picture-book,
Kit Carson had the open, simple look
Of folk inured to heed
The language of a wing, a rock, a fern
I saw him with a comrade at his side,
A wanderer too, though of a lettered turn,
Comely and slim, with eyes of luminous pride
And figure wary as a spring, who wore
Loose hair long-flowing, and a scraggly beard,
Felt hat and buckskin trousers, yet appeared

Perhaps too young, too elegantly reared.
"Fremont, I'll go. I'll help you to explore,"
Said Kit; and thus a lifelong tie was started
Between two men, both free and vagrant-hearted.

Then what a bright enchantment Fremont faced,
Such as no citizen of our tamer world
Ever can know again! — the chartless waste
Like a great tapestry, its art unfurled
In strange designs of wood, blue lake and hill,
Glassy ice-spire, flame-butte and red ravine,
Plum-purple tints, topaz and bronze and green —
Food for the hungry scientific eye
And the mapmaker's skill,
Though starred adventure still
Was riding high.

Along the Oregon Trail, where rocks are steep
And torrents foamy and deep,
Or where the migrant, with his mule-drawn team,
May lose his last dim dream
In sagebrush barrens or the brackish stream;
And through fast-shifting acts, and episodes
Of violet mesas and the black defile,
Scarred ochre lands unscratched by homes or roads,
And the curved canyon's mazy river aisle,
I see Fremont exploring. Where a fire
Leaps on the prairie like a racing doom,
And where, in ridges shouldering high and higher,
Tier after tier of tree-walled mountains loom
With iceberg cones, I watch him plodding on
Scornful of winter through Sierran blanks
Of rock and tall, blue-shadowed snow, forlorn
As Greenland's glacial banks.

"Turn back! Turn back, or die!" the Indians warn.
How pierce that many-turreted, craggy mass,
Bare as the moon-peaks — an unearthly realm
Where sudden blizzard gales may overwhelm
The midge who tries to pass?
But man's own will is fate. "We'll seek and find!"
Said Fremont; and across the pinnacled wild
One after one his men on snowshoes filed
In a white blaze that almost struck them blind.
Then, after chattering days and nights, at last
A gap among the Alpine ranges showed
A far oak-sprinkled valley, green and vast
Where the long, silvered Sacramento flowed.

And yet not always would the dial of chance
Be flicked to favor him.
The warders of the mountains grew more grim,
Gibing at his advance
When in the Rockies, in a later year,
He sought a path where untried peaks rose sheer.
All breathing things had fled
A winter universe grown weird and dead.
In new-piled hills and many a drifted heap
The snow was mounded deep,
And trees wore plumes of white
And twigs encased in sheaths of beady light.
Drooping, dull-eyed, dispirited and slow,
Their ribs protruding, laden mules were urged
Forward where sleet and gale and shadow merged
And gusts, in maniac dances, whirled and surged.
And some, from razor ledges, pitched below
To swallowing gulfs; and some, with sagging necks,
Drooped on the trail, and twitched, and then were still.

Cursing, with brows of death, pale hollowed wrecks,
The men dragged on, trudging against the chill
Of the blank storm, the crags, the beetling cliff.
Their breath congealed, and in the Polar air
Eyebrows and beards were bristles, sharp and stiff,
While cast-off packs and clothes lay everywhere.
Straggling ahead on bleeding feet, at last
They panted to the crest,
And groaned: beyond them, billowing far to west,
Valley on valley spread like frozen seas,
Peak after peak in iced immensities,
Range behind range, assembled giants massed
To mock their coming.
                "Back! We must go back!"
Said Fremont, for those high frost-gods would never
Yield to man's dwarf endeavor.
Yet as they stooped on their down-winding track,
Out of his weathered party one in three
Would leave his bones beneath some naked tree
Or under the nude rock-domes' cold glaring majesty.

Yet pioneers like Fremont, bravely striving
Even when failure glowered, showed the way
To a great West, where cities tall and thriving
Would mark a later day.

In vasts mysterious as a foreign planet,
Where danger was a love to be embraced,
He forced his way; and with a thrust of granite
Vanquished and tamed the waste.

Kin to the Jason of old song and fable!
Kin to those modern knights who, scorning bars,

Riding a capsule into space, are able
To wing their dream with stars!

XII

Like some antique Arabian wonder tale
Appears the vision seen by Joseph Smith.
And many said it was no dream or myth —
A miracle that never would grow pale.
When still a youth, he saw some golden plates
Marked with inscriptions, strangely unrevealed,
And over them all a magic sword and shield,
And magic spectacles to pass the gates
Of arcane wisdom. Thus he came to see
Deep in the heart of sacred mystery,
And from the lore he read — that part not lost —
The Mormon saints and prophets came to be.

Now, after search and pilgrimage and stress,
When Smith had perished, bullet-pierced in jail,
A more illustrious pilot won control —
A Moses leading in the wilderness,
Who guided his people on a hard, long trail
That gnarled the hands and tried the nerves and soul,
Until the Faithful, at the desert edge,
Looked on a lake more salt than ocean brine,
And high above, ledge upon riven ledge,
Beheld snow-mountains shine.

"This is the place!" decided Brigham Young,
Who, like some hairy patriarch long ago —
Jacob, or Joshua at Jericho —
Commanded with a dictatorial tongue.
And so the covered wagons creaked and halted,

And on the treeless flat men built a town,
Heaved at the spade and harrow, and assaulted
The virgin earth, and led fresh water down
In branching ditches. Yet their huts of clay,
Bowers of brushwood, and the squat log-fort,
Were only as gauze to keep the cold away;
And skull-marked faces told of food grown short.
And mountain lions and bears
Swooped out of canyon lairs,
And wolves devoured the cows; while, almost worse,
The desert mice in myriads, like a curse
Hatched by the devil, stole into the corn.

And after spring was burgeoning at last
And planted fields were green for hope reborn,
Fresh horror, suddenly as an earthquake blast,
Roared down upon them; all the sky grew dim,
And flying shapes, a dark continual rain
Of crickets, droned into the bursting grain.
Grimly outmatched as ants that fight a gale,
The frightened people rushed, with prayer and hymn —
Women and children, with the men beside them —
To battle with open ditch and fire and flail.
Now, after all their trials, did God deride them?
And then — the miracle! From Great Salt Lake
Legions of sea-gulls, greedy as lean hounds,
Pounced on the insect millions, fierce to slake
Their hunger in such fruitful hunting grounds.
Thus providentially, when hope seemed gone,
The settlers saved wide acres of their corn.

Now granaries and shops arose to bless,
And though, stiff-seated in an iron State,

The Elders were endowed to legislate
The people's thought and faith — their joys, their dress;
And though the outer world would gasp at lives
Of men with harem-like arrays of wives,
Still they would foster empires in the West,
And nourish cities where the sagebrush spread,
And even while politics and dogmas wed,
Win pears and honey from the desert's breast.

XIII

"Gold! See, it's gold! Gold! Gold!"
Youthful San Brannan, with blue eyes afire,
Ranged through the city like an old town crier,
And from his tongue the syllables boomed and rolled,
"Gold! See, it's gold! Gold! Gold!"
In his right hand he waved a wide-brimmed hat,
And flourished in his left a twinkling glass
Of orange-yellow. "Look, it's gold, not brass!
True Western gold — the veins are rich and fat!"
Out on the dusty street, whose rude plank-shacks
Straggled beneath round San Francisco hills,
The hairy residents, in hope of thrills,
Came forth in boisterous packs.
"Gold! See, it's gold! Gold! Gold!" they gasped and
          cried;
And some were crimson-faced and bulging-eyed.
And thus Pandora's box was opened wide.

If some invading army had appeared
With aimed artillery, the startled port
Could not have been more drained, more suddenly sheared
Of citizens, who with one nervous thought
Were scurrying away

On sailboats and canoes they crossed the bay,
Horseback and muleback and on carts they rode,
Long-haired, red-shirted, whipping on their teams
Through swamps and brushy plains and over streams
Forth to the foothills of the Mother Lode.
Hardly a man, upon once-bustling streets,
Was sighted now; the carpenter fled his bench,
The printer his press; the butcher left his meats,
The accountant his stool, the smith his forge and wrench.
Along abandoned docks, the bags and bales,
Unclaimed, unguarded from the plunderer's hand,
Were strewn like cargo wrecked on desert sand,
And in the bay a wilderness of sails
Rose from forsaken vessels. Thus began
One of the epic flights of modern man.

"Gold! It is gold! Gold! Gold!"
Bright with a nimbused glow,
Like a contagion it would flame and grow,
While radiant dust still called the stout and bold.
"Gold! It is gold! Gold! Gold!"
Out of New England farms the young men streamed,
Sacks upon shoulders, pushing to embark
On any leaky craft that sailed or steamed —
Valiant adventurers diving in the dark!
Jammed in a rotting hold,
Pitched round the Horn in sleet-swept agonies,
Nibbling at biscuits shared with worm and mold,
Groaning below in hollowing disease,
Lying becalmed for hot eternities,
Tortured by tedium as weeks crawled past,
Racked with homesickness, thousands still went on

Through solitudes where never a cheering mast
Hailed them from dawn to dawn.

    Others I followed through the snaky green
Of jungles, persecuted by the stings
Of insects in the humid palm-ravine,
While buzzards looped above on spiralling wings.
Across malarial lakes and swamps they trailed,
And over ridges to the southern shore;
Then waited, waited, tossed the dice, and swore
At tardy vessels, which too often sailed
So laden that even food and water failed.
Ah, many as the stars the griefs they told,
Who voyaged forth to look for gold, gold, gold!

    But crueller, sadder yet
The trials of wanderers by foot or wheel.
I see them trekking to the long ordeal
Where, near the Mississippi, crowds have met,
Bearing the stacked and bundled household goods.
In wagons with the round wide canvas tops
I mark the bronzed explorers of the woods,
Breakers of trails, and harvesters of crops,
Hunters and trappers, farm-boys, merchants, clerks,
Men with torn lives, and men with lives to make,
And some within whose furtive glance there lurks
The memory of some shadowing old mistake.
Drawn by the crawling mule, the slow-limbed ox,
They plod across the flowering prairie spaces,
While far ahead a mounted sentry paces,
Searching for Indians hidden to harass,
Who, cunning as the fox,
Slant unsuspected arrows through the grass.

And then at night, with wagons ringed about
The dwindled fires of a sleeping host,
What terror of marauders that no scout
Has trailed, who, with the silence of a ghost,
Crouching in demon raids,
May sweep the camp and strike with scalping blades!

But gay is the prairie sun
And sweet is the prairie air,
And children rollick and run,
And ridged horizons have no shade of care.
And women, comely-featured, strong and young,
Dipping their garments in some reedy stream,
Warming their pans by fires of bison dung,
Are wistful with a wonder and a dream.
Not till the mountains, clustering bold and sheer,
Meet them with ramparts like the world's frontier,
Will they need courage steadfast as a rock,
And truly know the barbs of pain and fear.

I traced the ramblings of a wagon track
Far over bald plateaux and sagebrush plains,
And everywhere I gazed at rude remains
Scattered as by a hurricane's attack —
Paintings and pots and rusty kitchen wares;
Horned skulls of oxen whitening on the road;
Axles and broken wheels; a cast-off load
Of mattresses and chairs;
And now and then great canvas vehicles smashed
Or overturned where canyon torrents splashed.
Rude crosses told the tale
Of some whom cholera, cruel as a shark,
Felled in the night; and many made no mark

Save by their bones. But though a host must fail,
Bright as a sun-burst was the earned success
Of others, after famine, plundering blows,
Thirst in the glaring flat salt-wilderness,
Lost paths, and precipice walls, bogs and vertiginous snows.

Spread on the green Sierras' further slope,
Guarded by limpid rivers and tall pines,
Finally Eldorado, land of hope,
A blessed vision, shines.
And while the valleys and blue peaks unfold,
Still rings the cry, "Gold! It is gold! Gold! Gold!"

But who can scoop up gold in trowels like sand?
Even though some have struck
Nuggets and treasure veins of flashing luck,
Thousands must fish and sweat for metal panned
From hard stream bottoms. Watch the miner stand
Knee-deep or thigh-deep with the pick or spade,
Or sifting gravel where a torrid sun
Beats down without a heaven of cooling shade,
Seeking bright dust, more onerously won
Than many a plowman's pence. And after toil,
No home but flapping tents, or crude log-shacks,
A bottle the window, and for floor the soil,
A stump for table, and a rock for chair,
The bed a pile of straw, a mass of sacks
Or canvas. But what need to linger there
When the back-breaking, burning day was ended?
Repelled by scraps self-cooked, the bearded man
Would sling aside the kettle and frying pan,
While all the camp attended

The revels in the roistering saloon,
Where the dice glittered and a liquid boon
Purchased oblivion; slew memories
Of faces smoldering with ghostly pleas
From lanes and doors by other hills and seas.
But some looked sorrowful, and strangely old
To hear that call, "Gold! It is gold! Gold! Gold!"

* * *

I wandered down the billowing reach
Of valleys fair with streams and oaks,
The tawny hill, the long gray beach,
Meadows with golden poppy cloaks.
And fenceless was the cattle range
Where antlers nudged the chaparral,
And ages never seemed to change
The laurel clump or redwood hall.
There silence sang her dateless tune,
And peace lay on the mountain's face,
The choiring grove, the gorge and dune,
Where beauty made her nesting-place.

But like a cannonade
Booming above the summer song of bees,
Uproarious hosts invade
And batter down the old simplicities.
They slash the canyons; and the ancient trees,
Great-boled sequoias, shiver and topple down,
Till rivers that of old poured diamond-clear
Are trickling chocolate-brown.
The condor and the grizzly disappear,
And bare white tailings heap their barren stone
Where the pink mallow or tall fern had grown.

And riot crackles, pestilence spreads a shroud;
Bandits, black-masquing, in a galloping raid,
Dash on the road, or wheel against the camp;
And the bared pistol and the driven blade
Are legislators for the blatant crowd;
While in the "diggings," when spilt blood is damp,
The ragged-faced, red-shirted miners swarm
Round a rope-dangling tree, a bleak tied form.

    Like an explosion, rather than a stream
Of regular flow, the mining hordes were cast
Too fast, an age too fast
Into a West where chaos was the scheme
Of evolution, while all men outran
The molded structure and the patterned plan.
Mighty the cities that would lift their towers,
And vast the land of peach and almond flowers,
And rich the fields of grain that would unfold.
But where Sierran torn escarpments spread,
Where the prospector fell, the townsman bled,
From graves of yellow men, and white, and red,
Still sounds the call, "Gold! It is gold! Gold! Gold!"

VII. Oracles of Freedom

". . . across cities and fields of a widening nation"

High in the clouds that bounded the halves of the
    planet,
I looked again upon beings who, mistily stirring,
With figures mighty as gods, and patriarch faces,
Were mantled in light, with trailing garments of vapor.
And one, with the whiteness of years on his Jovian features,
Who seemed as the soul of the ages, thus uttered his wisdom:

"O Man, in the greatness of time are no viewers and
    judges
To decree like a court on the doings of peoples and nations.
But the law of the cosmos, exempting not even a pebble
From falling by regular laws, has enclosed and embraced you.
And the law of the cosmos ordains that the seeds you have
    scattered
Shall grow like the broom or the briar; and each, by its
    species,
Shall burgeon with spines or with blossoms, and none are
    excepted.
Thus you shall pluck what you planted through past
    generations,
Whether harvests of cherries or grapes or baskets of thistles.
By the hand you extend to your staggering comrade, you
    gather
New strength to hold you erect when the road spirals
    steeply;

165

By the hand you refuse, or that preys on the sweat of your
    fellows
Or binds them with slave-yokes, you pass a self-judgment,
And your skin shall be pierced by the thorns, and recoil from
    the lashes."

High in the clouds that bounded the halves of the planet
I looked again upon beings who, mistily stirring,
With figures mighty as gods and patriarch faces,
Were mantled in light, with trailing garments of vapor.
And now, once again with a sense of fate that unfolded
From the tangles and knots of the past to the maze of
        tomorrow,
I peered across cities and fields of a widening nation.

* * *

Like a dull sullen coppery glow that fills
The far recesses of the evening sky
Above a ridge of fast-approaching hills
While low storm-voices moan and multiply —
Like such a presage, in the gale or smoke,
Angry with flush of warning through the years,
The coming struggle of the States awoke
Premonitory rumblings in men's ears,
Which, rising with the distant thunder's roar,
Sensitive nerves could mark from long before.

Around, around, around,
With screeches, howls and screams,
As on a battleground
In hot, torrential streams,
Around, around, around,
With hardly a check or bound,
The mob, with swaying hands and wildman faces,

Is ravenous as a hound
For the rabbit that it chases.
Around, around, around
I watched it charging like a bull that rages
At a red rag, whose owner it engages
With blood and pain, with pain and blood for wages.

    As onward it staggered, mighty and unseeing,
With jaws and teeth of dinosaurian size,
I saw it merged into one passionate being,
One beast of many legs and arms and eyes.
Against the timbers of a barred school-door
I heard it batter, entering with a din
Where dusky cowering figures shrank within
And rubble of desks and papers strewed the floor.
I heard the axes thump, the crowbars pound,
Cracking a press that resolutely had spoken,
"Freedom for slaves!" I looked on type-fonts broken
And the torn fragments dashed on trampled ground.
And then a shot — and one who shrieked and fell
And lay stone-silent.
                    Not only in the South
But northward even to Boston rose the yell
Of rabbles roaring like a lion's mouth.
I heard a crackling Abolitionist
With Ciceronian fire and swinging fist
Raise the stout cry,
"Off with all shackles!"; and the mob's reply
Was prompt and grim:
"Down with the devil! Tar and feather him!"
Then a mock gallows mounted to the sky,
And a long rope was wound
On the crusader's waist, who, struck and bound,

Was dragged away.
                      Yet bullying force once more
Unbared its weakness. For a day or hour
The blunt club-wielder may be perched in power,
But cannot beat at life's immutable core.
He may slay men, and hammer into dust
Gardens and temples, but can never smash
That soul, unreachable by the goad or lash,
Which holds like mountain rock when sabres thrust
At palisades of truth. No power exists
To quell the live idea, which still persists
While the illumined mind of man resists.

II

    Under the starlit night the vessel rode
Into a bayou fringed with inky trees;
And anchored near a reddish lamp that glowed
Where the dim shore's immense leaf-draperies
Made phantom towers. From the deck a line
Of fettered forms was loosed, and boats beneath
Bore them through darkness dense as in a mine,
Until they passed the forest's tall vague sheath.
But few would give a thought
And fewer yet relate
That one more ship had brought
Illegal living freight;
That now the market block
Would show, at trade's demands,
A fresh imported stock
Of black plantation hands.

    How would it feel, ah, how, to be a slave?
Though not of those uprooted as by tongs

From huts and dear ones — shipped with herded throngs
To alien fields across the white-jawed wave —
Even so, how would it feel? Always to be
Like a young child that orders circumscribe,
Hearing the prince and owner's least decree
Uttered as though to an unreasoning tribe;
With reverential nods
To honor the coming of the brusque white gods;
And even when warm eyes shine,
To bow like worshippers at Pharaoh's shrine,
And all because of a dark-pigmented skin
You chose no more than cattle pick their kin,
Which haunts you like an old ancestral sin.

Love, which can overleap all gaps of race
Where kinky-haired old servants walk content,
Often will radiate the dear home-place,
While laughter and soft tunes are eloquent.
But not all bondage is so kindly meant —
Not where the scourges fly for masters harsh
As ever the Romans on the great slave-farms,
When, amid snarled alarms,
Bloodhounds and guns pursue the fugitive's track
Into a wood or marsh,
And drive the cringing, whimpering captive back.
And what of auction stalls where women moan,
Clinging to small black shapes that moan replies,
While the gruff lord who buys
Snaps them apart with a squad commander's tone?
Truly, in selling sheep,
None wonder if the ewe or lamp may weep.
The butcher has one interest — coins to reap.

But more and more, contemptuous of rebuffs,
The oracles of freedom raised their call;
Modern Demosthenes, in many a hall,
Defied the bladed stare, the threats and cuffs,
Flint-willed for liberation. There was one
Of the rebellious projects that I viewed,
Which could not be displayed beneath the sun,
Yet fired a host, and blest a multitude.

  Low in the starless night,
A crawling shape on an unlanterned lane,
Furtively as a criminal in flight,
Creeps forth, creeps forth to gain
A waiting door. Pale welcoming hands inside
Receive the worn black figure; bring him bread,
Replace his muddy rags, give drink and bed,
While, trembling and with dark eyes moist and wide,
He pants his thanks. Behind him winds a track
Over whole states, through swamps and piny deeps,
Where, quaking, he draws back
At a leaf's flutter; when, by fits, he sleeps,
Bloodhounds invade his dreams — the master's growl,
And whips loud-whistling. He has pushed his way
Through backwoods like a lynx upon the prowl,
Making brief pauses, each precarious stay
Planned by the Underground, whose beckoning crew
Guide him between the stations, fully knowing
What slippery risks they too are undergoing —
Mobbing or prison cells, which not a few
Already have suffered. But the chance is taken;
No runaway, hard pressed, can be forsaken.
Strangely reborn one morning, he may waken
In Canada, unfettered.

                                   Thus the scourge
That kindled frenzies while the shackled groaned,
Has also prompted an heroic surge
Of brotherhood, as though a few atoned
For the world's ill beneath a saintly urge.
And man, composite formed of heaven and earth,
Of clay, rose-petals and fire, again unbared
What all the ages and all lands declared —
His hybrid spirit, his queer divided birth.

    Even for those who plead the angels' cause,
Passion may counsel maniac extremes,
While tongues that sizzle on fanatic themes
Are scornful of the mind that counsels, "Pause!"
The new religion, Abolition, spread
Till violence, nurtured in the heart and head,
Challenged with brands and fists, and South and North
Alike saw blue as black and white as red.
To men who, all their segregated years,
Had dwelt where cotton and tobacco waved,
It seemed predestined as the orbiting spheres
That Negroes be enslaved.
And fools to north who haughtily intruded
In saner folks' affairs, so far deluded
They never guessed their fault — could these explain
How, with no slaves to plow or reap, the South
Would not be as a field stripped clean of grain,
And seared by drouth?

    Fitfully here and there
I saw new sparks, a red foreboding flare
When lightning streaked the clouds and thunder crashed.
I heard shrill mutinous voices, in a gale

Loud-clamoring, when storm-emotions flashed
And shackled men broke free
Upon the slaver *Creole,* under sail
To bear her prisoners over vasts of sea
From port to Southern port.
                                But more malign,
More sinister, more of a warning sign,
Even as slave-revolts in ancient Rome
That sent long shudders down the empire's spine,
One portent flooded every Southern home
With hate and horror. As so many a time
When in the name of heaven's high intent
Men scatter hellish crime
And hold the heinousness divinely meant,
So the black minister Nat Turner smote,
Hurling his henchmen, like Comanche braves,
Screaming, half drunken, at the unshielded throat
Of man and child and woman. Fifty graves
Of innocents told the tale, before he too
Paid with a noose. But tumult he inflamed
Was like a shaft of terror driven through
The country's heart, with freedom scarred and maimed.

III

        Morosely swinging rifles, squatters paced
Where the grass-matted Kansan prairie spread.
And not desire for homes nor need of bread
Bade them patrol the waste.
Out of Missouri, in raw companies,
Rode "Border Ruffians" with shot and brand,
Scorching a way for Southern hosts to seize
The scarcely opened land;

And made elections safe with guns and staves
For all whose vote would favor Kansan slaves.

But hear! a thrust and tramp
Out of the rival camp,
First without arms . . . till, as a last resource,
Metal of naked force meets naked force.
See here a champion time will long remember,
With face so battle-gnarled men think him aged
Though still a season from his frayed December.
He's not forgotten how in youth, enraged,
He saw a slave-boy whom he called his friend
Whipped and insulted. Then it was he swore
The infamy of man-sell-man must end.
Then he, John Brown, resolved he would descend
Well-armed upon the South, until he tore
All chains asunder. Tragic contradiction!
Faith in the Bible, love of spotless right,
Yet warrior passions, and the hot conviction
Black fury may create things pure and white!

Late in the night, he weaves a catlike way
While mute, arms-carrying comrades trail behind
For vengeance that his broiling wrath designed
Against a chosen prey.
Silent the cabins where the slave-men sleep,
And silently through the dark the raiders creep,
And sullenly with one hand Brown thumbs the list
Of strangers he has doomed. Then weapons leap
Like horrors in a nightmare. Startled awake,
Wrenched out of bed too suddenly to resist,
The victims, gasping, see the knife-blades rake
Their homes, their comrades. Five, mowed down in blood,

Yield the last tribute.
                                    Vain as a Borgia's deed
Of murder, letting loose a sulphurous flood
Of greater murder! Dashing with wolfish speed
The Ruffians scour the land, and slay and burn,
Till John and Jason, Brown's two guiltless sons,
Sink groaning beneath the guns.
And then the bolts of shrivelling hatred turn
On huge Fred Brown as on a cornered hare;
And battle blazes; looters of barns and stores
And horse-thrieves scuttle like Vandals everywhere.
But how this opens any wider doors
For the slave stooping in the cotton field,
Alas, no story-teller has revealed.

       Upon some incidents, themselves not great,
Vast consequences, like a tower, may rest.
So, as he dares the grinding ultimate test,
John Brown can surely little estimate
How he will pile foundation stones of fate
When in a deed so rash
Its crazed extravagance will startle time,
And with a fervor that may have seemed sublime,
He plans a smoking dash
Against an arsenal among the hills
At Harper's Ferry. After this assault,
Not his will be the fault
If crowds of black men, fleeing from old ills,
Do not triumphantly join him. Well supplied
With weapons, they will storm the countryside,
Till by God's wish and with God's holy power
The last of their dark brothers are untied!

Creeping like brigands where two rivers run
Under dim mountains in the screening night,
The band steals forth — so few, but twenty-one!
They take the town, more by surprise than might.
And see the train they halt! the huddled throng
Of prisoners they surround! The bearlike fight
Continues, two days long,
And rifles of the famed Virginia Guard
Must battle fierce and hard,
While rebels, pressed together, backs to wall,
Locked in a firehouse, crouch with gritted teeth,
Ready to slay and fall,
Like Greeks in the pass where Persian spearmen spill.
And shells scream by; and ever more hot, beneath,
The struggle blazes; like a battering-ram
A ladder swings against the door, until
With a wild lunge and slam
It yields, and men rush in, and shoot and shout,
And in the grappling bout
John Brown is seized and bludgeoned and knocked out
And captured.
                Mirroring the moods that swept
A shaken land, the fallen chief became
For various eyes a torch, a signal flame,
A demon, one of Satan's most adept,
A saint, a Galahad. For he had blazed
His name in crimson on the nation's sky;
Bewilderingly, in his defeat, he raised
A fiery "We defy!"
Pointing at chains. With trembling lips that curst,
Incendiaries, swinging vehement arms,
Raced through the South to clamors and alarms,
And charged, "This devils' blow is but the first

Of Lucifer's invasions!" Soon the thud
Of Minute Men, exhibiting blue cocades,
Drilling, and flaunting arms in trim parades,
Spoke preparation for the trial by blood.
And vigilante mobs, with mad-dog eyes,
Self-made police, a state above the state,
Gathered to terrorize,
And sick suspicion whittled clubs of hate.
Folk from the North — the teacher with her classes,
The traveler on the road — might gasp to see
Onrushing foes in waves, in gibbering masses;
And after a trial's delirious travesty,
When tongues of vitriol seared the innocent air,
Whips crackled down on shoulders striped and bare;
And bleeding victims, ordered, "Go elsewhere!",
Seldom would tarry. On a leap and surge
Of schizophrenic passion, men were hurled
Impetuously across a slippery verge;
While giant-high, above the quaking world,
John Brown was glaring, and he seemed to glower
Bearded and stormy-browed, with eyes of baleful power.

   So he was more than man. When he was tried
Not he but slavery's black image stood
Bowed at the bench. And on his grim last ride,
When underfoot he felt the coffin wood
Yet noted the laughing beauty of the day,
He went like some old martyr to receive
The crushing rope, knowing he'd had his say
And soon the very earth would shudder and heave
And terrors he'd unchained
Would rise, and crackle in a conflagration,

Till in the fields and dooryards of the nation
Never a yoke remained.

IV

A ball of reddish fire above the fort
Curved in a semicircle, plunged and burst,
And repercussions of that one report
Would stir the fibres of man's best and worst
And shake the whole Republic. In the shot
Discharged at Sumter and the Union forces,
Time wove the meshes of a tragic plot
For clashing millions shorn of all resources
Save blood and terror. Hate, on buzzard wings
Swooping for carrion feasts; and haste, whose eyes
Observe the face but rarely the core of things,
Were frantic to advise,
"To arms! To arms!" Bristling and iron-walled,
The Southern fervor, spiked with spiny pride,
Left the vociferous multitude enthralled,
Although the promised price was fratricide.

When the world-rousing news
From Charleston drummed a plea in rebel ears,
Loud were the yells and cheers,
Many the pulses dancing, the glad views
Of watchers blinded to the flame ahead,
The graves fresh-dug, the smoke where homes had been,
And women sobbing. In all lanes the tread
Of marching squadrons made a rhythmic din,
And motley young recruits
Bustled to volunteer — in homespun gray,
Or with rag-carpet blankets, rawhide boots
Or beaver hats; while, leading the strange array,

Were officers in black-trimmed cassimere,
Spurred, and with hats that sported ostrich plumes.
And bugles, sounding arrogant and clear,
Proclaimed the cocky confidence youth assumes.
Strutting and swaggering in brisk parades,
The fighters formed their squadrons and brigades;
And ladies, waving kerchiefs, cheered them forth;
And death looked on with bare, invisible blades.

        Far over the North as well,
When from the lips of Lincoln flew a plea
For volunteers, frenzy began to swell
The veins of men, who met life's cruel decree
With hearts that bounded. Once again they felt
That intoxication of adventurous chance,
That thrilled excitement which has always dwelt
With war, and made its tragedy seem romance,
And been a prime recruiter. Everywhere
Packed meetings, with their loud "Hurrahs!", awoke
The breath of glamour; brilliant posters spoke,
And the bands playing, and the trumpets' blare,
And streamers floating, and the flash and flare
Of uniforms. Not that, in sober minds,
Fear of the sanguinary rising threat
Struck no grave note, nor grief for lives upset;
But war, for most, is a drawing down of blinds,
And the dazed legions of its devotees
Look not beyond the cannon's boom and crash
But stagger, drunken on unrealities,
Heedless of broken skulls and gore and ash.
So, of the hosts who went
Carelessly, even gaily forth to fight,

How few foresaw the actual event
Of four tempestuous years of long and anguished night!

V

Sadly, with lingering gaze, he looked his last
On the old office and his Springfield home,
Soon to to be drowned forever in the past
In a far city, where the unfinished dome
Of the new capitol rose wide and high —
Imprisoning him, for now, wherever he went,
Hearing a soulless "Mister President,"
He'd stand unbared before the nation's eye.
On the long trial of his inaugural trip,
With brass receptions, speeches without end,
And when, at Baltimore, he had to slip
Disguised into a Pullman with a friend
Lest a fanatic's dagger-point descend,
Perhaps he summoned back in clear review
The years that raised him to his perilous post,
Asking, "Abe Lincoln, is it truly you,
Or do you only dream the blare and boast
Of fame and office?"
                              Surely, men adjust
To most ascents and turns the world creates,
Though few, from bare log cabins, ever thrust
Their way to domination over states.
But I imagine many a well-lived scene
Returned in flashbacks — that Kentucky wild
Where cedared hillsides called him, lushly green,
And he went shouting as a fenceless child;
And woodlands further west
That saw a gaunt frontiersman spike his way
Bravely to meet the test,

With mail to carry, acres to survey,
Rails to be split, and farming chores to share,
And nights when by the fire's red fitful flare
He thumbed old dogeared pages. Then the years
As lawyer —pleading in a spellbound room,
His own eyes bright with tears,
Or circuit-rider where the sunflowers bloom
On rimless prairies or the frost-winds blow;
And squally politics, whose puffs and bouts
Lift him steep rungs, only to dash him low
When he assails invulnerable redoubts
Of the ducal Senate; and those famed debates
With Douglas, the brooding and portentous-browed,
When rockets sparkle, serenaders sing,
And bunting hangs gay-colored, while the fates
Show a new actor to the close-packed crowd
That cheers as for a king.

Surely all this the tall, droll, sad-faced man
Would recollect, and surely had to ask,
Was it all part of some predestined plan
Or chance alone that time's spotlighting choice
Should point to him — that his should be the task
To save a cloven nation — his the voice
To trumpet vast decisions? Who could say?
Observing the war-smoke gather, grim and gray,
He could but lift deep anxious eyes, and pray.

Low on the roofs the riflemen were crouched,
Watching the nearer windows; while, beneath,
Into the square the cavalry debouched
And squat artillery made a guardian sheath.
Attired in black, with shirt of formal white,

Dangling a stovepipe hat and gold-tipped cane,
Rough-hewn and lean and homely, the new chief
Spoke words which, had men heard with crystal sight,
Soon might have won the bilious times relief.
This vision, to his mind, was starkly plain:
The breaks that spread like cracks in battered glass
When from the Union seven states withdrew,
Had split the land in two —
Now it must grope as in a blind morass,
In need of climbing tackle. His own hands
Must weave, from rotting cords, the rescuing strands.

Of all who heard with wrinklings of contempt,
Sparkles of hope or love, or flailing cries,
"Yokel!", "Gorilla!", was there one who dreamt
What fires had stirred the man, his actual size?
Could he himself, untested, recognize
His own great courage — what God-forces pressed
In trial and storm against his burdened breast?
I looked on countless pictures, like the scenes
On fluctuating screens,
When bleakly he would come to understand
The pain of power, the heart-stabs of command,
The irony of renown. Watching him pace
Disconsolately apart, in grief and prayer,
More deeply, season by season, I could trace
In the large scrawlings of his tortured face,
The signature of agony and despair.
I saw him, tense-eyed, at the conflict's start,
Scan the unguarded walls of Washington;
And knew the passion of pity in his heart
When in the rain, after the first Bull Run,
Fugitives plodded through a soggy dawn,

Mud-soaked, dishevelled, many with blankets tossed
Over wet shoulders, some with knapsacks lost,
Some gunless, all with faces taut and drawn,
While women, huddled on the storm-swept streets,
Poured out hot coffee. I observed him stride
In midnight rooms alone, when late report
Told of new losses, dallyings and defeats,
Dreading the Union's cords would be untied
Before campaigns he plotted could be fought.

    Few even of the great
Have felt, against their heads, this challenge smite:
"You, only you, must save the tottering State!
You, only you, must guard the law and light
Or sink in chaos!" Few must tread that road,
Bitter as crucifixion, sentenced to bear
A generation's grief, a people's load,
Knowing their own decision will prepare
Glory or doom. Some unsuspected spring
Deep in himself had overflowed, with force
To guide the nation on tomorrow's course
More regally than a coronated king.

    Yet humbling himself, how meekly he would stand,
For his dear country's good forgetting pride,
Waiting with hat in hand
That a curt general might be pacified.
Then on the battlefield, behold him loom
Deep-trenched of countenance, tragic of eye,
Yet scattering trust above the laden gloom.
And though his desk held documents piled high,
And diplomats besieged his door, and guns
Snarled in his ear, still he could spare a sigh

Of tenderness for her who gave five sons
On the red field; his fathering sympathy
Could save the drummer lad a fierce decree
Condemned to shooting. When a man humane
As even Saint Francis must direct a war
Of talon, beak and claw,
Of showering misery and heaped-up slain,
Then here was Abel reluctantly playing Cain.
And stranger yet, that with astute control
He should devise the master strategy
With vision for the whole,
While he, beyond all men, molded the victory.

V

To us who view the entire picture plain
Down the long vistas of receding time,
It seems he faced a cliff-like barricade.
While patriots agonized and boys were slain
To save the Union, how the rats of crime
Chewed at the ramparts loyal thousands made!
And oh, the crates stacked high with wormy beef!
The shoddy cloaks falling apart like straw!
The ships with beams decayed beyond relief,
Sold to transport our gallant youth to war!
Worlds might be crashing, but a lush career
Drew the black vulture and clawed profiteer.

And now, beside the faithful and the brave,
Mammon in uniform! Look! For a fee
He seeks the recruiting offices, to save
The shuddering wretch conspiring to be free
Of drill and peril. And of those in camp
Or marching to battle for the Blue or Gray,

How many, in dark swamps, would steal away,
Or, tattered and hungry, desolately tramp
To far-off home! In straggling pairs and groups
Sometimes they fled; and close upon their trail
Came galloping troops.
Often I heard the women scream and wail
When, from dim crannies, cringing shapes were borne;
Often, too often spoke
The rattle and snap of firing squads at dawn —
Stray tragedies soon lost amid the smoke,
The ruin and terror. When the true and tried
Lay bleeding or dismembered, who could care
For one more Kate's or Mary's lone despair,
Or some poor quivering John or Joe who died?

But one within the White House cared indeed;
With every open wound he too would bleed;
And while new crosses rose on many a hill,
A proclamation — "Let the slaves be freed!" —
Electrified the country. Words alone
Might loosen not one fetter, yet that call
Moved men like their own conscience; and a wall
Of old iniquity was overthrown
As by a shell-blast. In man's long ordeal
Against the squeezing gyre, the trampling heel,
Mark one more victory, though still the States
Grappled on scarlet trails with fire and steel.

Strangely, the battles seem, in retrospect,
To merge into one vari-colored whole,
One stormy whirl and pandemonium —
The ash of broken trees and batteries wrecked,
Red puddles, seepage of a ghastly scum,

And scattered limbs and bodies — charnel toll
Of men and horses. I perused once more
The sad, dark tale all ancient annals bore
Of wounds and groans and gore,
Now magnified by man's new-found reliance
On man-destroying science.
And where the tents in straggly lines were strewn
And the sick man lay squirming on his cot,
I saw the shaveless, soapless multitude,
Rag-clad and vermin-bitten, dusty hot
Or numb with cold —too often meagerly fed
On blue salt beef; or foraging, band on band,
For nuts or berries over a plundered land,
Snatching stray fowl, or plucking fruit or bread
From orchards or houses. In a barn or shed,
Mansion or church or school, how many a row
Of soldiers writhed in fever! — some whose arms
Or legs had felt the amputating blow,
While white-robed sisters, with compassionate charms
As of angelic healers, rustled past
And touched them with new hope. Cruel the fate
Of those war-captives cast
Behind the doors of prisons — doomed to wait
Twiddling their fingers through blank, loitering time,
For though their jailors might not contemplate
Barbarian torture, still war's filth and grime,
Flat tedium and want and stringencies
Must in themselves beget barbarities.

   In battle, as in day-to-day events,
Can one be two, or two or four be five?
Yet by such mathematics we contrive
To fan the mood that marshals armaments.

Each stroke of ours outscores the enemy's ten,
But their misdeeds rebuke them fifty times —
Therefore we know that we are righteous men,
And they the authors of black-handed crimes.
So, in the struggling States
The same arithmetic, too well applied,
Has made each side indict the other side,
And, judge in its own court, win all debates,
While both, in tremulous sincerity,
Rebut the foe by counting two as three.

   Thus the white ardor of the Southern dames,
Sewing and knitting, prodding the men, "Enlist!",
Or gambling their young lives by playing spy.
Thus with their foes, impassioned to resist
And plunge into the annihilating flames,
With seldom a panted "Why?"
Thus with the valiant sacrificial horde
Charging in droves of glittering bayonets
At Gettysburg, their only sure reward
That of a sun which sets.
And thus with eerier battles; thus at sea
When slim dark vessels dodge by night to pierce
The North's blockade. Thus when the *Monitor*,
Her turret like a pill-shaped fantasy,
Duels a ramming ironclad, a fierce
Apostle of new mechanistic war.
Thus when the rebels portentously contrive
A plunging death-machine,
The *H. L. Huntley*, midget submarine
Which drowns its crew — precursor of a scourge
Of deep-sea predators — steel sharks that dive
With doom's torpedoes under the blanketing surge,

While great masts topple.
                     Even when a swath
Of ruin rips through Georgia's deep-red soil,
The ravagers see but reason in their wrath.
And while they round up cows and sheep for spoil,
And shorn Atlanta's smoke curls high and gray,
And the charred skeletons of water-tanks
And embers of barns and bridges line their way,
Still the long vans and brisk, blue-uniformed ranks
Hear chants of "John Brown's Body!" through a din
Exultant with victory. So had it been
When Sargon led his swarms and Rameses
Rode forth with lions and chariots to win
Fat dividends from neighbors' granaries.
For he whose arm is strong
Is master of right and wrong,
And triumph, joy and pride command his trampling throng.

VI

    Rumblings of conflagration smote my ears
Amid the storm-blasts on a Richmond street
Where after jubilations, burdens, fears,
Men saw the sparks and cinders of defeat.
Over the housetops, twists and curls of smoke
Spread a large smudgy cloak
Across the brilliance of the April air,
And dust and acrid smells were everywhere.
Women, uprising in a panicky tide,
Their long hair waving, beat at storehouse gates,
Then bustled out with bulging arms flung wide
Round plundered bags and crates.
And the ground heaved in sharp, reverberant throes
From gunboats shattered at the riverbank,

And into the heavens fire and soot-clouds rose
When the ironclad *Virginia* burst and sank.
And forth from the city trundling wagons streamed,
A bedlam of horses, carriages and carts,
While at their side dishevelled people ran,
And men were shouting oaths, and children screamed,
And flame was rocketing in orange darts
Above the long and shuddering caravan.

Next morning, when the stride
Of Union troops exacted gasps and stares
From those sad remnants who still occupied
The gutted homes and smoldering thoroughfares,
The sky and water showed dull sultry glares,
And the deep rubble piles, a twisted blight,
Fumed as dark spokesmen, asking, "Why the fight?"

But, to the north, a wan and weary smile
Softened the plowed-up Presidential face.
How long the torment! An Herculean trial!
Four years of nightmare! But his hands were raised
Gratefully to some Power in unseen space
Whom with moist eyes and swelling breast he praised,
Viewing, in ash of Richmond homes and piers,
Pledge of a Union safe through distant years.

VII

His hair was silver-gray. And silver-gray
His full thick beard; and shining gray the sheen
Of his trim uniform; and gray his mien
When he put on his officer's array,
His spurs, his gauntlets, and the sword he tied
Almost flamboyantly with sash of red,

Pending that interview of which he said,
"Sooner a thousand deaths!" Now, mystified,
Gravely he probed the past. "You, Robert Lee,
A captain under Scott in Mexico,
How many years ago
Brushed elbows with Grant! What breed of man was he?"
But sieve-like memory
Had let him slip, and could no more recall
Than if the two had never met at all.

The hamlet chosen for a chance renown
Claimed half a dozen buildings in a row,
Perched on a small hill's crown
That scanned a valley stretching miles below,
Where guns and wagons of two armies stared.
Straight to a high-stooped porch the victor rode,
And Lee, awaiting him inside the house,
Taut-faced as though he dared
Hell's barricaded gateway, crisply strode
Forward, and hid the bleeding pride he bore.
The younger man, nut-brown of hair and beard,
Swordless and spurless, with blue open blouse
And mud-splashed clothes that casually he wore,
And trousers tucked in boots, might have appeared
A friend who merely happened by the door
To seek a moment's chat. He gave his hand,
And watching the pair, you never would have known
One was the Union general in command,
And one a sovereign driven from his throne
In stark surrender. You might half believe,
Hearing Grant reminisce of old war days,
His tall, chill rival waited to receive
A foe's capitulation. Only praise

Surrounds the conqueror, who could resist
The acid of the withering years, and met
His vanquished rival with no flourished fist,
But like a neighbor come to pay a debt,
With kind compassion, as for one akin,
One who had offered his whole heart to win,
And fought with honor.
                                        Yet, the meeting past,
Observe how, like a panther in a cage,
With fulminating glares and speechless rage,
Striding beneath nude apple boughs, Lee cast
Scarcely a word at comrades come to ease
His grief, his crucifying agonies,
His wounds now doused with acid. He could hear
The tumult in the Union lines, the blare
Of bands, and many a booming yell and cheer
As flags were waved and hats were tossed in air
And singers chorused. With a mute, fixed stare,
Oblivious to the hoofs that pranced and raced,
The Stars and Stripes raised high with applauded haste,
The General paced, and paced, and paced, and paced.

VIII

Clutched in a dream, he heard a sobbing sound
As all alone he walked the White House floors,
And everywhere the grief appeared profound,
And everywhere ran empty corridors,
No man or woman visible, though the din
Of mourning still vibrated through the gloom.
And then he wandered to the large East Room
And saw a catafalque, a corpse within,
Draped in dark funeral vestments. "Who has died?"
He asked a guard; and, like a known event,

The tidings smote him as a voice replied,
"An assassin's blow has felled the President."

Such was the nightmare Lincoln would report,
Holding some dreams are warning blasts of fate.
And oh, that they who heard had taken thought
Before too late!
Now, at the thankful season
Of the war's ending and the nation saved,
Peace had unloosed the hounds of wild unreason
And mad dogs foamed and raved.
And one there was, dark brooding-eyed, dark-haired,
Long nursed by rebel furies, in whose mind
Chaotic passions flared —
An actor who, spurred by a Cassius rage,
Was blackly self-assigned
To an immortal stage.
For John Wilkes Booth would live in evil fame
As long as eyes could weep or tongues exclaim.

Swaggering at the bar, he fortified
His weak intentions from a brandy flask;
And bolstered thus for his arch-villain's task,
Rapidly changing roles, began to glide
On dim theatre aisles, where, still and tense,
The audience, spellbound by Laura Keene,
Was blind to drama dwarfing the acted scene.
Abandoned without defense
While his one guard stole to a seat apart,
The President, swinging in his rocking chair,
Little could guess whose eyes, with sultry glare,
Peeped through a gimlet hole that pierced the door.
Soon, with a lunge and dart,

A shadow invaded the box; a bullet tore
Into a great bowed head, which sagged and fell;
And with a roar, a yell,
"Sic semper tyrannis!", the slayer leapt away.
Then, while the people, in a startled hush,
Rose like one man, abruptly to end the play,
A burst of hoofbeats, with a clatter and rush,
Sounded outside, and sharp bewildering cries,
"The President — he's shot! He falls! He dies!"

Now the great spirit, after storms and strains
That saved the nation, would at last be free
From the immense harassment of his chains.
But though time blunts the edge of tragedy,
The shot that felled him never ceased its flight;
Even now the loss remains.
And eyes, in reminiscence, still are bright
And sparkle moistly for that dread last night.

VIII. Tragedy and Conquest

". . . widening plains, and peoples expanding"

And what is the measure and law of the greatness of
    nations?
The fields that they sow, or the shops and the towers they
    fashion?
Or the pictures they paint, and their rainbowed and intricate
    structures?
By a sword or a brush or a hammer or pen do they triumph,
By an engine that roars over peaks or a thought that can
    travel
To comets and suns and the caves of their own deeper being?

Oh, what is the measure and law of the greatness of
    nations?
The missiles we hurl, or the creeds and the councils of justice?
As I gazed upon widening plains, and peoples expanding,
And watched the New World that was growing as pivot
    and focus
And lantern and magnet for millions on shores widely
    scattered,
I asked, Will the dream of the founders of states be
    transcended
By the vision of those that inherit? Ah, what of tomorrow?
And how will the measure and law of the greatness of nations
Appear in the eyes of new chiefs and the legions that serve
    them?

All black-apparelled, black of hair and eye,
In a black carriage, and with brow of tan
And stoic bearing, to the passer-by
He might not seem a dominating man —
Juarez, President of Mexico.
Bitter as brine the way he'd had to go,
Though in a country turbulent as the sea
None ever towered more upright than he.

Back through the years I gazed
To see an Indian lad, who moped forlorn,
An orphan hoeing his uncle's patch of corn
Or guarding sheep on hillsides while they grazed.
None, surely, would expect
The penniless youth, unfriended and unknown,
To rise among the shining and elect —
Or is it that destiny preserves her own?
As in an Alger story of success,
He ran away to town, and found employ;
And a rich merchant, watching the somber boy
Bustle at household tasks, perhaps could guess
Here was not one of the windy-headed throng.
And so he schooled the servant, till he came
To plead, as lawyer, fighting the piled-up wrong
That bowed his people. And he rose to fame
Not with an Alexander's blaze and flare,
But with a smoldering fire, a flint-edged will
That shot him from a solemn governor's chair
To the dank prison mold, and thence to flight
And exile, while he plotted to fulfill
His place as Launfal of the poor man's right.
Then sudden as thunder, with a growl and roar,
A menace darkened from a foreign shore.

Behold, at Vera Cruz, three fleets converge,
Waving the flags of England, Spain and France!
Look! from the gangplank sabred troops emerge
To take all Mexico in a swift advance
And rescue lost investments . . . . Two withdraw,
But iron fists of the third Napoleon,
Ready to beat at colonies new-won,
Reach out, reach out with hammer strokes of war.
Not yet has he discerned
What wiser men have learned:
That not by arms alone are empires earned.
And so he nonchalantly flicks a page
Grim with an episode not meant to be,
And sets the stage
For bleeding terror and black tragedy.

But tragedy, as often, clasped the hand
Of folly, and disaster walked with pride,
Picking an Austrian Hapsburg to command
The realm where Montezuma ruled and died.
Sardonic was the choice
Of fortune when she named her instrument,
Not a new Caesar with a bull-toned voice,
But one of smiling mien and mild intent.
The Archduke Maximilian, young and fair,
With bland full-bearded face and courtly ways,
Sought to escape the lap of purring praise,
The feline lushness of a royal heir.
And those exotic syllables, *Mexico,*
Provoked and charmed him. With a self-esteem
That made him prisoner of his own bright dream,
He held a borrowed sovereign might bestow
A benediction on the sore-oppressed.

And wheedling followers urged him, "Seize your chance!"
And the noble visionary never guessed
He looked through mist-banks silvered with romance.

    Yet long, as though forewarned, he hesitated:
"Now do the Mexicans want me for their throne?"
And then he clasped his hands, cried out, elated —
Their preference was shown
By ballots counted in a plebiscite!
(Which would have brought him rather less delight
Could he have known the fraud — could he have known!).
But why should humble Mexicans evince
Love of Vienna's prince?
Ah, did he ever question? Far the worst
Was this: no glass could show him, clear as flame,
Juarez, and his life's implacable thirst
For freedom as a high religious aim.
Not even half perceiving
The patriot's rage at regiments from abroad,
He poured sweet oil in rifts beyond retrieving:
"Let's join our hands in brotherly accord!"
No! there are wrongs, the President replied,
On which no voice but history's can decide.
With his guerrilla band
In rough back country he must patiently bide
The sure predestined liberating stand.

    Carlotta, daughter of the Belgian king,
Was young and radiant, with keen comely face,
When, wearing Maximilian's wedding ring,
She sailed beside him for the dreamt-of place.
But where was the festive crowd anticipated
After the long, hope-tingling cruise was done?

What! were they not applauded, wined and feted?
Why had no plumed official party waited,
And why no blare of horns, no welcoming gun?
Next day, through streets forbiddingly deserted,
They rode to Vera Cruz; while, close to tears,
Carlotta knew! the populace asserted
Its passions starkly as by hurtled spears.
Then, in the mountains, warning growls of thunder,
A broken carriage wheel, a night delay,
As though the fates advised, "Redeem your blunder
Before the reckoning day!"
But in the murmurous Indian crowds that saw
The great pale chief whom ancient myths foretold;
And in the city, where the troops were law
To hurtle back the muttering and bold,
The imperial couple glowed at cheers and shouts
That lit the sun again, and cancelled doubts.

    Like watchers of rose-templed cloud who build
Cities and capes from mist afloat in air
Till fog seems golden fact, the royal pair
Toyed with a bubble that they loved to gild.
To clip the hawk-claws of a preying church,
To feed the pauper hunched in sleeveless rags,
Shelter the roofless, and inspire the search
For justice, and a lamp when learning lags —
These were illumined aims. But to control
The deep heart-stirrings of the tattered mass
In wars of beggars and barons, class and class,
Required a Christly role.
And theirs was not the starred, world-rousing deed,
But only a colored mask; and they must dwell
Apart, as in a cracking rainbowed shell,

For they were led who had assumed to lead,
Napoleon's bayonets their one firm shield.
And sometimes, when glad ballroom music played,
From the city edge they heard a cannonade.
Before the guerrilla thrust, the armed horse-raid,
They lived as on a close-pressed battlefield.

    Yet he, who looked for peace in lovely things —
Blue distances of plain, the bald white peak,
Sunsets, and hummingbirds' vibrating wings —
Was not a Nero burning the frail and meek.
Often, with free benevolence, he'd save
Convicted wretches from an open grave.
Then harsher voices spoke: unless he lifted
A club to smash, the land would soon have drifted
To flame-throes of rebellion. Once again
Salvation by the slashing blade and noose —
The devil's most adroit bequest to men,
And, age on age, a fulcrum of abuse
For red-dyed Sullas — was revived to cure
The ills of Mexico. And he who reigned,
Deaf to his deep self-councils, saw the lure
Of royal strength and majesty attained
With scaffolds and bullets. Therefore he decreed
That rebels — which, by kingly logic, meant
All followers of the legal President —
Might be court-martialled. Thousands now would bleed
Unknown to Maximilian, their one fault
That they had struck the invaders of their soil.
But in a swift recoil,
Men rose in answer to the new assault;
A horde, dark-bodied and with hot black eyes,
Gathered as sworn allies

Against the intruder; fought with unsheathed claws
On fields wherein the captured won no quarter
And hatred, calloused and blinded, claimed no laws
But ruin and slaughter.

Whom was the Emperor shielding? Time can see
What his beclouded eyes appeared to miss:
That bladed power courts a nemesis
Of fear and quaking insecurity,
And often not the strong man but the weak
Will shout with steel and flame,
For genuine strength has not the need to speak
Or bugle forth its claim.

And what of the French aggressor, who had borne
Once more the Old World's culture to the New?
As in a vise, his hands were gripped and torn;
Along a wide frontier
Troops with the Stars and Stripes blocked his career —
He'd lost the game. So hastily he withdrew,
Leaving bewildered Maximilian caught —
A foe beleaguered in a crumbling fort.

By some keen-sighted flash, from deep within,
There burst on him the impulse: Abdicate!
But stanch Carlotta would not merely grin
And bow to fate.
"What!" she exhorted. "Will you crawl aside,
Weak-limbed and cowering? Have you no pride,
No resolution fitting for a king?
Come, hear me! Hear! I'll hasten overseas,
Plead with Napoleon, and bid him bring
Squadrons to smite the rebels to their knees!"

Ah, passionate dreamer! She could not untie
The meshes wound about two continents,
Nor dam the engulfing stream of world events.
Little she guessed, bidding her spouse good-bye,
Never again she'd feel his arms, his kiss.
Little she could foresee her eyelids wet
As she pitched sharply down a black abyss
Of madness and regret.
Rebuffed alike by Emperor and Pope,
At the last cliff-edge of hope
She tottered; and beneath the pummeling strain
Shadows and crazed illusions packed her brain,
Though still for sixty years her body would remain.

To Maximilian once again it seemed
That some sagacious guardian power spoke.
His crown was lost, never to be redeemed —
Let him escape before the tempest broke!
The boat was waiting; he'd already piled
Bundles of private papers safe aboard.
And then, mercurial as a frantic child,
He shifted ground. He'd keep his throne and sword!
And what if death would be his quick, his sure reward?

They say that sufferers, glimpsing just ahead
The gray, mysterious Gate,
By their own attitude will demonstrate
Whether the heart inside be gold or lead.
And Maximilian, perishing like a prince,
Would meet the test. "Look!" he heard friends advise.
"The guards, well paid, stand with averted eyes!"
He shook his head. Not his to quail or wince,
Or court escape while loyal followers fell.

And on the fatal day, when he was led
In black apparel from the red-tiled cell,
"Ah, what a glorious afternoon!" he said.
Long, with contemplative and wistful gaze,
He scanned the enclosing hills, the warm blue sky.
"Truly, a perfect day on which to die!" . . .
Short minutes later, one could see a blaze
Of rifle fire.
         And now, aloof and grim,
Juarez, safe again as President,
Who by one pardoning compassionate phrase
Might have forestalled the tragical event,
Came as if driven by some grisly whim
To see the enemy whose living gaze
Never had met his own. And as he viewed
The form embalmed, the mute and frozen face,
Perhaps he felt his pulses leap to know
That he, sprung of the Indian multitude,
Was perched supreme above the haughty race
That conquered Mexico.

II

    Not at the final trumpet blast
The battle ends, the tumult fades.
For the long fury of the past
Cannot be sheathed like dagger blades.

    Not with the pen inscribing, "Peace!",
Nor with the weary homeward tramp,
The havoc passes, rancors cease,
And reason rules the town and camp.

    But while dismantled hearths remain
And while storm-passions fume and foam,

Old battle fiends will not be slain,
And in the night old ghosts will roam.

What prophet had foreseen the dazed dismay
And disillusionment of a broken world
For many a soldier of the Blue and Gray,
Disbanded when Confederate flags were furled?
The war was over, but the wartime debt
In falterings and frustrations, lives and land,
Teardrops and sighs and bitters of regret,
Made an immense usurious demand.
The ragged homing Southerners, bowed with packs,
Halting aghast where bridgeless rivers flowed
Or where the weed-grown miry wagon tracks
Bore memories of a road,
Would unbelievingly stare, like men betrayed,
At shambles of a country they recalled:
Flattened old fences; hogs and cattle strayed;
Barns charred and doorless; houses half unwalled;
Stumps where a grove had raised green needled arms;
And on forsaken farms
The briars spreading. Then, should they proceed
Back to the cities — Charleston or Mobile,
Atlanta, Richmond — they might almost feel
The earth grown strange as Mars or Ganymede,
With homes deserted; wharves whose rotting planks
The scurrying rats possessed; streets deep in grass;
Warehouses empty; and long skeleton ranks
Of blackened shops and dwellings, mass on mass
Of rubble and ruins! If the mingled might
Of ten Pelées erupting joined to smite
And wither the country, surely the devastation
Would not have equalled man's self-wrought damnation.

Now hunger, battle's favorite son and heir,
And sharp-ribbed destitution prowl abroad.
Statesmen and generals, suddenly stripped bare,
Must drudge like serfs to fill their empty board.
One, whose great-columned mansion proudly rose,
Hawking tobacco, strains to keep alive;
And one, on whose plantation thistles thrive,
Seems a rude hired man that plows and hoes.
Then some, wry-featured, snatch their bags in flight,
With dreams of Europe or the Mexican shore;
Others, beneath the challenge, "Die — or fight!",
With heaving shoulders struggle to restore
Remembered fortunes, though there is no way
To the bright palace gates of yesterday.

And what of humbler folk — the widow left
Blue-lipped and roofless, begging meat and bread,
And orphans so bereft
They crouch in pine-branch hovels, scarcely fed,
And Negro babes that famine and disease
Pluck like the frost-nipped fruit of autumn trees?
What of the dusky throngs, with chains cut off,
Caught in the war-wave's rude receding trough?
Rag-girt, in squalid packs,
Like children fleeing home,
The loose plantation blacks
Confusedly drift and roam.
"Free as a bird!" they cry,
Though birds are lords of air
Whom rarely the gods deny
Nests and a daily fare.
But freedom, like contentment, has its price,
Paid in invisible coin more dear than gold;

And hosts, who in snug cabin walls of old
Drew food and shelter, never thinking twice,
Are suddenly, harshly hurled
Among the markets of a raucous world.
Some make the transformation. Others still
Stoop in the field, or shuffle round indoors,
Serving, for wages, their old owners' will,
Or with the shovel or axe find menial chores.

But see the crowds who, sporting in the sun,
Laughing and lounging, toy and stretch and bask,
Deliverance made complete — exemption won
From every task.
With Freedmen's Bureaux open to provide
Corn for his bowl, why should a man be tied?
But some, like brigands, range the countryside
For hogs and calves and chickens. They who toil
Often will yawn and loiter, masters state.
And how the people's bins are sucked for spoil
By northern sharks, while poor ex-slaves debate
In plush and gold of legislative halls!
So hatreds scores of years will not erase
Mark all horizons with long tarry scrawls
And curse the colored race.

Then I survey, sheeted like vengeful ghosts,
Hooded night-riders, goblin shapes of fear,
With horns stuck out and spectral masks that leer.
And victims' cries are shrill
When shirtless blacks writhe on the whipping posts;
And lit by crosses blazing on a hill,
Bodies swing lifelessly. And shots ring loud
Where flogged men scream amid the clamoring crowd,
And homes and barns puff forth a sanguinary cloud.

III

His square and chunky face, not warm or bright,
Though with a stubborn strength like weathered wood,
Cast no reflections of a starry light,
But told the firm, ground-rooted hardihood
Of Andrew Johnson — not a man you'd choose
To climb a tightrope path as President
And mount precarious rungs in Lincoln's shoes —
A leader few foresaw and none had meant.
Bristly with spikes and hard
Had been his road, a trail that struggle scarred
And twisted. Back through time he often peered
And saw, inside a small clothes-littered shop,
The needles he darted and the cloth he sheared
As tailor's apprentice — one who could not write
But recognized no voice demanding, "Stop!"
Then some beneficent chance
Gave him a wife who, with deep-piercing sight,
Could look inside, and pilot his advance
In brawling politics of Tennessee.
And when war rumbled through the border state,
As Governor, in oak-ribbed loyalty
He risked the assassin's shot; and random fate,
Almost as though
It picked a common crow
To flutter in an eagle's habitat,
Lifted him to the perch where Lincoln sat.

Never did time more sharply prove how men
Command events; how destiny is contrived
By hearts and brains. Had Lincoln but survived,
What different lines might issue from this pen!
Conquests his wisdom might have nobly made,

Leading with him a people well prepared,
Now had been yielded to a tyro's blade
In a war still undeclared.
Not with clear gaze had Johnson estimated
How passion, with shut eyes, retaliated
For aching wounds, and fear still unabated.
What! pardon traitors, murderers whose guns
Slew their own kin in treacherous Bull Runs
And felled great Lincoln like a gang of Huns!
And when, with snickering disdain, the South
Sent her prime rebels to Congressional posts,
Johnson, with puckered lines about his mouth,
Was startled at the insolence of their boasts.
And now, with a faculty
For stinging like a bee,
Accusing immoderately,
He was himself the butt
In a new war of states
When condemnation, knife-edged, lashed and cut
And men were torn in scorpion debates.

I noted, in a hushed, stone-solemn hall,
The Senatorial desks that filled the room
In a half circle; at a forward stand
The black-robed leader waited, while a call
Of names was ominous with threat of doom
And the country walked on shoals and sinking sand.
"Shall we impeach him? hold the President
Traitor to his high oath?" Now to invite
A judgment that the wise might long repent!
While rapiers clashed unseen, the brooding fight,
Close as a pinpoint, in a house divided,
Was sultry and undecided.

Breathless, men watched; then, by a single voice,
The nation made its choice.
Johnson remained — mate of a weakened ship
With riggings blown away and bulkheads smashed,
While skipper Congress, tied and blinded, steered.
And had one voice preserved us from a slip
To gulfs where union would have disappeared
And anarchy in stormy zigzags flashed?
Happily, when we pass the precipice,
An inch-escape is sure as a ten-mile miss.

IV

On a low ridge the tribesmen stood, and strained
Dark eyes along the blue horizon-line.
Silent as death the distances remained,
And the wide prairie twinkled with no sign
Of mighty moving shapes. "Where have they gone?"
The bronze-skinned watchers wondered. "Tell us, where
The humped and shaggy thousands?" Every dawn
They'd come to watch; and, every dawn, despair
Had chilled them. Always, with the budding year,
Since even the driest toothless crone could say,
The swishing herds were punctual to appear
In multitudes flowing far and far away,
Man's friends although his prey,
Whom the Great Spirit sent to give him meat,
Walls for his lodges, robes against the snow.
Lacking this help, how could the people eat?
Where could the hunters go?
Like men who blink in paralyzed surprise
One morning when the sun forgets to rise,
They watched and watched — and still no buffalo.

Then had the paleface raiders, with their din,
Frightened the creatures to some far-off plain?
More tragical the truth, blacker the sin
Than ever the wailing tribe could ascertain!
Crawling on grassy heights
Or through the bushes of some hill-ravine,
Were men who moved unseen,
Red murder in their eyes, and fixed the sights
Of long, thick-barreled guns upon the herds
Foraging calmly as seed-pecking birds.
A shot rang out; a great maned creature sank,
Stamping the dust; and other beasts drew round,
And sniffed the blood; but that strange cracking sound
Left their unpracticed wits confused and blank,
Not sparking the rush, the galloping escape
That might have saved them. Further shots streaked forth,
And at each shot a ponderous furry shape
Writhed to the earth, with lips of reddening froth,
Till the whole nearer prairie bulged with swarms
Of still and gory forms.

Then, from the windows of the new-built trains,
What pleasure, ah, what pleasure might be won!
Rifles of passengers were aimed for fun,
While over the miles the bloated, strewn remains
Stank in the wind and sun.
See the huge bales of hides transported east!
See the tanned hunter, claiming tongues alone,
Bequeathing the bodies for the coyotes' feast!
How many were slain? This only can be known:
More than the citizens that congregate
In modern Florida or New York State.

"And thus, O Man, like a pirate reeling and drunken,
A fox as it drools and slays all the geese in a barnyard,
You have looted the world and yourself, and plundered your
    children.
Thus you have emptied," a voice from the silence was saying,
"The waters that gathered their strength for the founts of
    tomorrow,
And poorer the planet will be, and poorer your spirits,
And bitter the price which time, with usurious fingers,
Shall exact in the deserts new-made, where dust-storms are
    blowing,
When at last, from the earth and her stream-beds and valleys
    forever
Shall have vanished a wonder of life and a joy of creation."

V

After the buffalo, the cattle king
In ranges ampler than whole Eastern states!
Look how the ponies dash, the lariats swing,
The herd of pawing longhorns snorts and waits!
In buckskin garments, with wide giant hat,
Around his neck a red bandanna flung,
And a huge holster slung
About his hips, and visage gaunt and browned,
A creature fashioned by his habitat,
Whom legend has renowned,
Behold the cowboy on the trail alone
In a world of grass unmarred by house or fence,
Far to the west a blue-beaked mountain cone,
And elsewhere space without circumference.

And how he rocks upon a bucking steed!
Witness the round-up, calves and heifers lowing,
Oxen and cows, a mass of horns and flanks,

As he whirls around to check the dread stampede,
And coyotes warily nose the further ranks!
And mark the cruel branding iron glowing
While victims bawl in anguish. After weeks
Riding the trail, frying his own flat food,
Sleeping by campfires in a solitude
Pierced by the long wolf-howl, perhaps he seeks
The solace of a town, and eagerly
As a sailor new-returning from the sea
Drowns his long abstinence in a foamy flood
Where the blank shanties of the frontier stare;
Carelessly flings his coin where cards are flashing;
Woos the soiled dame who smiles, with bosom bare;
Or, quick to take a dare,
Whips out his pistol to a spurt of blood
And sound of shattered lamps and tables crashing.

Then on the range, at times, cracklings of war
When sheepmen with gray nibbling myriads pass,
Which, devastating as a power-saw,
Crop every blade, tear out the rooted grass.
And fights with rustlers raiding
In cantering careers,
Who seek a fruitful trading
In stolen calves and steers!
And bouts with Indians banded
To drive the herds away,
When bold rides are demanded
To capture the beasts astray!
And worse, worse still — the ultimate enemy! —
The blunt gun-wielding farmer has imposed
Barbed-wire that bristles with a spiny might.
As when the English common land, enclosed,

Utterly ceased to be,
So by degrees the range would pass from sight
And wavy wheat and orderly corn would grow
And windmills turn to tap earth's underflow,
Where cowboys and their bronchos have become
Colorful pictures out of long ago.

VI

    At Fort Phil Kearney, volleying snow piled deep
In a night-blizzard cold as Labrador.
Soldiers with shovels strained against a heap
Raised in the darkness like a mounting floor,
Making a stair the lurking foe without
Might climb, and suddenly take the whole redoubt.
Hunched where the firelight puffed and flared inside,
The men, teeth chattering, made a dreary crowd,
And women wept apart, and children cried,
And one blue-lipped and bowed
Muttered, "We must have help!", and dismally eyed
Dismal companions, while the gale swept in
Through chinks and knotholes with a whoop and howl.
What earthly man could go
For help in that demoniacal din
Where feet and noses froze beneath the snow,
And skirmishing man-wolves stooped upon the prowl,
And flitted for scalps. Two hundred thirty miles
Across the shrieking waste, Fort Laramie
Might send relief. But through those spectral aisles,
Bleak as an iceberg sea,
Legs could not travel. Still the blizzard swirled,
Whistling and jeering; and two words were hurled
Into the company like shafts of flame,
"I'll go!" And every eye was fixed on one

Of huge, bull-shouldered frame,
"Portuguee" Phillips, trapper and Indian scout.
"Give me a horse and gun,"
He muttered, "and I'll break a pathway out!"

Too well he knew the odds. Who could outlast
That rioting, lunging blast?
Gauging how weak the fort, with line on line
Of their best men lost in an ambuscade;
And groaning as shivers crawled along his spine
At pictures of babes and women in a raid
Of screaming redmen, he could not debate,
Nor shrink, nor bow to fate.
Through a side gate he stalked into the storm,
With the commandant's horse, the blooded best,
In a bison robe that barely kept him warm,
While prayers and blessings showered upon his quest.
Snow whipped into his face; the wind that sneered
Cut like flung blades as quickly every light
Of the frosted fort behind him disappeared
Into a cave of night.
Yet more than the reeling gusts, far more he feared
Cheyenne attackers as he picked his way
By some old instinct geese and dogs obey
But wall-bound man has lost. At first he led
His beast by hand; then, feeling no redmen close,
Leapt to the saddle; and away he sped
Into a tumult growing more morose,
While from the Big Horn Mountains, fiends with flails
Drove at him with a rain of icy nails.

Days had gone by, and Christmas Eve had come.
At Laramie glad violins were playing,

And officers and girls were merrily swaying
In the ballroom's boisterous delirium.
Then suddenly, from without,
A rattling, a yell, a shout!
And as the confusion and noises multiplied,
A sentry's challenge, sharp as a striking knout,
While revelers jammed the windows. What they viewed
Abruptly closed the evening's festal mood.
There on the snowy ground a great horse lay,
Kicking his last; and near him, swaying and weird,
A fur-clad shape with icicles in his beard
And nose quite frozen away.
He tottered, he staggered in. "The fort! The fort!
Kearney! Phil Kearney!" he gasped, like one who raved.
"Send reinforcements!" His immense arms waved;
He stumbled and sank, and food and bed were brought,
And he could rest. By his blood-won report
Not only his own life but many more were saved.

VII

Perched on his pony with a conqueror's air,
He rode with haughty vehemence of command.
Broad-faced, with big hooked nose, and falcon stare
From eyes of bloodshot black
That served as law for his admiring band,
He wore the great war-bonnet of the Sioux,
With long brown feathers covering all his back,
And trimmed and beaded leggings, white and blue,
And delicate fringed shirt. At once I knew
The dreaded Sitting Bull, a warrior famed
Since his May-season. I observed him stride
With quick gesticulating arms beside
The council fire, and brooding dark-limbed groups

Were tense as he exclaimed,
"Hear me! No more we'll be the paleface dupes,
Nor trust to promises wild as rain that fills
The deep dry gully with a slaughtering flood!
No more, like the loud wind that whirls and kills,
The foe shall hurl us down in storm and blood!
Wolf-hungry, they have slain the buffalo,
And trapped away the beaver, and dispersed
The elk and deer, and fouled the streams that flow
From the Earth Mother's breast. But this the worst:
Crazy for yellow stone, they tramp upon
The oath they gave in the Great Father's name!"

    He paused, and the dark glitter of his scorn
Could not conceal the bedrock of his aim.
"Till the last sun has set, their treaty ran,
Here in these loved Black Hills, our hunting grounds,
Never shall come unasked a paleface man —
These promises are coyotes' wind-borne sounds,
Lost in the night! How well, my friends, you know
That with their mules and horses, pans and spades,
Beast-eyed inspectors, noisier than the crow,
Trample the country, plundering us in raids
On our fast-thinning game. If we protest,
They shoot us as a hunter shoots a bear!
Great is their power, but shall we let them wrest
Our fathers' land away, and never dare
Strike out like men?"
              But simple his request:
"Keep off our land!" And they who would not heed
Would finally have to bleed,
As Custer learned, when from a gullied hill
Riflemen charged him in a galloping swarm,

And after a panic rout, a fiery storm,
The General and his soldiers all lay still,
With Sitting Bull above them.
                          Yet he waged
A war to halt Niagara. Still the whites
Would come and come, and no victorious fights
Could check their cataracts, which crashed and raged
And rose, and ever rose
Despite all compacts and all counter-blows,
When cannon fire and numbers would possess
The gateways of the western wilderness.
And Sitting Bull? I saw him wander forth,
An exile far astray
Deep in the dark pine-forests of the north;
And then, one fateful day,
Tricked into prison, while the war-whoops screeched
And shouts were dinned and he was urged to go
With his white wasters, "No!" he challenged. "No!"
And guns retorted, and a bullet reached
The great chief's heart.
                    And as they struck him low
An epoch passed. I saw the old tribes fall
To white men moving like a tidal wall —
To white men like an inundating wave,
Sweeping alike the craven and the brave
From camps and lodges lost beyond recall.

VIII

Out of the night a sob, an incantation,
Voices of women, weird and long and shrill,
As though all peoples' ancient lamentation
Reverberated still.
And the witch-doctor, with his drums deep-rumbling,

His muttered spells to drive the fiends away,
While in a hut, despite the chants and mumbling,
An old man, groaning, feebly stirs to say,
"Bring me my son!" And when the youth looms high
Against the firelight, arrow-straight of limb,
The sufferer's withered features grow less grim
And pride still glitters from one half-shut eye.

"Hear me, my son! The earth will swiftly take
My broken body, and my soul will go
Home to the great First Spirit. But I ache
For you who stay below.
Palefaces, hungry as the hawk in air,
Greedily swoop for land. So hear me, son!
A Nez Percé is not a cowering hare
That shadows cause to run.
For many seasons have I lived as chief,
Herding our people on the bison trail.
Take, then, my robe! I'll die with blest belief
You will not flinch or fail!
Live on in peace! But if men bid you sign
Your fathers' earth to strangers, then decline!
Give not away our heritage — yours and mine!"

The speaker ends. He's made his will and deed.
And young Chief Joseph, a Washington to lead,
Not cruel like the wasp, but eagle-wise,
By birth and death is chosen to succeed
And earn great reverence in his people's eyes.

Years pass. But long before the son is old,
His father's dire presentiment comes true.
"You will not sell? Ah, but the land is sold!"

Challenge some men, with eyes of icy blue
And manners blunt and bold.
And sharp is his reply:
"If I've a pony that you wish to buy
But I esteem as friend and crave to keep,
You tell my neighbor, 'Here! I'll take that horse!',
And give him coin, and to its back you leap,
And leave on a dashing course —
That's how you've bought my land!"

As well appeal
To the wind or lightning, "Spare that great old oak!"
Joseph, a stranger to the hot ordeal
Of battle, might have bowed beneath the stroke
Of fortune, and with torn and burdened heart
Beheld his tribe depart
To seek a reservation's channeled bounds —
They who had ranged in fenceless hunting grounds,
Their only wall the mountains. But wry fate
Tripped them on treacherous passions. Spurred to act
By old iniquities and soured hate,
Some of the tribe, in secret fury, hacked
At white man's flesh. And scourging as a whip
The white reprisals lashed them.

Now began
An odyssey not often matched by man,
When Joseph and his followers schemed to slip
Far-off to Canada, where freedom smiled.
And oh, the pilgrimage with herds and flocks,
Squaws and papooses and the old and ill
Over two thousand miles of jumbled wild!
And oh, the battles among woods and rocks
When stanchly, with a Garibaldi's skill,
Chief Joseph led! And oh, the hard ascent

Across Montana's stony Lo-lo Trail,
With echoing gulfs beneath, and winds that rent
The half-bare climbers, when they had to scale
Cliffs slippery as tightropes! Close behind
The paleface soldiers followed, vengeance-bent.
And still they had to wind
Through measureless wastes, and often had to fight
And always won, while hearing death-drums roll . . .
Till, in a northern land,
One glad but weary day they came in sight
Of the Bear Claw Mountains, knowing that their goal
Shone just beyond.
                    Then destiny took a hand.
Resting that day in camp, a gaunt, grim host,
Too long they waited. A tragical *almost*
Would haunt the survivors. From the filed ravine
In which they loitered, suddenly they saw
Cavalry squadrons closing like a fan,
To whirl upon them. Then a shriek! a scene
Of pandemonium! when every man
Fought like a grizzly trapped, knowing the war
Had reached its desperate close.
At last Chief Joseph, ringed about by foes,
Bowed and surrendered. "Tell the Big White Chief,"
He pleaded, "that I want no further fight.
My children die. My heart is sick with grief
For the good comrades who have taken flight
And I shall never see till I have gone
To the great spirit-lodge."
                    So finally, borne
Into a reservation far away
In Indian Territory, see him stride,
Still with stern eyes of pride,

Showing the scars of many a long affray,
While in the land he knew as his no more,
Conquerors came with picks, and scraped for shining ore.

IX

Before my mind a thousand pictures flashed
Of warriors bright with feathers, paint and beads,
Who in the forest, field or canyon clashed
With shots or arrows in disastrous deeds.
I looked upon swamp-threading Seminoles
Deep in palmettos of the Everglades,
Fending for home, and taking blood-red tolls
Of troopers and artillery brigades.
I watched the Modocs range the lava beds
Among torn hillocks bladed like a knife,
Where hidden marksmen, in unequal strife,
Cut staggering corps to shreds.
I saw Apaches sweeping
On quiet villages with a lunge and yell,
Leaving a trail of fire and smoke, and reaping
In screams and gore while settlers fought and fell.
I gazed at scalping whites
Hunting for redmen as for ducks or geese,
Who shot down squaws and babes in running fights,
And viewed, by their queer lights,
Extermination as the way to peace.

But even when the friendly pipe was passed
And hands were joined and honest hopes were given,
The gulf between the peoples was so vast!
Misunderstanding was a spearhead driven
Into their councils. Never in all time
Had strong invaders and a conquered race

Blended like chime with chime
Or the weaker found an equal dwelling-place.
As when a Mississippi overflows
And tranquil swards along its banks are drowned,
So the white inundation rose and rose
Above the green of Indian hunting ground.
Two types, two cultures, and two ways of thought!
Two histories and two ancestral codes!
But since the intruder, in the last resort,
Must have prevailed no matter what his roads,
Why all the ash, the terror and the pain,
The smoldering towns, the hillocks of the slain?
Ask man's old warrior mood, the spears high-stacked,
The lances swung ever since Troy was sacked
And Nineveh was levelled with the plain!

   "But more than the thrust of the arms of your sons and
       your brothers
Has opened the trail to luminous lands of the sunset.
When the West was a wilderness still of tenantless spaces,
The wizard of steam spouted forth, and electrical witches.
And how could the Yuma or Ute, from the trail or the
       wigwam,
Compete with these gifts, as strange as a magical carpet
Traversing the clouds, and rich as a fabled Aladdin?
And how would it be if you, in your highways and cities,
Must battle invaders tall-armored from Venus or Saturn,
Who could dive with the lightning, and race like a storm-gale
       and thunder?

   " . . . Who could dive with the lightning, and race like
       the storm-gale and thunder?"
A voice was repeating; and hearing no answer, I hastened
Again to the vastness that glimmered from ocean to ocean.

IX. As From A Penthouse Window

"When the New World, transformed by sharp degrees,
Was beating at its insulating wall."

Over the prairie ruts, with jerks and lunges,
The stagecoach wallows like a raft at sea.
Down a long bowl, in squalls of dust, it plunges,
Then, with six horses laboring heavily,
Rocks slowly upward. At the driver's side
Three men are jolted; several more within,
Close to the wheels' continual crunching din,
Share with some sacks of mail the jarring ride.
Caught in a mud-hole of the roadless plain,
The vehicle sinks and stops; with groans and curses,
Aiding the hard-whipped beasts, the passengers strain
To pull it free, knowing that new reverses
Hide just ahead. A stream compels a halt,
Grudging a ford along its soft sand-banks;
Fleet mounted Indians, in a dusk-assault,
Whirl round, and bandits gallop along their flanks.
And oh, the many days
Of cold and thirst and heat,
When the weary rover sways,
Tied often to his seat!
With worse than prison fare,
And never a bed for rest,
What trials men gladly bear
To cross the continent, and reach the West!

Now for a time, along the giant spread
Of mountains and valleys, deserts and plateaux,
Rush pony riders, like war couriers sped
To bring the mail, swift as the wheeling crow.
Forth on their missions weaponless they dash,
Dust rising and tails flying; and they hope
Their speed will more than cope
With robbers ambushed for a smoking clash.
Sometimes a horse, amid the brush or boulders,
Stumbles or trips, or spurred to panting haste,
Collapses; then, with mailbag swung on shoulders,
The messenger must trudge across the waste.

But soon the rider and his pony pass
Utterly as war-chariots of Greece;
Soon a soot-belching slave, an iron mass
With hoarse night-hootings breaks the ancient peace.
Ah, never a continent
In all the ages since the first men wandered,
Was crossed by such a magical event
As when this cindery goblin lurched and thundered!
I saw the long rails looping round the hills,
Through gorges, over mesas, swamps and streams,
And into tunnels straight and sharp as drills,
And out in cuts among the tall rock-seams,
Mastering plains and mountains. Then at last,
Near the blue waters of the Great Salt Lake,
While crowds applaud a nation-bridging feat,
A golden spike is driven — fit to make
The triumph over time and space complete
And cleave the future sharply from the past.
No longer will the fruitful West be far
As some strange country on another star.

II

Making a glimmering floor without a break,
Mile upon mile is wavy green with grass,
Except where fences bristle, "None shall pass!",
With barbed-wire warnings for the farmer's sake.
Behind the barricade, a windmill turns,
Drawing dear water from the under-soil.
A sod-house rises, and a family earns
Precarious bread by slow, back-stooping toil.
Harder is life than in the tree-green East;
The ridgeless flats oppress like plains of lead;
Winter swirls down in blizzards, and the dread
Of white and Indian foe, bandit and beast,
Has never wholly ceased.
But worse! the twisting hurricanes that roar
As though all heaven, with sledgehammers, struck;
And locusts that, in shadowing torrents, pour
Over the fields, incarnate evil luck,
Which crops away the last live stalk and seed;
And drought, starvation's bony old ally,
When the lean settler grimly strives to read
Rain-portents in a bare and brassy sky,
But never once, through dust of withering weeks,
Receives the boon he seeks.
Then often the westward-faring pioneer
Nudges another, with his cows and horses,
Wagons and babes and piled domestic gear,
East-bound, abandoning blood-earned resources.
But many stay, to sweat and dig and strain,
And cursing the weather, sow and reap their grain,
And build, with calloused hands, a great new farm domain.

Still pressures grow, and hunger

For land, for land, more land.
The bolder men and younger
Shout in a mass demand.
And the wide western regions
That seemed immense as space
Are swallowed by the legions
Of an unnumbered race.
Districts that oath-bound treaties sanctified,
Sacred forever as the redman's dwelling,
Are nibbled off, or covetously eyed
While migrant swarms are swelling, swelling, swelling.
And when, in Oklahoma, fertile strips
Fall to the taker by official order,
It seems as though a cyclone whirls and rips,
And madness shakes the border.
On the appointed day, long waiting trains,
Packed with adventurers greedy for the boom,
Disgorge dark human crowds that cross the plains
As though in marathons with the dogs of doom.
Mounted men gallop; wagons heave and lurch;
Careening carriages tangle and collide;
A few, in river mud-holes, end their search;
A few, with whoops and yells and gunshot, ride
Forth to good claims, reaching them yards ahead
Of panting rivals. Others, tight-jawed, stare
Into steel muzzles; shrink away, and swear
At squatters cheating. Soon the hut and shed,
Low-roofed where all had been green wilderness,
Shall cry man's will to harvest and possess.

III

Along white passes under pyramid peaks
And in the desert sink and firred ravine,

And where the great-horned mountain sheep are seen,
He wanders with his pack-mule; and he seeks
Glistening fortune with the pick and pan —
Lonely prospector, like a link between
The ancient nomad and the modern man.
I traced him on all slopes
Of western canyons where a river turned,
A tanned and rangy form, with eyes that burned
In ever-rekindled hopes.
Hotly to any rock-scarred ridge he raced,
And fought with oven heat and Polar cold,
And pitched his tent upon the gravelly waste
When rumor breathed the witching syllable, "Gold!"

A hundred camps I viewed,
Hovels of logs and brush or canvas shacks
Where lately, in a tall leaf-solitude,
Were wolf-prints, trails of elk, and grizzly tracks.
Often, as in Montana's battered wild,
Bannack, or Last Chance Gulch, were men marooned
Through months long-crawling, whom the snow enisled
And greed had driven and fury had attuned.
Great-booted, and with bulging guns and knives,
The bearded rogues caroused where guns were flashing
And bottles frothed in gaudily lanterned dives,
With red-daubed harlots round them, while the crashing
Of bullets made uproarious interludes
To voice their feral moods.
He who has gold-dust, earned on bleeding knees
With sweat and blisters — let him guard it well!
And if he packs his horse and starts away,
Beware! a galloping sudden gang may seize
The plunder, making sure he will not tell;

And where he lies no tongue will ever say.

    Worse yet! the hounds of crime may be the law.
Swaggering in goatee and sailor's tie,
Here is bluff Henry Plummer, bandit chief,
Named sheriff! much as though a tiger jaw
Had swung to give imperilled lambs relief;
While still, in fights and holds-ups, men would die.
But terror in the end
Will lose its head, will overtop its mark;
And, hovering in the dark,
Justice will wait her summons and descend.
Grim-lipped and rifled, vigilante bands,
Ropes dangling, crowd about a gibbet tree;
And Plummer's brigands, clamped in manacling hands,
Squirming and cursing, begging to go free,
Are swung aloft. Long after they are gone,
The wild life of the camp will still rage on.
Sometimes large towns will rise
Where gilded dance-halls, lewd as temptress eyes,
Have glittered, loud with song and bawdy cries;
And sometimes all returns to rock and thorn.

IV

    The knights and barons of the world today
Have never a thought of castles ringed by moats.
They flaunt no halberds, clank no iron coats,
Shine in no mailed array.
In suits of wool or dacron, from the throne
Of some ungarnished office, they preside
Darkly above a planetary zone
Of oil and coal, of quarries, dams and mines,

Of smelters, mills and transportation lines;
And grow the mightier for the strength they hide.
Nature, the great creator,
Within the New World's soil
Like some benign testator
Has left unmeasured spoil —
Minerals and streams for power,
Copper and zinc and lead,
Forests that crowd and tower,
Fish-bank and oyster bed.
And some beholders, with the shoving might
That built old states and principalities,
Moved as blind architects of destinies,
Spurred by man's ancient drive to dare and fight,
And sent the churning ship
Round iced Tierran shoals to find the West,
And dug the shafts that dip
Deep in earth's undercore, the spouts that wrest
Gold out of quartz. They made the dredge, the flume,
Oil-pump and powerhouse and cotton loom,
And with audacious arms they cleared a track
For engines and dynamos, the belching stack
In glass-walled towns and sulphurous countrysides,
Where the great noble of the modern earth,
Though often of common birth,
Reverenced like a marquis, proudly strides,
Well knowing that, without his mastering will,
Factories might not rise, but men be horse-drawn still.

I saw the new aristocrats, with faces
Wide-jawed and square, or slim and weasel-sly,
Not with chivalric mien or knightly graces,
But with a pushing nose, a measuring eye,

An armored penetration that could scan
A drill, a motor, or a stock report,
But, baffled, would stop short
Before a lily or the heart of man.
I gazed on Astor, with his traps that spread
Far over woods and hills, while gold clinked high
From mangled furry millions, squeezed and red,
Depopulating thus the life-supply
Of teeming regions, faithful to that creed
Of topless gain whose truer name is greed.
I looked on Vanderbilt, from New York docks
Climbing to dukedom of a shipping throne.
"The public — public good be damned!" he mocks.
"Have I not made my own?"
I stared upon a one-time bobbin boy,
Who, wandering with bare pockets from abroad,
Had found, among bedraggled waifs, employ
Beside a cotton reel, but now was lord
Of blazing steel mills. Both in youth and age,
"What need," he asks, "of fortune's piled-up gifts?",
Though his own laborers, on twelve-hour shifts,
Bake where the furnace demons glare and rage.
But public libraries, in days to be,
Will bless the name of Andrew Carnegie.

There was another, who was pitched to fame
By a dark ooze that subterranean tanks
Through long rock-guarded ages had concealed.
Oil, fierce progenitor of speed and flame,
More precious than the gold in all our banks,
Would shower forth a variegated yield,
More blessing or curse? What man can rank its worth,
Who sees tall foundries, with their fires full-blown,

Nursed on this humor of the under-earth,
Yet scans the roads where thousands yearly moan
In screaming wrecks? and shudders at the raids
On Coventries by wheeling bomb-brigades?
But who foresaw these woes
When first the viscid treasure welled to sight?
Derricks, like gaunt and leafless woods, arose;
Meadows were splashed with squirts of black; a flight
As to a gold-field called adventurers out
Where towns, like mining camps, would suddenly sprout
And red-faced speculators gauged the spout
Of each new gusher with a fox-surmise.

    Elbowing from the throng
With hands of agile weaving enterprise,
A close-eyed schemer would not dally long
To corner the central spoil
Of all those springs and cataracts of oil —
John Rockefeller. In the twisting school
Of poverty, he rose by spurts and bounds
From an accountant's stool
To hunt in wide industrial gaming grounds.
Wolf-keen, and long of nose,
Wedge-featured, wizened in his riper years,
He was not one of those
Whose conquering charm illumines their careers.
But in the church he sat devout and proud,
And regal fountains of philanthropy
Were eloquent of his creed: the man endowed
With flowing millions was the world's trustee.
And how you view him, most of all depends
Upon your vantage-point. In all the roll
Of rivals who, while paying grudging toll,

Were clubbed or crowded to the precipice,
Stood few admirers, and fewer friends.
And yet — he saw no blot or blame in this.
"I'll do the right," he said. "Let that suffice."
But some see right in fire, and some in ice.

Just as the prairie favors blowing grass
And southern shores are bright with figs and limes,
So he and all the captains of his class
Were molded by the climate of the times.
From vast new empires, wealthier than Rome
Had ever won, spreading in plain and height;
From science, opening her portentous tome
Of wizardry and might;
From creeds aggressive centuries had woven,
"Possess! Possess, though neighbors' hearts be cloven!";
From old stone-barricaded ducal ways
And from new titles of nobility,
The modern barons, whether for scorn or praise,
Drew power to shake the land and bridge the sea.

"They are only the heirs of the ages, their idols and
        spokesmen,"
A voice from the void was proclaiming. "They mirror the
        millions!
For see how the many bow down and salute and applaud
        them!
And all that they are, the legions of lesser contenders
Would gladly become; and all that they seem, in their
        castles,
Appears to the crowd a haloed, a godly attainment.
And if they have plaudits no Plato or Milton is granted,
And if, while they glide in their yachts or glow in their
        salons,

There wells from the springs of the land no Mozartian
      music,
No surge of Vergilian verse, no colors of Rembrandt,
No Angelo's art, and no thoughts of a second Spinoza,
Not they are the culprits to lash, for the moods of a people
And the tides of a time and a world have in them an
      expression,
And they are ourselves, though framed in a larger
      perspective;
They have reached what we hunger to be, with our earth-
      clinging vision
And our wires, computers and bulbs, and the courage
      creating
Our brick-towered cities, and airdromes and turbines and
      motors
That never a Troy could have dreamed of, a Babylon
      pictured."

V

To spreading lands of buff and brown and green
Where all was natural as the swallow's flight,
There came the whirring of the wheeled machine,
The boiler's hiss, the boom of dynamite.
In the new cities, as across the sea
In sooty Birmingham and Liverpool,
The miracle that was to set man free
Clamped him the tighter on a bench or stool.
I saw pale women and thin children hunched
Low in the crashing factory's lint-choked air,
And men with picks that crunched
Through coal-shafts, blinking in the lantern flare.
I saw the miners' houses, row on row
In some blank valley or the gray gouged hill,

Whose fumes would blight and kill
Till not a petal bloomed, a blade would grow.
And in the cities I observed a mass
Of pinch-cheeked immigrants in dust and glooms
Of reeking lofts or moldly basement rooms,
Stitching and sweating under spouts of gas
Half the long hours of the long, tedious week,
Or dingily windowed in a shade so bleak
The sunlight scarcely made a passing streak.
And when the niggard gods of toil withhold
Even a stale hard crust, then mark the cries
Of children wailing for bread! the haunted eyes
Of ragged youths already gaunt and old,
And the bowed figure slouching through the cold
With hands upraised for work a fastened latch denies.

        And did the beaten then
Dare to link arms with comrades, and unite?
From the stone mansions of trim-tailored men
Came yells of pain and fright.
Stamp on the vipers! Throw them from the gates!
Yet from repression rage sucks nourishment,
And steam too tightly pent
But broods and waits.
I saw the secret "Knights of Labor," meeting
In clandestine basements, like conspirators;
Heard passwords mumbled; noted signs of greeting
In solemn ritual beside their doors.
And then the symbol — of a ring enclosing
Five stars, within a triangle's embrace —
Stared upon walls and sidewalks, so imposing
That apprehension furrowed many a face.

Yet theirs no crueller purpose than to call
All working men to seek the good of all.

  Even in lordly Rome the slaves had risen;
Even old Europe's whip-marked peasantry,
With rakes and pitchforks, in the *Jacquerie,*
Lashed out, though vainly, at their lifelong prison.
And men obliged to dwell
At Company prices in a clapboard town,
Seeing balloonlike profits bulge and swell
While their thin wage was sliced abruptly down,
Might grumble and rebel.
Many a wild, arm-waving scene I saw
Of howling strikes and lockouts that exploded
With the brute turbulence of private war,
When hired assassins charged with rifles loaded
Or fell beneath the snarling massed attack
Of hungry men who swarmed in desperation
Where the squat steel-mill, with the smokeless stack,
Stood silent, cold and black,
While oaths and mutterings growled across the nation.

  Not less the passion as, from coast to coast,
Reckless as hurricane waves that pound a dike,
Wrathful as men the scorpion fates betray,
With coinless pockets and deep-shrunken pay,
The workers gathered in a squally host:
"Our side must strike! Let's strike!"
"But no!" Balking the hammers of their rage,
Pleaded a smoldering-eyed, lean-featured man,
Eugene V. Debs. "We'll fight by reasoned plan,
Not on a lawless stage!"

Still, anger crackled — anger, twinned with hate
Against the brassy Boss, who snapped dissent
At envoys begging a peaceful settlement:
"Be gone! There's nothing here to arbitrate!"
Indeed, was hunger subject to debate?
"I'll smash the Railway Union," Pullman swore,
"Like a glass bowl!" Hard-bitten men and strong,
His hirelings, came to settle an old score,
Convening, throng on throng,
With clubs and bottles, ominously gunned.
Must toilers then be dovelike, while the foe
Pounced with assassin blades and privilege struck them low?

See now the flames that sweep
From shops, from rows of cars, from signal towers,
The wrenched-up rails flung in a twisted heap
Where crowbars pound and sparks are blown in showers!
And whose the stroke that fired the demonstrations?
Ask not the workers where they dourly stand
With desolate stares while two-men bouts are fought —
Ask Pullman's mercenaries! Accusations
Scatter abroad: this ruin all was sought
By some vile strikers' band!
Promptly will sound an order from a court:
"Beware! No interference with the mails!
No blocking Company business!" . . . Down a track
A chugging locomotive slowly steams;
And while the crowd pulls back,
Drawn-faced and glowering, with shouts and screams,
From the cab-roof a bullet-burst assails
The watchers, spattering in a brusque attack.
Blood gushes; women stumble, shriek and run,
And men slump down . . . and when the fight is done,

Look! Management has won,
Though not till companies of blue-clad troops
Dash in to hurl aside the working groups.

And Debs, the leader? As slow months drag by,
Bleakly he broods among the grilled, dim walls.
"Why am I here, a prisoner? Tell me, why?"
Then, like a mockery, the judgment falls,
"Contempt of court!" They know he broke no law.
His crime was courage — daring to defy
A power voracious as the Minotaur.
Now, a live martyr moping in a cage,
He sorrows for his people — blue-lipped mothers,
Wan babes, and shattered men. But he must wage
Fresh battle for his bruised and trampled brothers!
Fanned by abusive winds and gusts of scorn,
A new crusading fire, a rebel flame is born.

VI

While gilt and marble courts, like halls of state,
Were sumptuous with tiles and tapestries,
And carven chairs or desks or antique plate
Were purchased at the price of baronies;
While some set diamonds in their teeth, and some
Served pearls in oysters for their dining thrills,
And others, with a flick, a casual thumb,
Lit cigarettes from hundred-dollar bills —
Within a mile of where the lordlings sat,
I roamed a less resplendent habitat.
I saw old five-floored gloomy boxes stare —
Brick tenements of smudgy gray or red,
A Tartarus wherein the breathing dead
Wandered in rags and squalor and despair.

With iron fire escapes where blankets lay
And refuse piled until no man could pass,
These dreary squat Bastiles stood mass on mass
Like cell-blocks waiting for the Judgment Day,
Loaded with tortured souls. Inside their glooms,
Where God's great blessing of the air and light
Was barred from all but two of seven rooms,
Or where vague basement caves
Were grisly living graves,
Sometimes whole families shared the rot and blight
Of dens too foul for dogs — folk with the night
Of prison in fogged eyes and doughy cheeks,
While from the pushcarts and the alley grime
Arose few skyways for the mind that seeks
Escape from dirt and crime.

If from the brawling ancient Roman mart
Opulent Crassus came to earth again
And scrutinized Manhattan's huddled men
In old-style tenements, would he not start,
Throbbing at sights familiar, thinking how
From rickety frames erected floor on floor,
He'd mowed sweet dividends, even as now
The fat slum landlord? As so long before,
Money was First Preceptor over man,
And time retained its predatory creed,
"Praise self-desire! Ignore a brother's need!",
And "Capture what you can!"
Yet, mounting above the darker centuries,
We'd not await hot tongues of conflagration
To cleanse the human waste, the soul disease,
But conscience, yawning awake throughout the nation,
Would lash against the piled iniquities.

Slowly, as when small cells, in darkness, build
Tissue to heal a wounded wrist or knee,
Some sure regenerative spirit willed
More healthy things to be —
Not at all points, or succoring every neighbor,
Yet with a hope, a father-wise intent,
When cities, after long debate and labor,
Knock down the cockroach-ridden tenement.
And great new towers soared,
With lawns and lilies, sunlit spots between,
That man, if only in part, might be restored
To the world of blue and green.

Then pity, strangely, in her devious course,
Forming societies where men might plead
For the whipped dog, the worn and beaten horse,
Crept through back windows to a human need.
The shrunken mill-girl, timed
With rushing fingers to a rushed machine,
Capping tin cans, and cans, and cans all day;
The beaker boy, begrimed
Where down a chute the chunks of coal careen,
While torn, bruised hands pull barbs of slate away;
The blue waifs withering in the loft, who stoop
At pale and waxen blooms they limply make
By toil unnatural as their man-made flowers;
The ten-year-olds, who droop
In red infernos where they wilt and bake
And molten glass is rained in scintillant showers —
All these, and more than these,
Prey of man's greed, his dollar-clutching claw
And the brute precedent of centuries,
Are reached by mothering thoughts and salving law.

VII

Like one who, from a penthouse window, stares
Over a city's rush and swirl and flow,
Its parks and churches, monuments and squares,
I saw far-stretching time that spread below
With a great people's feuds and destinies,
More varied than a quilt of leaves in fall,
When the New World, transformed by sharp degrees,
Was beating at its insulating wall.

I watched the rangers of the last frontier
Fade in a mist of far and fabulous things;
Observed the vast free farm-lands disappear
In homesteads and baronial plunderings.
And cities, east and west,
Stone-walled or wooden, grew,
High-chimneyed to attest
Industries bold and new.
And glistening rails were laid
Through desert bluffs to south,
And where the salmon strayed
Along the broad Columbia's fir-grown mouth.
And honor and corruption, while the light
Was dim on courts and halls and domes of state,
Made once again their never-settled fight
As wolves or watchdogs of the people's fate,
As when a "Boss" who sucked Manhattan dry
Fell from silk-curtained rooms
Where diamonds glittered on Fifth Avenue,
And heard the packs of outraged law pursue,
And came at last to die
In Ludlow Jail's stern, barricaded glooms.

The lordly Union of the States, which spread
Between two oceans on a swelling tide,
Would still expand, as though the way were led
By forces vast and unidentified.
Stern with the treeless tundra's lichened gray
And long saw-mountains where the ice was piled,
There was a northern wild
That seemed unreachable as the Milky Way.
And when an envoy of the Czar proposed
To sell this deathly blank of snow and peak,
Mumblings were heard, and doubts; fears were disclosed
Greenland was not so Polar-bare or bleak.
Yet through tense sessions, all one fateful night
Almost till morning, statehouse lamps shone bright,
While for a bargain fee
Forests and mineral wealth none could foresee
Yielded their treasure to a far-flung State.
And none conjectured how the aftermath
Would plant, as though by some percipient fate,
Alaskan bases in the Soviet path.

Over the New World's shore
A tainted wind was blowing from the Old,
With greedy hoots and screeches, "Take and hold!",
As squadrons marched and skirmished more and more
For place and empire. Soon the thought became
Contagious as the measles — hot as flame
Crackling in oil and lumber; and men's glance
Was darted covetously overseas.
And where warm sparkling waters flashed romance
And smoking cones surmounted mango trees
Of charmed Hawaii, and a luminous land
Smiled on a people varied and complex,

Ringed by pineapples, flowers and coral sand,
Manipulators plotted to annex
The groves and peaks of earthly paradise.
Some, in tall sugar-cane, saw profits rise;
And some, whose faith was stout
And fervid, saw the Stars and Stripes reach out
Until all rival flags were put to rout;
And some, with naval zest,
Proclaimed, "Here is the key to East and West!
Give us this base, and we'll be first and best!"
And when men reason thus, and stride in might,
Their means to power will soon be lost to sight.
More by the mood and will than by the hand
That raised the emblem, we achieved command
And moored our sloops against the tropic night.

VIII

Where deep-blue Caribbean billows broke,
Old sputtering revolution hissed and flamed
On Cuba's palm-lined beaches; fire and smoke
Of Spanish mortars raked the long green isle,
Blackening fields, and marksmen charged and aimed
And the helpless moaned beneath war's ancient trial.
I saw a ragged crowd
Of farm-folk herded where the rifles gleamed,
Jammed into garrisons, while cries were loud
And women prayed and wept and children screamed,
And infants howled for bread,
Shivering in the jail-like glooms and damps,
And daily carriers bore the sheeted dead
From the foul sheds and concentration camps . . .

And now a screen descended, and I viewed

Warriors of a brisk commercial breed,
Who made of man's deep sorrow meat to feed
Their private hunger. On Manhattan's shore,
Two large newspapers, in a poisonous feud,
Courted the multitude
With snarls of "Cuba! Cuba!" . . . More and more,
Each grappled for a match to light the fire
Of a roused people's ire.
Oh, vast the virtues of a chainless press,
To bare one's heart without the law's redress!
Yet, ah, the leech-jaws sucking on distress!
On both great journals burst a revelation:
A war to titillate and stir the nation
And wave its flags, was grist for circulation —
A short, small war, of course. And it was plain
The made-to-order enemy was Spain,
Which could be spat upon in holy wrath
And crushed in high disdain.

But first to spur the people! For the fight,
Though plotted like a novel, must invite
Millions to cheer the grand, heroic right.
Talk boldly, nobly! Though the truth may be
An incidental little casualty,
Lash out, lash out at foreign butchery!
Tell how the vampire foe
Strips women bare (a lurid bit of fiction),
And in a gaudy horror-story, show
The heroine's affliction
Behind the villain's cell-bars. Better yet,
Bid a reporter seek the Cuban jail,
Climb on the roof, if feebler tactics fail,
And, like a fireman ready with a net,

Rescue the victim! Then, with shouts and cheers,
Call loud flag-wavers! bring a song and band!
Gather in greeting on the streets and piers
Of Freedom's waiting land!
Thus may a gallant people be incited
At tyrant ways, and nations be ignited!

The plans went smoothly as a butterball,
And one could almost smell the battle smoke,
Until the Spaniards basely donned a cloak
Of Peace, and came with bows, and granted all
Our country asked. Against such meek compliance,
How marshal troops? How bluster in defiance?
Almost, alas! it seemed one side alone
Could not arrange a war. Our President
Achieved, at times, a non-belligerent tone,
And all might soon have passed without event,
Had venomous destiny
Not coiled and waited where no eye could see.

Tossing at anchor in Havana Bay,
With all her crew retired in bunks below,
An iron-turreted colossus lay,
The U. S. *Maine*, which many years ago
Would be forgotten, had no freakish fame
Dealt her the death-stroke that preserved her name.
Suddenly through the night
A flare arose, as though an entire world
Erupted sunny bright.
Skyward huge meteoric chunks were hurled
With peals and booms of thunder
And screams, unheard, of mortal pain and fright;
And the great vessel, like a writhing beast,

Shuddered and heaved. When the convulsion ceased,
Her hulk lay settled under
The red-lit water. In the attendant gloom
Hundreds went mangled to a salt-sea tomb.

Then frenzy, spurred and blindfold, stormed abroad,
Her long arms waving in a dance of hate.
"Betrayal! Murder! Infamy!" men roared.
"A crime for which we must retaliate!
The Spaniards mined the ship! The Spaniards aimed
To sink our seamen, with a snake's deceit!
So let our President," the mob exclaimed,
"Summon our forces! mobilize our fleet!"
And there were hot-eyed volunteers, with none
To marshal them; and zealots in parade
Shouldered the flag and gun,
Dinning, "Hurrah! We go to Cuba's aid!"
And rallying calls resounded in a blare,
"Remember the Maine! The Maine! Remember the
        Maine!",
Though never anywhere
Had pleaders shown that saboteurs of Spain
Had sunk the ship. But when men rise in passion,
Fact becomes fiction, truth is out of fashion.

So visions of mephitic treachery
Blazed up in minds grown sick with fantasy,
And fed the war-urge. And the war we sought,
Lit by a fanned emotion, not by need,
Came in a puff, and zestfully was fought,
And patriots, with chests thrown out, could read
Of San Juan Hill, which our roughriders took,
And Spanish warships in Manila Bay

Burning and smashed, or shattered in the fray
At Santiago, while our shell-fire shook
The foe as when a terrier shakes a rat.
Therefore the war was won
To booming bands, the raised and waving hat,
And millions shouting cheers in unison.

But had men looked upon the triumph twice,
Beyond the wild éclat, the flags and glory,
They might have heard again the timeless story
All Caesars learn: that victory has its price.
Launched forth at last beyond the New World's gates,
Where the blind Titan, world dominion, waits,
We would be central actors on a stage
Of smoldering empires and flame-blackened states,
Never to know again the plain content
Of unpresumptuous folk upon one continent.

Far over isles and seas
I watched the feelers of the New World grow,
Not by stark pressure of necessities,
But since ambitious minds desired it so.
One third around the globe
I gazed on vessels crowded with Marines,
And watched their rifles probe
Among rice paddies of the Philippines.
And vexed debates were heard: "And is it wise,
And is it right and best
To weave our shadow over foreign coasts?"
And some exclaimed: "Both need and enterprise
Compel! our destiny is manifest!" . . .
"Who rules the fleet is master of the hosts
Of the world's power!" Admiral Mahan said.
"For us the only course is straight ahead!"

Then fair, blue-circling atolls heard the tread
Of marching columns, though in jungle lands
Not all the black or ochre-colored men
Looked on with thankful lips or clasping hands.
But snarling like the cougar in its den,
Rebels would strike, with red barbarities
Returned in crimson, following the law
Of ripping javelin and clutching claw
Known since the armed Sumerian centuries.
But he who founds an empire must expect
That some he rams or tramples will object.

IX

Far in the south, where once Balboa stood
Watching as white Pacific breakers curled,
A neck of hills and thick primeval wood
Parted two oceans covering half the world.
But surely he, as with bright eyes he gazed
On rumpled waters glimmering in the sun,
Would have observed man's later dream amazed:
To make both oceans one.

Theodore Roosevelt, President, a bolt
Of push and flame, desired a waterway
Through Panama; impetuous as a colt,
He would not brook delay.
I saw his square, firm face ignite with rage.
"So, then? Colombia has scorned the pact
And flings her challenge? Now's our time to act!"
And action followed on a sudden stage
Behind a curtain. Almost in an hour
The revolution burst. A fire brigade
And railway workers furnished soldierly power;

A northern warship bristled near to aid;
And in less time than would be used to win
A football game, they shouted, "Victory!"
Then, with a jubilant din,
And a wild dance of glee
They surged through Panama in celebration,
And spilled champagne, and capped their exultation
A few days later when a treaty saved
The epochal canal that Roosevelt craved.

        Thus, in the trial of states
The earthy god Success
Ordains and legislates,
And but one title is observed: Possess!
Still, though we took a tunnel lane, who might
Have traveled roads of clear and open light,
Our feat had dwarfed all Babylons time could cite.
Deep in the mountain flank
The straight, long ditch is driven,
High-walled and wide and blank,
Where sweaty years are given!
The spreading lake! the locks,
Lifting great ocean steamers,
Though still a peril mocks
The vision of the dreamers —
Small insects, buzzing through the marsh in swarms
With stings more terrible than snakes or storms!
But all is conquered, and a channeled way
Opens in jungle cuts from shore to shore,
And freighters, bound for Bristol or Bombay,
Foochow or Hamburg, Rio, Singapore,
The lean dark tanker with its one rear-stack,
The glistening cruise ship and white pleasure boat,

The slate-gray collier and the fishing smack,
Trail down the salty highway's shining throat.

One of the wonders of the world, this deed,
Beyond the power that raised the Pyramids!
But he who would succeed
Often must open unsuspected lids
Guarding Pandoras' boxes. We possess,
And are possessed by what we call our own.
And few the men whose shirt-clad selves express
That which they are when naked and alone.
Thus the Canal, which aimed its Titan shield
To make the entire continent secure,
Might tempt assailants like a baited lure,
Compelling us to wield
Great-turreted fleets and cannon in defense
Of our defender. So we trod a course
Still further from our first simplicities,
And draining new power and magnificence
From that colossal gash between the seas,
Rode on with ever-gathering armored force.

Like a giant that slumbers, as yet unaware of its muscles,
And tosses and turns and stretches in drowsy confusion,
The nation was swelling in strength, and its movements
        were echoed
Afar through the audience halls of a listening planet.
But was it aware of the iron and flame of its greatness?
And could it perceive, through the eyes of its lords and
        lieutenants
How the shadows it cast, and the flares and the lanterns
        it lighted

Would illumine the cabins, the camps and the domes of
    tomorrow?
Did it see, in a vision, the column of tribes and of peoples
That would wander before it in legions like ants as they
    skirmish?
Could it look with a widening gaze that crosses the ridges
To a world more content, where machine-guns and mortars
    are melted?

    While ships with their cargoes of sugar and cotton were
        steaming,
And derricks rose somber with oil, and soldiers bright-sabred
Disembarked upon beaches and capes, what voice had asserted
How the mantle of time would be thrown by the fingers of
    fortune
On the shoulders that heaved in the dark? — the task and
    the burden,
The glory and privilege and awe of a leader of nations?

    But none could foresee; the future was vague as an
        island
With headlands half muffled in fog in the silence of night-
    time,
While onward we moved over ranges that beckoned and
    towered
Beyond the predictions of seers and the sight of our pilots.

X. A World Comes of Age

". . . shadows of a giant transformation"

Floating like petals, flocks of butterflies
Circle against the sun in sparkling blue.
And bright enameled things of thumbnail size
Flutter and whizz with every gemlike hue.
And birds of flashing red,
Orange and indigo,
Are streaking overhead,
Brilliant as flowers; while the world below
Is shadowed by the fronded jungle green
And long lianas looping. Here and there,
Through river gaps, or looking out between
Tall rows of palms, the wanderer's gaze may stare
At peaks far-off, azure or olive-rimmed
Or violet where the morning mist has dimmed
Their jutting vastness. In this gracious land
All should be peaceful as a summer dream.
Yet here is heard the snap of snarled command,
Sobbing of women, and the whipped man's scream,
Where, bristling with a feudal sovereignty,
The *hacienda*, like a barony,
Bespeaks the grim old Mexican regime.

Thick earthen-walled, the manor house spreads out
With barns and stables and a church and shops,
And verdant acres billowing far about
With corn and cotton crops,

249

And woods beyond. In clusters, bare and blank,
Floorless and windowless, of sun-dried clay,
The peons' hovels stand minute and gray;
Or thatched low huts, ill-smelling rank on rank,
Shelter the workers. In the yard a crowd
Of mules and swarthy men and jangling carts
Are bright with color, and the din is loud;
And on the land, unhelped by modern arts,
The laborer jogs with oxen; swings the hoe
And flail; drudges behind the wooden plow;
Strikes with the long brush-cleaving knife, as though
Time has not moved from yesterday to now.

As sharp as ever in man's jagged past,
The chasm between the lordly and the frail!
Look at the Church, whose servants have amassed
Treasure as in some fabulous Mammon-tale!
Mitres with diamonds! robes of velvet white
All gold-adorned! the jeweled vase and dress
Beneath the arched and vaulted holiness
Of the great cathedral's forest-solemn height,
Where ragged Indians, with matted hair
All dirty black, devoutly come to share
The sacred presence! . . . Then, behold the State!
Porfirio Diaz, in proud control,
Masters a mighty goal:
Currents of commerce freely circulate.
Now, where the foreign banker counts his loan,
Bandits no longer pounce with mask and steel.
The grand dictator, in a princely reign
Far from the capital of Mexico,
Regales his guests with caviar and champagne.
So what if still the cutlass and spiked heel

Ever more sharply cleave where poor men moan,
And mutterings of revolution grow?

    Zapata, one among the multitude
Of humble sugar-croppers, lit the spark,
When with curled lip, in an ironic mood,
He happened to remark
How sumptuous the stables, rich in tile,
That housed the masters' racing horses, while
The laborers' huts were dirt-paved, squalid, vile.
So batter down the rule
Of the strutting landed lord!
Why be the rich man's mule,
Earning a mule's reward?
With his guerrilla horsemen, seizing arms,
Zapata wandered through the pass and plain;
And smoke of smoldering sugar racks and farms
Trailed just behind, and shapes of foremen slain,
While, to the landless, land was given to plow
And guard and cherish as their own.

                 And now
A weirder, half unearthly rebel rose.
I saw him with great bulging head flung high,
Brown beard, a pygmy size, a flattened nose
And voice high-pitched, yet prophet's lighted eye —
Madero, dreamer marvelously born
To mines and lands, a reader of the stars
Who thought to speak with spirits, and was torn
By speared desire to snap the poor man's bars —
Plantation manager who spent his gains
To feed the peons and dislodge their chains.

    Daring the fangs of fate,

He entered the wild-beast den as candidate
Against imperial Diaz . . . Like a screen
Swiftly revolving, all the world was changing.
Before the President's mansion, mobs were ranging
With hoots and hisses, in a mutinous scene.
"Down, down with our exploiter!" . . . Shots rang out
And hundreds pitched and fell,
While like a tide the rabble surged about,
Ebbed and re-surged. And Diaz read too well
The immutable signature of destiny,
But doggedly, while he struggled, sick abed,
He fended off the swords of things-to-be,
Then doffed his mantle and his rod, and fled
To a refuge oversea.
Thus, after thirty-six commanding years
He heard the satyr tongue of time, its sneers
At mighty arms brought low and drowned careers.

        As though the angel Gabriel had come
With trumpet, harp and drum,
And chanted jubilantly, "Rejoice! Rejoice!",
In every city where Madero passed
The crowds were glad and vast,
And thousands lifted one exultant voice,
"Long may he live!" And palm-fronds waved in air,
Idolatrous hosannas swelled with praise,
And women with their babies came to stare
As at a patriarch from Bible days.
Some who, with worship in their glances, bore
The shrivelled and the sick, grew strangely calm.
The lame, the hurt, the purulent and sore
Struggled to touch his sleeve, whose wizard balm
Dissolved all ills.

Alas, no god was he
But merely a man! And though no man was ever
More spotless, reverence and idolatry
Are but as wind in freedom's great endeavor.
Only with muscles taut, and nerves of steel,
The faithful could endure the brusque ordeal
Of rebel cannon. In that tortured state
The bandit and the angel were at strife,
And who can wonder that the bandit's knife
Ripped out a scorching trail of stealth and hate,
And that the angel, facing prison gloom,
Foully was felled, and staggered to his doom?

II

Perched in a back saloon whose walls were streaked
With bullet scars from past habitués,
He sipped of cognac, and his gunmen wreaked
The vengeance of his laws in red affrays.
Why such a gangster ruled as President
(As Huerta ruled) may best be solved by those
Who've fathomed why old Roman Clodius rose
Or cat-claws of the Borgias slashed and rent.
Sad, bullied Mexico
Was fated still to know
The robber captain; see blood-torrents flow.
I watched, in later scenes,
Long columns of Marines
Landing at Vera Cruz with gunboat screens.
I followed Pancho Villa, brigand head,
Leading his dark, sombrero-wearing band
Of horsemen near the torrid Rio Grande,
And striking, while the earth beneath him bled,
In a small border town. Soon, hitting back,

Came General Pershing with his troops that thrust
Far through the cactus waste of heat and dust
But only wandered on a dead-end track.

    Then rancor, like a flame
Nourished on oil, sizzled and hissed and flared;
Havoc and riot blared;
Pistols erupted fire, to kill or maim
Mexican settlers. Far to south meantime
Resentment smoked at Pershing's scouting force,
While northern throats were hoarse
And vehement to answer crime with crime:
"Take over Mexico!"
                        But in the east
A blacker cloud had lowered, where the roar
From Europe's forts and trenches never ceased,
And growing closer, rumbled more and more.
And scarlet flags of her dire tragedy
Warned us from Mexican catastrophe.

    The drummings of the far-off storm, its ruddy flashes
        grew,
And called the mother to the son, the Old World to the New,
While forth to Flanders mud and cold, the Meuse, the Marne
        and Aisne
The progeny of a continent were sucked as through a drain.
Fury had splintered cliffs and woods and crimsoned towns
        with fire,
And launched the battering barrage, and sparked the
        raiding flier;
And terror, close ally of doom, had loosed the submarine;
And arms of foundering seamen waved in a gray Dantean
        scene.

Alas, alas, for brave, star-searching man
And his indomitable climb of ages,
That council rooms should plan
The beaked torpedo's rush, the nightmare rages
Of steel-girt goblins, and of gas that drifted
Chokingly through the air . . . whereby our kind,
Which through long sweaty striving had been lifted
To leave the wolf-pack and the cave behind,
Now had descended, by precipitate bounds,
To slashing throats like mad embattled hounds.

But far aloof as from some agitation
Shaking the Gracchi's Rome
Were we who, walled beyond Atlantic foam,
Saw sparks and cinders of the conflagration.
Not yet we read the message: this small world
No longer stretched to safe infinity,
But any pebble hurled
In any pond might ruffle every sea.
And man, with cables, dynamite and steam,
Shrivelled the earth by each ingenious scheme
To master wave or fire.
                                        And so the heat
Of Europe's blazes soon began to scorch
Our clothes, and burn our feet,
And blister the paint upon our own front porch.
And though we might have winced, and turned aside,
What of our name, our pride?
What of the voices bellowing, "Fight!" — the shrieks
Of outrage and horror when we saw, dismayed,
Wreckers of ships that prowled with iron beaks,
Shark-silent in the underwater raid,
While seamen yelled and sank into the cold

Of the gray Atlantic? Then that dire attack
When the great *Lusitania* pitched and rolled
With the torn bulwark and down-slanting stack,
And plummeted bottomward amid the wails
Of women, shouts of men, and children's cries —
Innocent hosts whose drowned, weed-covered eyes
Would weep in lingering tales.

III

Huge as a mountain stared the irony.
The daily stretcher-bearing caravan
Was loosed by one who slaved to make us free
And seal the immortal fellowship of man.
I saw a thinker's face,
Bespectacled and scholarly and long,
Wherein I read no trace
Of fluttering aims, or cross-winds of the throng.
But sturdy as a pine-tree on a hill,
Stout-limbed, and fortress-walled
With pillared judgment and basaltic will,
Would be the Woodrow Wilson men recalled.
Not that, beneath his patriarchal mask,
No twinkling syllable flowed, no jest or gibe,
But that he bore to his illumined task
The consecration of the priest and scribe.
As when he lectured to brow-wrinkling classes
At Wesleyan or Princeton, so he brought
A teacher's message to the listening masses.
And if the waves and currents of his thought
Rippled unseen as breezes, still he loomed
As a new Moses where the Promised Land
Of milk and honey bloomed,
A prophet whom not all could understand

But many worshipped.
                              Was it chance that raised
This staid professor to a rocket height
Where staggering power blazed?
I saw his tired eyes that, late at night,
Followed the lines of some close-lettered tome
Of statecraft, while he strove to comprehend
Meshes of politics in Greece or Rome.
But many have pursued a kindred end,
To earn — at most, a pedagogue's repute.
And why should he, of all the crowd, attain
The jealously clutched at, fiercely envied fruit?
Surely, his bursting force, his spacious brain
Not fully can explain
His starred ascent. Did he not climb, in part,
Thanks to the screen about his mind and heart?
Slick politicians, in New Jersey halls,
Thinking to pull a puppet on a string,
Would meet some jarring falls.
What! did he mean this nonsense? that he'd bring
Honesty, like fresh verdure of the spring,
To politics' moldy basement? Such a man
Dismays the Boss, upsets the ruling clan,
Which soon may rule no longer. Even so,
From Governor's mansion to a White House chair
Was far as from a Trenton thoroughfare
To Jungfrau's rock and snow.
Then was it a random shot or fate's intent
That picked this quite unlikely President?

* * *

The granite armory at Baltimore
Baked in the summer heat; its spacious spread

Shook with a great convention's battle roar,
Where delegates were packed, and hope and dread
Were alternating, and it scarcely seemed,
While in dim hallways men conferred and schemed,
The name of Wilson would be most esteemed.

And then one rose in an imperial rage,
And tremors traveled through the multitude.
William J. Bryan, in a czar-like mood,
Stood scowling on the stage,
With palm-leaf fan and an alpaca coat,
To conjure forth an unpredicted vote.
In the electric tenseness that ensued
Men guessed what this old party prince would say.
At the press table, wry reporters slid
Low in their chairs, fearing a dangerous lid
Was off, and not excluding pistol-play.
Ballot on ballot, every watcher knew,
Had wearily passed, without a nominee.
But Clark, House Speaker, might have broken through
Had not his managers courted Tammany.

Still, all the rules and tricks
Traditional in the dark
And cellars of politics,
Should have elected Clark,
Had Bryan, glaring down
From a crag of moral force,
Not smashed the proferred crown
And changed the nation's course.
"I switch allegiance!" his full tones boomed out
In Periclean gusts. "A liberal cause
Would faint for breath in Tammany's hawk-claws!" . . .

His words were swallowed by a howl and shout,
And pandemonium stormed across the hall.
The deadlock broke, and history changed her face;
The forty-sixth roll call
Gave Wilson the nomination's fateful race.

    Thus in the open forum, by a blast
Of pointed anger and lance-swinging right,
The cloakroom plotters, dextrous in the past,
Had been bowled over by a charging knight.
And greater safety would all free men win
If he had many kin.

IV

    Stooped in a White House room, where none could see,
The President, like any lettered man,
Tapped at his own typewriter thoughtfully,
For in his working plan
No ghost-tongue chattered, hired and insincere —
Which may be why his individual speech,
Reverberant as a bell, and deep and clear,
Spoke to the depths of man; contrived to reach
A world's attentive ear.

    Even in some less tempest-riven day,
Led by the mind that plumbs, the hand that dares,
He might — who knows? — have climbed resplendent
    stairs.
Yet his to see a planet crack and sway,
And meet the challenge. When whole lands exploded,
And Europe quivered and tossed,
And spires were splintered, lakes of blood were lost,
And nations ran amuck, with rifles loaded,

We in America scanned the graying sky
Like random watchers on another world,
And few appraised the menace while it swirled
Closer, and closer still.
                              But Wilson's eye,
Ranging the dark horizon, plainly saw
No man is islanded from the human plight.
Though folly, leering with an idiot grin,
Babbled, "We'll crush the foe! We'll win! We'll win!",
Peace without victory must close the war.
For if one nation, swaggering in might,
Could lift a club above a neighbor's land,
Peace would come crashing down. And so he spoke
Like a Messiah, in whose outflung hand
A League was spread, a wide and mothering cloak
Mantling all peoples, shielding all alike.
And cannon would be melted, shells destroyed,
And warships sunk into a salt-sea void,
And never again a Belgium be invaded,
A Bonaparte or vixen Frederick strike,
Or steeled goosestepping legions be paraded.
If this was all a dream, a far ideal,
What nobler goal has man while hearths and empires reel?

          But first to tame the hurricane abroad!
After the long, wet trenches running red,
The homes bewailing for a son or head,
Now the belligerents must sheathe the sword
And sign a sane accord
That left no nation humbled! At our post
Of sad perspective in these soberer years,
We can observe from how immense a host
Of horrors, gutted churches, sunken piers,

Londons and Hamburgs smashed, we might be spared
If world diplomacy had only dared! —
Had ruled by judgment of the council room
And not by tanks and bombs!
                                        Whose then the fault
That both great factions let the pyres of doom
Blaze on and on and on without a halt?
Ask of the groaning past, the bulldog law
Of Roman duellists gripping Punic necks!
Ask those traditions of skull-cleaving war
Strewing all time with smoldering farms, and wrecks
Of ships and cities! Ask the lunatic lust
For triumph! for a spiky hell close-pressed
On a torn rival's chest!
Ask ancient robber lords, the gullible trust
In kings and ministers eyeless as the mole,
Who only see the mud beneath their feet
But not the brilliant, star-surrounded whole!
Ask autocrats enthroned in dread, deceit
And treachery — fear of the knife that slips
Slyly across the dark, the hand drawn tight
Round a convulsive throat! Ask of the lips
Chanting blood-anthems for the pride and might
Of Fatherland! the triumphs, bells and drums
Dinning the fervors and deliriums
Of strut and glory! Ask the minds that seethe
With hissing vengefulness and steaming hate,
Where rarely an air from wider spaces comes
And rarely man may pause, and freely breathe,
And scan himself, and judge, and contemplate!

The President, balked by these banded foes,
Might wave a wand of peace

And eloquently exhort, "Let conflict cease!",
But high above his head stone walls arose
Against his wisdom. So the fight went on.
And slowly, by a mocking paradox,
He who had sighed for quiet lanes was drawn
On a wild tide to war's tornado shocks.
I saw him face the Congress tense and gray,
With magisterial features, brooding stern
As one who picks a road of no return
And has himself decreed the Judgment Day.

Through all the years, as long as tongues debate,
Men will review the deep-sea plunge he took,
And question, Was there need for tempting fate?,
And wonder, Had he dared another look,
Might he have waited, and withheld the stroke
That, once delivered, echoed round the world;
And found in peace the knotted strength of oak,
And captained all lands, when flags of war were furled,
Into a sunned tomorrow? He no more
Than any man, could see the ash ahead
Through murk that deepened as the decades fled.
Not knowing that he stood upon a shore
Of chaos, he essayed the risk-all move —
And who can prove
What unfamiliar tides we'd sail today
Had he held out against the engulfing fray?

V

Black shadows of a stormy transformation
Fell on the land as from a cloud low-hung.
Khaki battalions drilled throughout the nation,
And camps were boisterous with the conscript young;

And banners floated high, and streets were flaming
With colored posters wooing volunteers,
And police swept down on dissidents proclaiming
Wartime resentments and resisters' fears.
And women rose in radiance and devotion,
White-gowned as nurses or in sewing groups;
And weird striped vessels wove across the ocean
In convoys, packed with freight of guns and troops.

And where the mortars and trench-cannon roared
And tanks were clattering and shrapnel poured
And spiralling planes shot terror overhead,
Ruddy young boys were led
Forth to ordeal by fire. I watched them crawl
Flat on their bellies, bayonets unbared,
Or dashing over a ridge or through a wall
Of blazing gas, or where the barbed wire stared
Amid dismembered comrades, or in glooms
Of the dank dugout, while the shell-stars burst
Above them, and they crouched like men accursed
Who lift vain fists, and swear in living tombs,
Or shake with nerves ripped ragged, yet display
Splendor and courage and the strength to pray
For yet one other dawn, one fighting day.

From bare Dakotan plains I saw them flock,
And out of Harlem's smudged, brick-girded streets,
And from New Hampshire slopes of pine and rock,
And blue-ridged California's palm-retreats.
From the deserts and the hills,
Ranches and shops and mines,
The tenements, the mills,
In never-ceasing lines

Flowed the recruits — from schools and village stores,
Mansions and huts and offices. And why
Should they be rushed away to far-off shores,
Perhaps to lose their limbs, or writhe and die?
Not many asked — the Lords of State decreed,
Orators dinned, "Now is the day of need!",
And ladies' fluttering kerchiefs waved them on
To the blind ending or heroic deed.

If he who captained the nation's destinies
Sorrowed to see the blood that spilled like rain,
And grieved to watch a long constricting chain
Clamped down on man to save man's liberties;
And if, with drawn, wry features, he recoiled
From censorship with her garrote and gag,
And propaganda, whose dark weavers toiled
Lest spirits should grow faint or fingers lag;
And if alarms and lightnings of regret
Stabbed in his mind to see the country held
Like a caught salmon in a squeezing net;
And if, become prophetic, he rebelled
At gathering specters of the black new night
Of total warfare and the total state,
Still passionately he must press on, in spite
Of terror, tyranny and tentacled might,
To one great goal that he would consummate.

All the long moaning travail, all the grief
Of mothers, all the holocaust of flame,
Could be redeemed, in Wilson's warm belief,
Only by one illuminated aim.
Again a hope burned hotly: for a League
Succoring in the shrine of its embrace

All lands and peoples, safe from snarled intrigue,
A port, a forum, and a rallying place
For every nation. This would spark the fire
When the white deathless lamp of peace was lit,
But lacking this retreat, we would retire
Into the brawling cave, the dragons' pit. —
Such was his faith. And in one bag were thrown
His fondest blueprints, fashioned to atone
For the deep scorching wrongs a brain-sick world
       had sown.

    And with this bag in hand, after the earth
Echoed with cheers and prayers beneath the bliss
Of stilled artillery and an Armistice,
He asked for man's rebirth.
I saw him mount a gangplank, taut and gray
As one who feels a patriarchal trust
For the long regiments of dead who lay
With vacant sockets pleading from the dust.
He must not fail them! Then, on streets abroad,
How the idolatrous, flag-waving throng
Presses around with shout and hail and song,
As though they greet no mortal, but the Lord!

    Often it has been said that, with a power
No Beaconsfield or Bismarck could command,
He might have ruled at that victorious hour
With torchlike vision and a kingly hand,
And won his pattern for a world reborn
A universal sanction. Who shall know?
But, balanced on a spiny summit, torn
By eddying gusts and whirlwinds from below,
He had the charm of no King Arthur's blade

To batter down the ancient barricade
Raised by old spitfire passions.
                                        I beheld
His hard colleagues — wry cynic Clemenceau
And dour Lloyd George, in whom raw hunger swelled
To drain the last life-juices from the foe.
And back of them were peoples battle-stunned,
Squirming for vengeance; back of them were all
The mad-beast centuries when man had gunned
In neighbors' yards for man, and sown with gall
And reaped in venom. Back of them were fears,
Blood feuds and raids and daggered jealousies,
Knifed animosities,
The thrust of Roons and Moltkes, and the spears
Of massed Napoleonic savageries.
And back of them the precedent loomed great
Of Peters, Marlboroughs, and chancellors
Masking and spurred to crush a rival state.
And spokesmen, gagged by sulphur fumes of hate
And shuddering still in war's old terror-throes,
Offered no hand to open novel doors
As the prophet from the New World might propose.
The aspirations of free peoples seemed
Only a bubble some idealist dreamed.

VI

Straining and wrinkled, deep into the night
The work-worn Prince of Peace had toiled intent,
Rapt inspiration in his eyes, to write
A deathless document,
The Covenant of the League. And did he see
That other chieftains lacked his crystal sight? —
Italians saw the peaks of Italy

Surmounting a continent; to France the power
Of resurrected, steel-armed Germany
Appeared to stretch and glower
And dwarf the shape of man;
And Japanese gains were pilots for Japan.
And since most captains of the nations peered
Through microscopes, and scanned the pebbly ground
But missed the galaxies as they careered
Across the Everlasting and Profound,
The marvel must remain
Less that one leader could not conquer all
Than that he scaled so mountainous a wall
And reaped so huge a gain.
And if the valley mists of compromise
Shadowed the road, how few can hold their way
Calm and unalterable as starlit skies
Against all snares, all snarls, all looped delay!
Much he had kept unsullied, though he braved
Nestfuls of hornets; high aloft he waved
Bright emblems of the League — the Cause was saved,
So he supposed!
                 But having valiantly sought
The Light abroad, with resonant victories,
He blundered into a trap; his feet were caught
In his own door as never overseas.
Say that he had no glib, back-thumping skill
To charm his foes, or soothe with sugary bait;
Say that his bladed drive, his rock-ridged will
Might fire resentment and its offspring, hate;
Say that he reared no altars to the pride
Of Senators where rage and envy strove;
Say that he may have seemed to override
His countrymen like some commanding Jove;

Say that, at his high rostrum's altitude,
Perhaps he stiffened with a God-complex;
Say this and more — and yet one must conclude,
Though flaws and errors might obstruct and vex,
His was the eagle's flight, and they who schemed
To break his wings, cursing him in their wrath,
Followed a flat earth-trail, and never dreamed
The radiance of his far, cloud-walking path,
And never knew or guessed
That the gun-barrel pointed at his breast
Was aimed at the world's heart.

                                    Like all the seers
And prophets who have preached to save mankind,
He built beyond his world by measureless years,
Spreading his nimbused tints before the blind.
Then, while his starred pavilions fell to dust,
Crass pride of party, clawing power-lust
Joined with complaining gales of fright and hate
To storm and agitate
With vulpine nip and slash and lunge and thrust.
Destroy the Treaty of Versailles! delay
The Covenant of the League by jabs and darts!
Slice off a hair, then hew a joint away,
And then an arm, until no living parts
Are left, and the great dream of banded nations
Collapses, killed by knifing reservations! —
Such was the plot of foes who would not dare
Aim frontal charges at the solid whole,
But creeping round the flanks, would dig a snare
To win their deadly goal.

So Wilson, furrowed from long toil abroad,

Returned to bear the saddest cross of man,
When his own people dashed away his sword
And spattered mud on his high-templed plan.
Discarded by its parents, like a child
Crippled at birth, tossed to an alien nurse,
The League would perish. But, unreconciled
To the gravediggers and the threatened hearse,
Scarred and still bleeding, gray and worn and old,
Yet with the vehemence of a jousting knight,
Once more the President rode forth to fight.
Far through the land, in listening towns, he told
The world's pre-eminent need
If continents were never again to bleed;
And in the West, spontaneous cheers were loud
From many a hailing crowd.
But for a blow of fate — though who can say? —
He might have won his way.
His spirit might be stout as Hercules
And resolute as Hector, but his frame
Wore human nerves and flesh — a moment came
When, in the knockout of a brute disease,
He gasped and staggered . . .

                Even now, in bed,
Disabled, he remained the chief who led,
Though from that death-marked face, that crumpled form,
That mind distracted as by squalls and fire,
How could commandments rise? How take by storm
A hesitant earth, and overwhelm the choir
Of shrieking enemies? . . . His wrecked physique
Was symbol of a world grown faint and weak,
Whose golden towers still were far to seek.

VII

After the luminous thinker, with his eyes
That searched forgotten scenes and spires to be,
A lacquered worldling, of the common size,
Was elevated for all lands to see.
Jesting and chatting with golf-playing friends
In parlors and the newsroom of his press,
He smiled with courtly charm and kindliness
Where falseface comrades diced for venal ends.
And why, amid the nominating swirl,
Was Harding named? They said he looked the part,
But must a President, like a poster girl,
Be picked for beauty? That he lacked the art
Of a new Solon; that, beneath his nose,
Like foulness wafted from a garbage van,
The stench of fat bribe-taking hands arose,
Was less the shame of one high-seated man
Than of a nation freed by sudden peace
From war's grim tyranny, to crave release
Where each might watch his gilded hours increase.

After the grind and drag
Of marching beneath the flag,
Come, gaily swing the arm, the flying heel!
Europe and Europe's plight?
Curtain them out of sight!
On with the song and jazz, the merry reel!
The tinselled youth who crowded tinselled dives,
Flaunting hip-flasks contemptuous of law;
And they who, in barred cellars, came to draw
The bolts of dim speakeasies, spoke of lives
Jangled and tossed. Sneaking in alley shade,
Stealthy as ferrets, heavy-jowled as swine,

The sly bootleggers slunk about their trade,
Dealing in more than whisky kegs and wine,
Hard eyes a-glitter as they silently paid
Dark debts to shadowy henchmen. Then the gang
Of liquor bandits as they swooped and preyed,
Often more deadly than a cobra's fang,
While with hoarse menace muttering in their ears
Merchants passed secret rolls to racketeers.

Where charred old towers of Chicago stand
I saw a bloated, scar-faced boss command
Like hell's high marshal — saw his followers, dressed
As policemen, make the blustering arrest
Of seven braves of an opposing band,
And watched the victims lined against the wall
Of a dim truck-garage. With flame and smoke
The rit-tat-tat of quick machine-guns spoke,
And when the screams and groans had ended, all
The foes lay still. Yet, strangely, I could trace
Invisible threads — tendrils that ran between
The terrorist skulking with his death-machine
And polished drinkers in the golfing place
Or cocktail club, whose clandestine desires
Gave sparks and fuel to the gangster's fires.

VIII

While chimneys multiplied and soot was poured
From barges, trains and sky-devouring mills,
And wealth, with diamond studs and silken frills,
Swaggered in velvet, spangled like a lord;
While cities shouldered high, and suburbs grew,
Millions acclaimed a god, unique and strange,
Who in one season raised more winds of change

Than centuries of Rome or Athens knew.
His limbs were wheels and tires,
His drink was gasoline,
His breath was blown by fires
Behind an iron screen;
His heart, a motor purring;
His eyes, two stabbing lights;
His blood-stream, power stirring
In lurching stops and flights.

Not all philosophers whose mellow lore
Kindled a glow across three thousand years;
Not all gold-miners who had scooped for ore,
Nor architects of mansions, castles, piers;
Not all the sowers and reapers as they strained
Through packed millennia, had brought to pass
A metamorphosis like that ordained
By this new Yahweh born of steel and gas.
No Solomon or Alexander planned,
No Amos, no Isaiah could foresee
The motor-god's trans-nation sovereignty,
The new cyclonic gales its worshippers fanned.
Worlds had been altered. Through red cactus vasts
I saw the serpentining highway crawl,
And over mountains striped by scarring blasts,
Whose canyons hid the high white waterfall.
And in trim factories where thousands stood
Like robots, posturing at assembly lines,
I watched the birth of engine, fender, hood,
While men with blueprints traced the late designs.
I marked the filling station, trailer camp,
Court and motel, the dusty parking lot
Where tulips used to wave, the curving ramp

And several-tiered garage, the wrecker's plot
Of rusted metal, and the tract-homes raised
Over the stumps of prune and orange trees
And poppied meadows. Then the fires that blazed
From many-stacked, smoke-belching industries,
Great rubber plants and oil refineries,
The mines where coal was torn
Out of a bakehouse cave to smelt the steel
That built the frame, the driving shaft, the wheel;
And makers of the radio, clock and horn.

But oh, the joy, the throb, the exultation
Of racing as on wings through roads and streets!
Of gliding birdlike far across the nation
To blue and distant coasts, high wood-retreats!
Spellbound as by a witch, and captivated
As by the kiss of love, how men would glow,
While on all lanes the speed-bolts congregated,
Row upon streaking row!
Then who will note the gray, eye-stinging blur
Of smog that dims the cities? — who take heed
That where the hurtling madcaps whizz and whirr
Sometimes will sound a screeching of brakes, a crashing
Of flying bodies and glass, and metal smashing,
And riders and passers-by will moan and bleed?
What matter the price? The great new deity
Spins round the earth to make his acolytes free,
And never a prince in Hindustan or France
Had such a royal mount before our day,
When rides beyond the wonders of romance
Are purchased by a clerk's or plumber's pay.

And while the millions dash as though to games
In similar cars that rush on similar springs
With similar motors caged in similar frames,
A common impress stamps all men and things.
In many a town the streets will duplicate
Patterns of towns a thousand miles removed;
The same jazz jangle-tunes will circulate,
With food and entertainment boxed and grooved.
Far-scattered men will wear
The same mass-tailored suits,
The same trim-parted hair —
Alike as drilled recruits.
And the large picture hat,
High heel and pointed toe,
Few women will combat
Beneath the enactment of the fashion show.
And the same notes, in pulpit, press and screen,
The same well-beaten froth across the air,
Are generated by a thought-machine
Whose parrot voices drone and drone and blare
From a loud-speaker, while its one worn creed
Re-echoes with a repetitious din:
"Succeed! Succeed!" And yet again, "Succeed!" —
Push is the law, failure the mortal sin.

And now a merry song is sung,
Its name, *Prosperity*,
Which pulses, for the old and young,
Of lyric things to be.

While credits still expand, expand,
And industry extends,
All hail our fair and blooming land

That grows in dividends!

All hail the bonds, all hail the stocks,
All hail the bank returns!
We build, as on eternal rocks,
A world that earns and earns!

And as this song makes music in the ears
Of would-be millionaires, of profiteers,
A crowd repeats the tune with chants and cheers.
Then speculation, like a pagan god,
Maddens the faithful at its merest nod,
And fraud stands by with priestly gown and rod
Where, reckless of the black impending crisis,
Conjurers raise and raise investment prices . . .

Then startlingly comes a day
When practical brokers of the marketplace,
Seeming impractical as a child at play,
Stagger, and cannot face
A too-revealing glare of morning light —
Sad dreamers blinking with bedazzled sight
At their own visions! Strangely, it is seen
The ramparts of the sworn materialist
Have masonry of mist,
And all his pinnacles are a bubble-screen.

IX

Crowded in surging swirls, with harsh alarms
While set eyes scanned the lagging ticker tape,
Men pushed and shouted, waving panic arms
Like shipwrecked passengers wrestling to escape.
Dismally, as a whole world staggered, sank,

They watched quotations fall, and fall, and fall,
Pale flinty-beaked, or flushed as though they drank
A choking draught of gall.
"Sell!" rang the order. "Sell!"
And from afar I seemed to hear a yell
Chorused by demons in a cave of hell.
"Sell! Sell! Oh, sell!" But there was not one cry
Of "Buy! Buy! Buy!"
Bright blood was gushing when the day was done:
Some tottered, hunched beneath a sodden load.
One man, with groping fingers, seized a gun;
Another wept, remembering debts he owed,
And all observed, beneath a shroud ahead,
Unborn tomorrow lying stark and dead.
The spires of trade, its gilt facade and dome,
But yesterday rock-based as ageless Rome,
Now seemed a will-o'-the-wisp, a tent of foam.

When shops or houses crumble in a gale,
We may more easily rear their roofs again
Than salvage broken trust or faiths that fail
Or heal the hearts of men.
Thus the dark malady of the marketplace
Was less than ailments of the fearstruck mind,
Which chilled all commerce to a beetle's pace
And proved the dukes of business lame and blind.
In streets, and leafy roads, and everywhere
Wheels grind and clatter to a halt. A mill
Where thousands bustled, suddenly is still;
While men, hands deep in pockets, slouch and stare
With baffled faces and dull stricken eyes,
Begging for work. Upon a brick-walled street
The apple vender, in the wind and sleet,

Slaps his numb hands, waits for the man who buys
The big red nickel fruit. And in a throng,
Massed on the sidewalks where employment signs
Are chalked and vanish, seekers pace day-long —
Suppliants craving help at unresponsive shrines.

Then, too, adrift in hosts,
Oppressed as with a purgatorial doom,
The homeless pass like ghosts
From factory door to door, from room to room
Of offices where laborer and clerk
Seek the dear phantom, work.
And as they hear a toneless "Not today.
Some other time, maybe," their faces grow
Peaked and more blue, their mien more blankly gray,
Their heads droop low,
And on and on, with meager food and rest,
They make the weary, ever wearier quest,
Seeing at first their stocking hoard stripped bare,
And then their shelves laid empty as their wives
Search for the job that never quite arrives,
Their sons vend papers while the street-horns blare.

Roaming the half-deserted town, I saw
Blind windows where the shopping crowd had flocked,
The architect and councillor-at-law
In dusty chambers where no client knocked,
And smokeless chimneys cold
Above rail sidings where no freight-car rolled.
And under shadows of Manhattan brick
On pavements whitened with new-fallen snow,
I saw the incarnation of all woe:
A family drooped where every pot and stick

Of their small household, from the parrot cage
To the old phonograph and dented chair,
The soiled brown lamp, ravelled in disrepair,
Had been flung out into the March wind's rage.
And, flanked by shanties of the great mid-West
I gazed as Negroes, packed in sullen bands,
Shouted and surged without a pause or rest
Against the deputies whose menacing hands
Dangled eviction papers. Drearily spread
Round a whole block, droop-necked and bristly-faced,
I watched petitioners for meat and bread
Slow-trailing down the gray, grim asphalt waste.
And men who once had sat
White-sleeved in editorial chairs, or made
Glistening brokers' aisles their habitat,
Now looking drawn and frayed,
Unshaved and ragged-shirted and unkempt,
Begging at restaurant doors
For scraps from plates, old crusts and apple cores,
Roved as beside the Styx — grim shades who dreamt
Of greener seasons, which had not denied
Warmth and a well-filled board and hope and pride.

And while apartments dangled signs, "For rent!",
Big huddled family groups would have to crowd
The foul old rooms of some lean tenement,
Where bawling of the hungry babes was loud
Above the sick man's moan. And some, who felt
The city, like a sinking deck, recede
And snatch away their foothold, met the need
By joining kin who dwelt
In great old houses where stone fences ran
Through scrubby fields; and with no pipes or wires

But only pumps and candles like their sires,
Must wrestle nature, even as early man.
And juveniles astray —
Road-battered youths, and girls attired as boys —
Straggled amid the noise
Of flat-cars where the rails curved far away,
Or rode the breakbeams, or in *jungle* camps,
With box-frames and old rusted iron sheets
Masking as huts, and rubbish fires as lamps,
And lying on discarded auto-seats,
Unwanted as vagrant dogs, appeared to mark
Disintegration of the world men knew,
As though life's grace and glory all withdrew
Backward and back into a primitive dark.

X

But as the ship was wallowing in the night
Through rough shoal-billows, with a listing freight,
Could not the captain turn the helm aright
And pass the perilous strait?
Ah, but the skipper did not know the sea,
And stumbling and groping on a foggy deck,
Heard no storm-voices of catastrophe
Screech of impending wreck.

When tongue-tied Coolidge, colorless as a yawn,
Chose not to run again, the way was clear
For one who beckoned like a brighter dawn.
Strange as a Launfal's tale was the career
Of Herbert Hoover — orphan lad who rose
To walk in mansion aisles, a millionaire,
Then wizard-lord of food for Europe's woes.
But this new captain, pudgy-faced and stern

In trim blue serge, white-collared and sedate,
Had not a Lincoln's fire and wit to earn
Men's sympathy, and charm away their hate.
Worse still! his shoulders stooped beneath the load
High-mounting from man's blind and drifting past.
His two dwarf predecessors had bestowed
A rudderless vessel with a tilting mast.

    Then his own faith, his gray cast-iron views,
Rusty old heritage of a simpler age,
Had made him stand arms folded and refuse
To reach for sword and armory, or engage
The emperors of private enterprise,
Or bend his ears to homeless wanderers' moans,
Mumblings of skull-faced women, old men's sighs,
Or wails of famished babes who gnawed on stones.
With cool eyes lowered, he could not foretell
How hungry folk rebel
And batter down the fairest citadel
And smash at temple doors. Though still no men
Lunged out with banners waving, I could hear
The thunder's growling den,
A snarl and rumbling through the atmosphere.
And while, from far, there came the beat and roll
And storm-notes of disaster,
A new and resolute master
Strode to the bridge, and seized a strong control.

XI

    Deposit books in hand, the people waited
Before the tellers' windows, line on line.
And some were red of face and agitated,
And others gave no sign

Except with tapping fingers and wry lips.
But customers who reached the windows cried,
"Withdraw — withdraw — withdraw my whole account!"
And muttering and swearing, men inside,
White-featured as the pilots of lost ships,
Bewailed, "We're not an ever-flowing fount!"
And down the windows slammed; and, from without,
There came a yell, a long complaining shout
Of crowds that milled and surged and swirled about,
Groaning for hard, blood-purchased savings, gone,
And all tomorrow shorn.

And how much longer could the land endure,
Watching its treasure drained, its heart-stream dried?
Many there were who cursed, and prophesied
That with the System's girders insecure,
Its stairs collapsing and its steeples battered,
Its ragged men like derelicts adrift,
Mad revolution, reddening in the rift,
Would swoop, and factories and halls be shattered.

Men now in life's late summer can recall
How a new President, by one swift stroke
Of leonine judgment, closed the doors of all
The nation's banks, so that the country woke
One morning shivering, without a cloak
Against the cold. Magnates who waved the keys
Of mills and office towers, walked abroad
Like kings divested of domains and fees,
And showed, of all their hoard,
A mere few pocket dollars. Trains ran bare
And boats half empty, and the wide-eyed mass
In stunning revelation was aware

Money was only grass
A drought might wither. Soon arrived a day
When bank-doors creaked again and checks were cashed;
And watchers, thinking of worlds that might have crashed,
Walked tearful-eyed, or solemnly bowed, to pray
In thanks for a skipper's hand to point the way.

But who was he, fresh-seated
High on a power-perch,
Whom cheering voices greeted
As the answer to a search?
To the perceiving ages
One leaves the last report,
But by all visible gauges
He saved a land distraught.
Looking at Franklin Roosevelt, one could see
A man ingratiating as a swallow,
Bubbling with wine of personality —
But under the smile, was he unskilled and hollow?
Many believed so; many held that here
Stood a mere groomer of his own career.

Yet few there are who own deep-sighted eyes
To pierce beneath a brother's words and mien
And probe his being's mazy vast, unseen
Even in self-surmise.
In the young climber of the sinuous years
Before he scaled a Presidential height,
Little beyond a grooved, gay man appears,
Deft-weaving, but not radiantly bright.
Many another might have won a role
As Governor, or even challenged fate
As a Vice-Presidential candidate

Without achieving that pre-eminent goal
Which thousands dream of and so few attain.

And then a drama, earthquake-sudden, showed
The gold deep-buried in a hidden lode,
When he was gouged and riven by a strain
Like some grim test the appraising gods had sent.
Why on his body, deadly as a kiss
Of vipers, should a swift paralysis
Have fallen, till his legs were shrunk and bent
And that great boon too few appreciate —
Of ambling and striding in the gale and sun —
Was taken from him? Life had closed a gate;
Smashed him, a cripple — was he then undone?
"Retire! Retire!" he heard his mother's voice.
"A country gentleman, in your estate
Henceforth you'll rest — my boy, you have no choice!"
And had he answered "Yes!", as many would,
Onlookers might have sighed, and understood
He really had no choice.
                                        But in his breast
A live compulsion flashed, a pulse and urge,
A prodding and a hope, a power and zest
Strong-walled to let no cuffs or kicks submerge
The fire within him. Torments such as those
Of Sisyphus, when all his sweat and skill
Never completely rolled his rock uphill,
Oppressed him in the weary, sad ordeal
Of trying to coax small wrigglings from his toes,
Or struggling with a vise-bound leg to feel
A tingle of action. Not in all his days
He'd know the suppleness of other men,
But finally, from a purgatorial phase,

He rose to lift his head and laugh again.
When coiled affliction smites
One either may lie down, with sobs and groans,
Or grope his way on hands and knees up flights
Of blood-bespattered stones,
Seeking the open sky — what path he picks
Will tell the stature of the self below,
For all men kindle their own spirit-wicks,
And most will follow where the tapers go,
And what they choose declares what they will be,
Becomes their nemesis or destiny,
Draws them to dusky caves of no-escape,
Or else, like Roosevelt, to life's apogee.

XII

What would we counsel, you and I, if given sudden
    command
Of a city that an earthquake ripped, or a whirlwind-battered
    land?
How would we move if a swelling tide billowed against the
    dike,
And greater waves from a vaster storm gathered like sharks
    to strike?

What would we do? What would we say if crowds
    stampeded round,
And dogs let out a terror howl and men had fallen and
    drowned?
Would we mumble, "All will heal in time!", or with
    sandbags, pick and spade
Hasten to hold the crumbling walls with a piled new
    barricade?

"Hear me, my friends! I promise you, I'll act!"
So the new President proclaimed; and so,
Not in speech only but in living fact,
He moved before one green new blade could grow.
Soon the astonished citizens would learn
There sat in Washington a novel chief,
Who with no high Olympian unconcern
Surveyed the people's grief.
It was as though a gale blew down on halls
Gray-layered with a generation's dust.
And none who felt that cleansing breath recalls
A swifter, more revivifying gust.
The blue-cheeked waif who lay
Tortured by hunger pangs, not knowing where
To find a crust for yet another day,
Might view a gleam through slits in his despair.
The farmer in the field,
Seeing a mortgage brooding like black thunder,
At last might have a shield
Lest he and all his nestlings be hurled under.
The city man who strained
To keep his keys out of the sheriff's grasp,
Might glimpse, through eyes deep-pained,
An arm reach out, a sudden rescuing clasp.
The youth whose fevered hands
Whittled a stick for want of things to do,
Might take a job in tall and timbered lands,
In work-camps of a world of green and blue.
And towering dams would rise
To prison the rippling vasts of man-filled lakes,
Where, castle-large, the powerhouse supplies
Invisible genii to a realm that wakes
With glad new life. And nursing currents flow

In irrigation channels, and bestow
Orchards and grain where sagebrush used to grow.

    Then, with the lifeline of a public grant,
The vacant-eyed, the bleak long-unemployed
Sprang as if rescued from a pit-black void
To swing the shovel on new roads, and plant
Hillsides of trees, and with the saw and rule
Labor to rear a stadium or school
Or build a wharf. And mass protection spread
Even to him who toiled with heart or head
At canvasses, or postured on a stage,
Or saw white scribbled pages mount, unread —
He who, but months before,
Cast off like some stale core,
Had seemed a sacrificial victim of the age.

    And though the cowed and famished still would droop,
And farmers grumbled, miners cursed their plight,
And shaveless thousands moped in line for soup,
What man could rear Jerusalem in a night?
What man, beneath the stress
Of an old system with fast-splitting seams,
Could mix the magic potion that redeems
As with a charmed redress?
It was as though a doctor were directed
To heal a patient whose inflamed disease
Other physicians long, too long neglected
Or treated with skin-tickling remedies.
The new practitioner, with salve of laws,
Might snatch the patient from destruction's claws,
But how to cure the malady's dark cause?

Soon, like the backhand stroke
Of a knifed assassin skulking in the brush,
New agonies awoke,
And smote as though all nature in a rush
Of anger had combined to castigate
Man's follies with a self-inflicted fate.
When planters, coveting war-needed grain,
Struck at the guardian topsoil, hacked it loose,
Ripped the long grass-roots of the western plain,
Oh, what a spined abuse
Our hands were seeding! In her silent wrath
The violated earth, across the years,
Awaited vengeance, and the aftermath
Smote like a rain of unexpected spears.
Far to the east one day
I stood astonished on a bridge that spanned
Manhattan's Harlem River; in dismay
I saw a screen of gray
Which blurred the sky and shrouded all the land,
Not knowing that, in this dull canopy,
Dakotan farms were blowing out to sea.

Black was the prairie-scouring storm, coal-black,
And chill the blast as though an Arctic doom
And all hell's demons gathered to attack;
And sudden midnight gloom
Eclipsed the day. Fine particles were shed
By the relentless slingshots of the gale,
A dense, fast-driving hail,
While frenziedly, in spasms and stabs of dread,
Choking and gasping, nearly suffocated
By all-consuming dirt, which fell and fell,
Men ran indoors, and shudderingly waited,

Or struggled, with wet towels, to dispel
The invading dust. They might almost as well
Have labored to halt night's coming! When at last
The storm surrendered, and they crept outdoors,
Never were hearts of watchers more harassed —
It was as though they stood on foreign shores,
Viewing a dried-up planet somehow grown
A thousand ages older. Over all
The heaped funereal wind-flung earth was thrown;
It covered the bushes, hid the porch and wall,
Obliterated the road, the fields, the fence,
The plow, the tractor, with high-swirling mounds;
And far as men could see once-fertile grounds,
A new Sahara spread grotesque, immense.

And time dragged past. And on the buried waste
Where long the redman and the bison flourished,
Often the poor white farmer was displaced
While dust-storms whirled as on a Mars that perished.
I saw abandoned farms, stripped nude and blank
As ruins of Tyre, the sheep and cattle gone,
The sagging windmill, empty watertank,
And house dark-windowed, silted and forlorn.
I saw old lunging cars, on rutted roads,
Jog through the desert flat and mountain aisle
With blankets, plates and work-clothes, pile on pile,
And children squirming on the roped-in loads.

But men would build torn lives anew,
Blest by Pacific sun and foam,
And find employment, and pursue
Hill-windings to a better home.

Ah, but too dimly could they see
They were but sand-motes in a swarm,
And rootless folk are rarely free
And seldom rich in bread or warm.

In flea-infected camps, and cabin shades
Wherein no lamp gave light, no water ran,
They were the helots of new work brigades,
The pilgrims of an endless caravan
Seeking the olive ranch, the walnut grove,
The pea-field, and the vineyard blue with grapes —
Importunate survivors, doomed to rove
Like foraging apes,
Too often jobless, or in picket lines
Or orchard roads in fire-hot August suns,
Protesting a starved man's wage with painted signs,
Till deputies closed round with fists and guns.

XIII

Nursing mute vengeance at the crimes of men
Like some sore-wounded but remembering beast,
Nature had brooded in her silent den
Among the forest ridges of the East.
Year after patient year
She had been waiting, biding her time in peace.
Since the first pioneer,
She had endured man's arrogance and caprice;
She had observed him striding axe in hand,
And heard the oak and maple moan and crash;
She had beheld him with a smoking brand,
Till woods were seared to ash;
She had seen gullies channeling the hills,
Rain leaching out the soil where pines had grown,

And watched small frisking tails and sportive bills
Annihilated, while her breast was sown
With corn that drained her. She had looked on streams
That, once pellucid as the sunlit air,
Flowed dirty yellow from earth's broken seams,
Or dried to trickles in a man-made glare.
And she at times had given
A warning in white thunderous freshets hurled
From the torn slope, the wood that saws had riven.
But man, like God's own viceroy, ruled the world;
Avid as always, still he slashed and slew,
Till nature, in a lightning burst, withdrew
Her old protection, and upon his head
Clapped retribution that he long would rue.

High-chimneyed cities with their schools and docks
Were sharers of the wide Ohio's flow,
And brawn and blood of many-towered blocks
Poured to the factory and dynamo.
And few who watched the waters swishing past
Like the long fringes of a land-bound sea,
Had nightmares of a power so swift and vast
It put their homes and lives in jeopardy.
Then, with a Cyclops' force,
Blustering loose upon a winter day,
The river leapt its course
And smashed far overland, rabid for prey.
Down, down, and down, from skies of pewter gray,
A drizzly rain, with steady drip, drip, drip,
Made a low undertone against the roar
Of currents that began to slash and rip
Across wide leagues of shore.
Soon, on the undulating valley miles,

The loamy brown wild torrents rose and raced,
Till fields were lost, and houses were but isles
Stuck in a wavy waste,
And streets were gurgling channels where a rush
Of rivers branched and spouted, while a lake,
With squirmings like a miry winding snake,
Reached far and far. And ripped-up trees and brush,
And drifting planks, torn porches, broken stairs,
And tables, bureaus, chairs,
And doors and fence-rails, and drowned pigs and sheep,
Dead cows and horses floated in the sweep
And lunge of waters, whose dark thoroughfares
Grew and still grew, with swishing and stench and mud.

    Now a long, deep alarm
Shrilled in the towns; on many a river-arm
Men toiled with sandbags, dashing to beat the flood,
Which churned against their ankles as they fought
To raise high bulwarks; meanwhile, in the gloom
From farms and villages, struggling half distraught,
I heard men wail and shout
As poles and wires splashed down and lights went out.
And here one battled in a basement room
Against a cave-cold deluge; here one fell
Beneath the streaming fury, with a tale
No chronicler would tell;
And here a fugitive, huddled in the jail
Of a slanting second story, hoarsely called
While the enormous turbulence swirled and squalled,
Hungry to wash him down. And here a boat
Bore an old woman from a roof, or cast
A line to save a family half afloat,
Clinging to driftwood. When the tide drew back

And men could scan their mud-caked floors at last,
With splintery havoc nudging foul disease,
And shops caved in and silent industries
Strewn on a giant track,
Survivors gaped and blinked, and saw, aghast,
Ruin as though the conquering Huns had passed.

XIV

Sharp was the waking in the dawn,
And dimly man perceived
That roots destroyed and hillsides shorn
Might never be retrieved.

And strangely on his mind there surged
The sense that all are one,
That pines and brooks and men are merged
In ageless unison.

And if you gouge a slope away
Or burn a forest black,
The whole creation has to pay
The price of your attack.

But if you spare a watershed
Or save a mossed ravine,
Then you may bless all time, and spread
Tomorrow's lap with green.

By corkscrew movements, improvised degrees,
The current of a mounting change was felt.
I saw bare mountains grow a robe of trees;
Heard prairies rustle with a long wood-belt.
I saw men plow the contoured, curving strip,

Zealous lest garden-lands be washed away,
Or fearfully check the sheep-jaws that would clip
Earth's skin of grass, till fields turned Gobi-gray.
I ranged the game-preserve where bright fawn-eyes
Peeped unmolested from the firs or fern,
And watched triangled wheeling wings arise
Over tall reeds, not as a gunner's prize;
And felt that we, though gropingly, would learn
All nature's ways are man's, and finally spurn
The nets that bloated avarice had spun,
And make the New World's life complete, and shun
The wastrel ways of Gath and Babylon.

* * *

High in the clouds that bounded the halves of the planet
It seemed that I gazed upon beings who, mistily stirring,
With figures mighty as gods, and patriarch faces,
Were mantled in light, with trailing garments of vapor.

"O Man," said a voice that was quiet as murmurs at
sleep-time,
Yet spoke in my breast with a warning of storm-gale
and lightning,
"Not yours is the earth, nor the creatures that scurry
and flutter
In the canyons and caves, and flash in the forests and
rivers.
For the oak on the hill, and the rushes that wave in
the valley,
The vine in the damps of the wood, and the moss on the
boulder,
Were shaped by the Master of All with a life and a
meaning

Which is other than man's, though man has a place and a
          portion
In all that they offer and are, and they are united
To you in the multiple web of your earthly existence.
Blight them or cause them to wilt
And something in you shall be shrivelled.
Greet them as parts of the whole
And something in you shall be lifted.
As the sun and the cloud and the dew and the ocean are
          mingled,
So man is received in the greatness of planets and epochs,
An atom subserving an end he but dimly surmises.
And aids on the way are the lakes and the streams and the
          cedars,
The glimmer of fur and of wings, and the grass on the hillside
And the sense of a measureless quest and an infinite
          joining."

     Mighty the voice, though its tones were as tranquil as
          moonlight,
And the vastness and peace and wonder and joy of the
          ageless
Made music within me as now, with a heart strangely lifted,
I glanced once again at the meadows and halls of a nation.

XI. Armageddon

"In the playhouse of ages, no drama so huge, so portentous"

Far-spread beyond the sunset waves, I viewed
The cherry-blossom cities of Japan,
And through the dark, small-bodied multitude
A long complaining sigh, a tremor ran.
Edged as with nettles, from the New World's shore,
Was flung an order that the dawn-wind bore:
"Let Orientals pass our gates no more!"
Here was a burning sting,
Thorn-wound to prick the pride,
Prompting a surge, a swing
Away from the New World's side.
What! must the ancient race
Of noble Nipponese
Be pushed to a backstage place
By upstarts overseas?
Blind bias, as so often, was requited
In bias; hatred and resentment gave
Fresh fuel where explosive fires were lighted,
For men despised must show that they are brave,
Strong-armed and able. Thus a moment came
When by the boatload, on Manchurian soil,
Yellow invaders snatched at foreign spoil —
First of those episodes of blood and flame
Which, hazily noted in the dozing West,
Poured oil for conflagrations to consume
Cities and thrones.

                              Had courage met the test,
Might not our smothering arms have quenched the doom
Beyond the horizon? But the seas were wide;
Safe as upon some transgalactic globe,
The watchers buttoned tight a shielding robe
Thick as an armadillo's, and denied
The grip of fellowship. Hearing a moan
Borne on a wind that blew across the sea,
They could not feel the sorrow as their own,
Nor guess they too must share the planet's malady.

                              II
         The spotted peace that lay upon the world
Recalled a garment stained by old disease,
In which, like undiscovered larvae, curled
The microbes of new wrongs and agonies.
Shadows of long portentous wings that fell
While hawk-beaks of depression tore the earth,
Reached over Europe like a witches' spell,
Not least on muttering crowds of German birth.
And in the dimness of that twilight time,
When skullbone famine slunk in rags and grime,
Life had been twisted into whorls of crime.
Proud in the battle's afterglare,
Sword-waving though without a crown,
Dictators marched with flame and flare,
Like buccaneers who cow a town.
And where the blood-flecked Czars had been,
A stealthy despot, bloodier yet,
Crouched like a spider, poised to spin
A new and empire-tangling net.
And in the Caesars' one-time land,
A scarecrow, preened in warrior dress,

Clamped down a smashing iron band,
While blackshirts ruled by gunned duress.

But more malevolent still to rip and slash
All nations and all continents alike,
Venomous as a copperhead to strike,
With cruel bead-eyes and hard, small moustached face,
Slithered a self-made king, insanely rash,
Who mangled nations under python bands,
And squeezed their people in a death-embrace,
Till when the thunderous terror which he shed
Had spread and spread
To steppes and jungles and Saharan sands,
Half of the planet had been splashed heart-red.

Big-jowled before their desks our magnates sat.
"Yes, we can trade with Hitler," they declared,
Yawning with oily smiles, like men who shared
A profitable business with a cat.
Meanwhile, with lips drawn tight, our statesmen gazed
Far from the madcap ruler's blood-designs.
When English eyes were fogged and France was dazed,
Should we anticipate, in staring lines,
The fire-swept future? Did our prophets guess
That the hooked blade of treachery, which sank
Deep in the Spanish back and Austrian flank
And bade the swastika-bearing brownshirts press
Down avenues of Prague, so soon would fell
Bulwarks of Europe, make the blood-tides swell,
And sweep our trans-Atlantic citadel
With hurricane gusts? Ah, yes, we saw by gleams,
Blinded by distance and bemused by dreams,
Like men at dusk where far sword-lightning streams.

Hearing the rasp and roar
Of steel-beaked squadrons from the Polish plain,
And tracing the bombers strewing ash and gore
From Narvik nearly to the peaks of Spain,
We rubbed our eyes, and noted more and more
Our own dire peril. And when France drooped low
Like a bull-fighter cloven to the heart,
And England saw night-raiders overflow
Her zenith — wheeling demons drilled to dart
While doom erupted — we foresaw a burst
Of winged marauders swarming across the sea,
Knowing how science sparked man's glory-thirst
To bloodier, ever bloodier butchery.
And our repeated cry, "Neutrality!",
But advertised a myth, now that the raw,
Slashing barbarians turned the German helm.
We too might founder should they overwhelm
The lights of England — should the land that saw
Shakespeare and Milton be but death-terrain
For a skull-pyramiding Tamerlane.

I watched the ships set sail
Across the Atlantic, riding low with piles
Of wheat and cotton for the imperilled isles;
And viewed the guns they pointed on the trail
Of the dread submarine; while far to north
In bleak Icelandish seas
The uniformed Americans marched forth,
Relieving the King's contingents. Moves like these
Might fortify weak spirits, and appear
Like posting of guards where bandits fired men's fear,
Though he was blind who could not look ahead
To Armadeggon's shells, and plains where thousands bled.

III

Now, while a lengthening glow,
Morosely crimson, lighted Europe's shore,
In the Far East I watched a smoke-cloud grow,
And sparks and cinders spout. Corps upon corps,
Through China's vastness, small intruders surged
In sabred columns. In that cloudy time
The cramped and handcuffed nation that emerged
After invasion, plundering and war,
Red revolution, horror and mass crime,
Was tragedy that few or none foresaw.
And few or none presaged an hour to be
When fliers from the East outrageously
Would strike against the West across the sea.

But some will say that only fate
Sounded the war command,
While man, the puppet and the bait,
Must do as fortune planned.
Yet ah, not by the stars above
The tank and gun were made —
Not these, forgetting faith and love,
Captained the bomb brigade.
For man was man's own enemy,
His nemesis and self-made tragedy.
Many and variegated were the hues
Twisted into one cord: hate's sultry red,
Ghost-white of fear, and pride's hard steely blues,
Flame-colored strut, and glory's purple thread,
Cold-gray of zinc and iron, planes and oil,
And inky black confusion, all combined
And knotted in a coil

That life would wind
Into a lariat to noose mankind.

IV

Blunt-nosed and turreted, the caravan
Of battleships and cruisers steamed southeast
Far from sequestered bases in Japan;
And bombers, like great dragonflies released,
Buzzed high in heaven on a raiders' plan
Of treachery and terror. They who schemed
The veiled attack, daring our mammoth hosts,
Not in their gaudiest vision could have dreamed
Of Western sentries drowsing at their posts.
True, we had hints and flares
Proving we need not yawn, all unawares:
A midget submarine
Startlingly seen;
And then, more ominous yet, Japan's war-fleet
Approaching — so declared a shocked report.
And one who broke a flight impulsively short
Swore he had chanced to meet
Wings of mysterious planes. Warningly thus
The descending storm sent rumblings far ahead.
But folly, dozing and incredulous,
Would shut her ears, deaf to the calls of dread;
Would loll, and close her eyes,
Then blink, and view disaster with surprise.

Like diving eagles drilled
To swoop upon a pebble-narrow goal,
Flight upon guided flight
Down from the morning blue the bombers shrilled.
Loud as volcanoes spouting, straight and fast

In meteor streaks of light,
They pounded with a detonating toll;
Explosions jarred the earth and heaved the sea
Almost in rhythm, regular blast on blast
Spinning a pattern for catastrophe.
And while the long reverberations roared,
Smoke-mantles billowed, spiralled, twisted, soared;
Far heavenward, in widening wreaths, they swirled
Like black last streamers of a dying world.
Now in Pearl Harbor, where an hour ago
Sleek battle craft of gray, a nation's pride,
Tossed on calm waters, surly swells were dyed
With blood and wreckage and the orange glow
Of oil-fires flaring. Sunk beneath the waves,
Helpless as tunny caught
By the fell torpedo's shattering onslaught,
Three thousand men lay sprawled in sudden graves.

Thus daggered stealth and sneaking butchery
Garnered what seemed to be
Triumph to dazzle awestruck history!
But time has ways that few beholders guess,
And it would come about
That the Mikado's blazing first success
Wove tangles for his cataclysmic rout.
Those bomb-proud lords of violence who designed
The brigand's strategy of slash-and-rip,
Ignored one sovereign power —the steel-girt mind,
On whose invisible bulwarks they would trip.
Not all the propagandists in the States,
Not all the preachments dinned by press and air,
Not all the warnings shouted in debates
Nor the rash counsels of resolve-and-dare,

Might have induced our people to unite
Vast-armied, with teeth gritted for the fight
Against a worldwide foe; but this great end
Our enemy accomplished by one flight.

V

Forth from the German shore
And out of the hills of Rome,
Sounded a whine, a roar
Of "War!", "War!", "War!", and then, deep-rumbling,
    "War!"
And suddenly, as if the shaken dome
Of heaven burned furnace-red, the conflagration
Swept nation after nation
To cindery chaos that self-stricken man
Never had seen before since storms of Mars began.

Like some wolf-hunted rover, who must fight
Monsters that skirmish to his left, and blows
Of sharp, sly fangs maneuvering to the right,
We were beleaguered by limb-ripping foes.
From the white ocean of the steppes to blanks
Of blown Saharan sand, and mesh-like green
Of Indo-Chinese jungles, our allies
Charged and recoiled with mortars, planes and tanks,
In clashes of steel machine and steel machine
More than of human brain and brawn and eyes.
I saw our troops meanwhile
In Burmese marshes, and the coral beach
Of many a cocoanut-encircled isle,
And where the chill Aleutian fog-banks reach,
And over snow-backed Himalayan chains,
And in Italian mountains, and bare plains

Of baked North Africa; the whizz and drone
Of bombers wheeling close in death campaigns
Would sound for Bremen, Dresden and Cologne,
When walls crashed down and men and women screamed,
Hunched beneath tumbling rubble. We would guide
The long zigzagging convoy as it steamed
Where raiders, in assassin packs, might glide
And transports pitched and listed. Far to west,
Where slate-gray carriers heaved in morning gloom,
Airplanes would buzz like hornets from their nest,
Rising in flocks; soar out across the vasts
Of shadowy waters with the shafts of doom
And strike with fire in blasts
That made the cruiser, smoke-wrapped, listing low,
Twist vainly to balk the annihilating blow.

VI

And when the frenzy was but half begun,
What blistering winds went hissing through the States!
On every street, grim placard of the fates,
The khaki-clad young soldier with a gun!
And shops roared late; and in a thousand mills
Steel torrents glared, and riveters rasped and clacked,
Women beside their brothers; blades attacked
And levelled down the hills.
And the wide dingy sheds of shipyards rose,
And pastures where last year the cattle browsed
Were clogged with wooden walls of shacks that housed
Drab-jacketed workers, while the old repose
Seemed far as Cromwell's England. Columned trees,
Rustling in canyons, listening to the psalm
Sung by clear streams for bright eternities,
Were suddenly smitten, and their ageless calm

Gave way to axe-thuds and the whine of saws,
For the insatiable devouring jaws
Must still be fed and fed.

                           But who could spare
Mere forests when men battered hearts of men? —
The drawn, pale mother whose tear-watered prayer
Throbbed for the son she might not see again;
The father with the features trenched and gray,
Gripping a note, grim-lipped for one afar,
With nightmares of a flaming sky foray;
The bride who bears the scar
Of parting as a martyr bears a cross;
The orphan wailing for the dear arms gone;
The lover's loneliness, the widow's loss —
Ah, who can say what sorrows must be borne,
Who can inquire or care
While still the guns boom forth by ocean, land and air?

       Then in a panic, in a puff of terror
As though at snake-fangs in a treasonous dark,
See the half-sighted army lords embark
Upon a tyrannous error
Engulfing countless lives! I can recall
How, in our friendly village of the West,
The old slant-eyed shoemaker who possessed,
Year after year, the kind regard of all,
Vanished with wife and young ones, nevermore
To walk our streets. And time would soon erase
Their very memory, a glass-front store
Supplant their vine-leafed, petalled dwelling-place.
Not many saw them as, without good-bye,
Sad-lipped and dazed, they trailed with bags in hand
To pay for wrongs they could not understand —

For birth beneath Japan's forgotten sky.
Bristling and tall, the barbed-wire fences spread
Over the desert, up the scarred rock-slope,
Where, cramped inside the hut, the raw plank-shed,
With rifled guards around them, they could hope
For the war's end . . . and fractured lives renewed,
Though few again would walk on paths they once pursued.

Across the land, while courage, strong and proud,
Companioned the marching squad, the brisk recruit,
Rumor was blowing in a murky cloud
And fear had shed a scarlet poison fruit.
Out of the clear deep blue,
High-circling above us in a wide array,
A hurtling murder crew
Would strike us any day —
So men believed. And now, on every block,
The air-raid warden; now at times, by night,
The siren, and the paralyzing shock
Of blackout windows blanketing every light,
Till cities were as sparkless and as dim
As when the mastodon roamed, and watchers stood
In the dark street, the still suburban wood,
Scanning the stars above a vague hill-rim
For glimpses of some meteoric bout
Of blazing fighter planes. How blest we were
Never at all to hear the approaching purr
Of bomber squadrons — that blood-chilling shout,
"Take cover!" Yet how sadly well we knew
That woes we but imagined, had come true
In many a jagged-walled and roofless town
Where sky-shells maimed and slew.
Wrily, ironically came the thought

That man, who through long laboring epochs, fought
To climb beyond the jungle and the cave,
Now, by man's own inventiveness, was taught
Barbarities the Stone Age never gave.

VII

While premonitions, cold as frost, were heaped
On more than one gray-haired official head,
The guarded papers that our chieftains read
Turned knees to putty. Terror stories seeped
Like muddy water through the censored screens,
Which even barred the weatherman's prediction.
And while we fed on bland official fiction,
We could but guess how skulking submarines
Sent vessels wallowing, with crews and freight,
Smoking and ripped, down to Atlantic deeps.
Secret as sin were records of the fate
Of airplanes splintered by daredevil sweeps
Over the Philippines; we could but curse
Weird fortune for the little that we knew
Of sour reverse that piled on sour reverse —
Prime British battleships sunk in the blue
Of South Pacific waters, and defeat
In China when armies faded out like ghosts
And a tired general straggled with worn troops
Through mountains and jungles in a frayed retreat
To far-off India. Bleaker still — the hosts
Of Russia, staggering under German swoops,
Tight-pressed at Stalingrad, might be knocked out
By swallowing tides of Panzas, in a rout
That left machine-like Nazi myriads free
To whirl against the West

In what might be
The ultimate, the catastrophic test.

Small wonder then if brows were wrinkle-lined
And lamps shone late in worried Washington.
And was it fluttery chance whose voice assigned
The seat of dread authority to one
Fitted to lead a world? Again I gazed
On the warm features of the President,
And saw the calm prophetic eyes, which blazed
Often with quips, and glowed with merriment,
Though his frail shoulders, even as Atlas, bore
The weight of every sea and every shore.
Hurricane-swept, like those illustrious two —
Lincoln and Wilson, who had fought before
On tempest-peaks of time — he sadly knew
The burden of blood and trouble, which would drain
His cheeks, and wrench him with a crowbar strain,
Until at last, with victory flags in sight,
Stricken one day by stabs of blinding pain,
He gasped and fell, a battle casualty
No less than any lad who went to fight
In cannonading bouts by land or sea.

VIII

I saw the brilliant-hued kaleidoscope
Of many wars erupting into one,
While slowly there appears a flush, a hope
From beaches seized and islands overrun.
But oh, the crimson and inexorable cost
No chronicler may tell or witness know,
Of wave-lashed sailors, and of fighters lost
When mountains blaze or cities crumble and glow!

The huts and steeples smashed! the cratered streets
Where men and women, shrivelling, moan as prey
Of conflagrations, whose bright rushing sheets
Roar down, until all breath is sucked away!
The refugees, dragging in hang-neck streams!
The troops that splash, under a red-hot spray,
To shores where decimating shell-fire screams;
The combats, cheek to cheek,
When steel rips flesh, and blood in gushers spills;
The Channel-vaulting monster bomb that kills
With random ruin, and terrors that bespeak
The infant rocket age! All this, and more —
Scenes that would startle Mephistopheles
And earn his envious praise — was etched in gore
By the black destinies
That raked the battle flames. The witnessing mind
No more imagines all the gloom and glare,
The sobs, the groans, the bravery, than the blind
Can paint a rainbowed cloud-fleet high in air.

　　　If scourging Attila, in ages past,
Had crushed all Europe with wild Hunnish forces,
Sent arrowed packs to leave all towns aghast,
And seized the continent's swords and battle horses,
Not slimmer would have seemed
The patriot's hope of liberty redeemed.
But even Attila, raiding with his hordes
Of brown barbarians drilled to rip and slaughter,
Was not more savage than the modern lords
Who blew up women and babes and gave no quarter.
Worse still! the Nazi ravagers, when they stormed
From Greece to Norway, strutting in defiance,
Had more than fighting men that snarled and swarmed,

But came stout-armed with science.
So who could pass where their steel bulwarks rose?
As soon, one might suppose,
Could Lilliput rout Brobdingagian foes.

Only by poring over Europe's map
Could the new architects of fate prepare;
The leap men take across an infinite gap
Must be protected with slow-footed care.
By blueprints, graphs and charts,
High-piled statistics and late-burning light,
With sunken eyes they plotted dubious starts
While months were lengthening and years took flight.
Yet at a puff of wind, the planned advance
Across the straits and over captured France
Might falter beneath the tricky hand of chance.

Squadrons and squadrons, far as eyes could see,
Destroyers and rusty hulls, the huge and small,
Stretched out unendingly down the Norman coast.
And where the choppy waves dashed spitefully
Caissons and spent old vessels reared a wall
As a rude harbor for the incoming host.
Beneath a sky whose thunder-bolts were loud
As threats from all the storms that hell could muster,
Out of the shaken landing craft a crowd
Of men with packs emerged; I saw them cluster
In many a splashing band, while overhead
Airplanes like buzzards spiralled, and long booms
Chorused the warships' ceaseless cannonade.
And shattering bombs made shooting stars of red;
And flaring against the shore's high smoky glooms,
Ramparts erupted, hails of flame were sprayed

High over the beach.
                    But doggedly on and on
The invaders pressed along the sand, although
A boat exploding like a living thing
Leapt from the waves, and in a flash was gone
Where the swung sea was dully smoldering,
And timbers tossed, and in the heave and flow
Men threshed around like spars; while, overturned
Into the spumy vast, another crew
Struggled, its agonies unobserved or spurned,
Then sank from sight — what man could pause to rue
The fate of comrades, when each hard-drawn breath
Blew from the shores of death?

       But up and up the beach,
Chests to the sand, the armies grope and crawl,
And hack and smash a breach
In armed Hitlerian hosts, while many fall
To blazing traps. Not in an hour or day
The New World myriads and their allies
Would batter down the fort and win that prize
For which slave-millions pray.
But persecuted by the tide and gale,
The secret swoops of night-planes planting mines,
Bomb-nests, concrete entrenchments, and barbed wire,
They must storm on, steel-breasted not to fail,
And with triumphant, ever-spreading lines,
Take ports and towns in face of snares and fire.

       Out of the sky, like raiding squads from Mars,
With great umbrellas opening overhead,
The paratroopers of the Stripes and Stars
Rained downward where the Norman beach was red.

And squat land warships, grayly fortified,
Bellowed with gun-blasts; clanking batteries fought
Among the hedgerows of the countryside,
Where every pockmarked yard was horror-bought.
And in a widening fan,
Under the fighter planes' swift-wheeling fleet,
The armored behemoths dashed, where Nazis ran
Backward, torn-bannered, in confused defeat.
Like streams converging to a central sea,
Fresh armies flowed, flags waving, from the south,
While the goosestepping thousands, in retreat,
Left boulevards of Paris suddenly free
As from a dragon's mouth.

Then far and fast, in many a driving line,
I watched the liberators plunging on;
Beheld them crowd a bridge above the Rhine,
And knew the oppressors' day was nearly gone.
Yet cornered bears may fight
More savagely after wounds have racked their flanks,
And still we'd reel beneath the dynamite
Of counter-attacking ranks,
Scattering crosses over hills and fields.
And prisoners, thick as plums in August yields,
Were garnered as converging troops and tanks
Went streaming east and west on bombed Berlin.
And there, joining the millions he had slain,
One day the Nazi despot wretchedly died,
The wild mass murderer a suicide,
Locked underground, nightmarishly shut in
Like a caught rat lashing its tail in vain.

* * *

Mighty the triumph, huge the feat, which time has not
    surpassed!
But was the conquest wholly ours when all was gauged
    at last?
For man, who mangles and tears in strife like a tigress
    for her brood,
Seldom will bring to calm white peace a war's devoted mood.
What of the treacherous years ahead? How lucidly did we
    plan
Those roads, still mapless, round whose turns we'd pilot the
    race of man?
How well did we see the sullen friend who soon would glower
    as foe
Though our fleets had filled his battle bins and helped his
    armies grow?
Did wisdom envisage a long Cold War of muffled threats
    and woe?

Ah, truly the bells were loud, were loud, and the
    cheering hosts were gay,
For a long and weary road was passed, and a yoke was tossed
    away.
And who would dim the victory glow, or look beyond the day?

IX

The modern war-chief is a more-than-king,
Emperor even over tongues and thought,
Sucking the flow from every living spring,
Measuring value by engagements fought.
The toiler in mole-galleries of the mine,
The planter where the wheat-field ripples green,
The robot of the rushed assembly-line,
Are gunless soldiers in war's mass-machine.

And one not less required,
Among his vials and beakers, white-attired,
Must make a screened report
On sputterings in the test-tube and retort —
The sorcerer of science, who may wield
Time's most miraculous wand to rule the battlefield.

In new Aladdin tales
Men were entranced by power like the sun's,
Star-hot, erupting in cyclonic gales,
Forever to muffle all our bombs and guns.
But that this genie from the caves of hell
Would make mere vapor of man's quivering flesh,
Was scarcely dreamt of . . . Then the doom befell
And we were tangled in a self-made mesh
Beyond our own conceiving.
If a race
Of invisible monsters, of Mount Etna's size,
Had glided down from planetary space
And struck with white-hot meteors, men's surprise
Could not be sharper than a gasping world
Witnessed one shuddery morning. Domed and tall
A cloud-puff over Hiroshima curled;
And lower, where the street and pier and wall
Vanished in storms of fire, more hideous harm
Went billowing up than arch-fiends could design.
The lives that tingled, even as yours and mine,
And then, as at a cosmic conjurer's charm,
All in one sun-bright instant were no more!
The wounded, when impalpable poison darts
Had left them withering, racked within and sore
From rays uncannily gnawing nerves and hearts!
And darker, grimmer still,

The death-example, the war-commanded will
To our own extirpation! black bequest
Soon to expand in flares no ruler guessed
And leave its dazed creator little rest
From trial and terror.

                              Yet we're told our side
Triumphed in war — her jugular pierced, Japan
Capitulated, torn and horrified.
And did the end not justify our plan?
Perhaps, as long as men have tongues and lips,
This theme will be debated, and until
War's fire-red planet meets her last eclipse,
Flingers of bombs will want the right to kill
Whole Tokios and Londons; some will claim
Threatened extermination's not a threat
But wise deterrence, albeit never yet
In all man's wasting years of blood and flame
Had frightfulness slain frightfulness before.

    But this at least we knew:
Monsters to dwarf the roc of Persian lore
Raged through the world. And this as well was true:
No longer the tribe of man could be destroyed
Only by burst volcanoes, plague or heat,
Mad comets, or the plummeting asteroid
Out of unhuman space; but our defeat
Might suddenly be complete
And black annihilation strike one day
By negligent chance, or from the poisoned mind
Of a crazed Hitler swearing to end mankind.
So, though we gained our way,
What if there still would be exorbitant bills to pay?

X

Yet many looked with glad and glowing eyes
Upon the years beyond.
"Whither?" they heard a questioning voice arise.
"To peace!" they would respond.
"To peace, bright peace! While man desires to live,
Its luminous citadels leave no alternative!"

If the wise soul of Wilson, from the height
Where all past councillors of nations meet,
Could witness, with a globe-encompassing sight,
His country's tumult and the foes' defeat,
Would he not smile to watch, in flame and gale,
His radiant world ideal, and hear men hail
His League again, and swear it must prevail? —
United Nations, pictured with a power
To build the peace as an impregnable tower!

Under blown hills beside the Golden Gate
I saw the chiefs of many lands convene.
Almost as though by ordinance of fate
A shining Western seaport was the scene,
Whence salt blue highways curved around the earth
To every tribe and people. Hard might be
The travail, and intense the pangs of birth,
And compromise might claim too high a fee;
But in the infant dangled to the view
Of an applauding world, there flashed a hope
The sad, ensanguined ages never knew:
To cage the wolf within man's breast, and cope
With the clawed demon, battle.
                              Was this dream
A rainbow bubble? As I stared ahead

To clouds low-drooping round the closed regime
Walled in far capitols, the flares that spread
Over the earth with rabble-maddening feuds,
And the Cold War that smokily burned on
From oily rubbish of false attitudes,
And invisible menace borne
On small death-rays polluting the atmosphere,
And goblin weapons challenging airless space,
I sighed, and called on faith to answer fear,
And some protective genius of the race
To succor man, whose reasons for alarm
Were his own brain, and his own eyes and arm.

      As in a lens, I viewed the approaching years,
The New World cities sparkling and bizarre,
Their high glass-breasted towers, tiers on tiers
Like giant hives on some fantastic star.
I saw gray hills reach out
In long expanding sheds, where sulphurous smoke
Puffed from the pipe-like spout,
And millions in the working cap and cloak
Rattled in timed group-labor; millions bowed
At the same altar-rail of get-and-gain
As even their bosses. Then I watched the crowd
Swish down the windowed, wheel-congested lane,
And far across the wide, once-open vast,
Bewilderingly massed
As black ant-columns. Luxury, like a sheen,
Would garnish even the toiler with a gloss,
Though many still, where huts were low and mean,
Must dine on dross.
Now a crusading faith, the creed of Things,
Would beckon where idolatrous legions knelt,

While less and less one heard the whirr of wings
Or dreamt in halls where love and music dwelt.
Where did it point? And whither moved the land,
Swung on a gale-whipped new momentous tide?
Tomorrow loomed too vast to understand.
One could but bow his head, and let the years decide.

* * *

High in the clouds that bounded the halves of the planet
It seemed that I gazed upon beings who, mistily stirring,
With figures mighty as gods, and patriarch faces,
Were mantled in light, with trailing garments of vapor.

"O Man," said a voice, "you have witnessed a blaze,
        an adventure
Unexampled in time, and not to be rivalled tomorrow.
You have seen the explorers in caravels bravely embarking
For the rim of the West; you have peered at the rovers
        and raiders
As they burst like a storm on the shores of a virgin dominion.
You have followed the settlers in forests and ranges and
        wheat-lands,
And watched as they labored and sowed and erected new
        nations,
And fought with the redman, and slaughtered the bison and
        grizzly,
And hammered out rails, and lifted their bridges and towers,
The stacks of their mills, and their schools and asylums
        and churches.
And you have observed as with strength and confusion and
        valor
The arm of America waved over Europe and Asia.
In the playhouse of ages, no drama so huge, so portentous

Was ever enacted before, and the spectacle flashes
From islands remote in blue seas, and malarial jungles,
And pinnacled cities, their future still dim in a dawn-mist.

"Oh, whither the route over ridges of time still
   untraveled?
For what all the strain, all the trial, the shouts and the
   sobbing,
The dream of Columbus, the quest of La Salle and Mackenzie,
The daring of Franklin and Penn, and the courage of
   Lincoln?
Oh, pray that the genius of time, which moves forward
   forever,
Will carry you forth to white summits, and summits beyond
   them,
To dazzle the eyes of your children in years still
   undreamt-of!"

High in the clouds that bounded the halves of the
   planet
It seemed that I gazed upon beings who, mistily stirring,
With figures mighty as gods, and patriarch faces,
Were mantled in light, with trailing garments of vapor.
But suddenly these, like fog-wisps, had dwindled and
   vanished,
To leave me a sense of greatness, and epics unfolded
Where deep in the west there sparkled the star of the morning.

THE END